International Trade and Political Conflict

D1416838

For all references to www.pup.org please substitute
www.people.fas.harvard.edu/~hiscox/Trade_and_
Political_Conflict.html

International Trade and Political Conflict

COMMERCE, COALITIONS, AND MOBILITY

MICHAEL J. HISCOX

PRINCETON UNIVERSITY PRESS

PRINCETON AND OXFORD

Library of Congress Cataloging-in-Publication Data

Hiscox, Michael J., 1966–
International trade and political conflict : commerce, coalitions, and mobility /
Michael J. Hiscox.
p. cm.
Includes bibliographical references and index.
ISBN 0-691-08854-3 (alk. paper) — ISBN 0-691-08855-1 (pbk. : alk. paper)
1. International trade—Political aspects—History.   2. Commercial policy—
History.   3. Coalition (Social sciences).   4. Migration, Internal.   5. International
economic relations.   6. United States—Commercial policy—History.   I. Title.
HF1379 H57 2001
382'.3—dc21   2001021463

British Library Cataloging-in-Publication Data is available

This book has been composed in Times Roman

Printed on acid-free paper.∞

www.pup.princeton.edu

Printed in the United States of America

10   9   8   7   6   5   4   3   2   1

10   9   8   7   6   5   4   3   2   1
(Pbk.)

FOR JOHN AND PEG HISCOX

CONTENTS

LIST OF TABLES AND FIGURES

Tables

Figures

This is a study of the politics of international trade. As someone who grew up in a wheat and wool-growing district in rural Australia, where fortunes fluctuated in line with world prices for agricultural commodities and trade policies at home and abroad, this topic has long held a special appeal for me. Historically, trade has always served as a lightning rod for political conflict. In the nineteenth century, in many places, it was often *the* central political issue over which political parties squared off in election campaigns and legislative battles and which caused protestors to take to the streets. Indeed, the first organized political parties in all the former Australian colonies in the 1880s and 1890s were Free Trade and Protectionist parties. In our own times, as political conflict over globalization has begun to spill over into demonstrations in the streets of Seattle, Davos, Melbourne, and Montreal, and as governments in the advanced economies debate about whether or how they ought to proceed with future trade negotiations, it seems just as important as ever to examine the political schisms generated by the trade issue.

I have attempted here to provide a general study of the types of political cleavages and conflicts created by international trade. The political battles that have been fought over the trade issue have actually been quite different in different historical settings. In particular, the extent to which conflict over trade policy has led to major clashes between broad-based class coalitions has varied significantly across time and place. I suggest that a good deal of this variation can be explained by the degree to which individual economic agents are mobile between different industries or productive activities in the economy. When it comes to determining the effects of international trade on incomes, such mobility tends to make class distinctions among agents more salient than ties to particular industries; this shapes the political contest over trade with profound effects not only for the evolution of trade policy itself but for the distribution of incomes, for economic growth rates, and for the development of political parties and other institutions.

I have incurred many debts while working on this project. Generous financial support was provided by the Robert G. Menzies Fund of Australia, which granted the scholarship in 1990 that allowed me to give up a very good job in Sydney to pursue a graduate degree in the United States. The Harvard Sheldon Fund also provided funding during the 1990–1991 and 1991–1992 academic years, and the Mellon Foundation supported me with generous grants in 1993–1994 and 1994–1995. The Research Training Group in Positive Political Economy at Harvard and MIT supported me during my last semester at Harvard in 1996.

I owe a large debt of gratitude to many friends and advisers who helped me during the course of this research. Jim Alt, first and foremost, has been a constant source of support and wise counsel over the years. I feel extremely fortunate to be able to count myself as one of his students. Lawrence Broz, Jeff Frieden, and Alberto Alesina also provided valuable advice during the development of the project at Harvard, and I owe a special debt to Bob Keohane, who encouraged my early graduate work and provided much sound guidance and instruction. At Harvard I also benefited from helpful comments at various stages from Carles Boix, Brian Burgoon, Marc Busch, Jon Crystal, Gary King, Henry Laurence, Lisa Martin, Andrew Moravcsik, Ken Shepsle, and Kip Wennerlund.

At the University of California, San Diego, I have been very fortunate to be surrounded by terrific colleagues. In particular, Neal Beck, Ellen Comisso, Gary Cox, Liz Gerber, Peter Gourevitch, Steph Haggard, Harry Hirsch, Gary Jacobsen, Miles Kahler, Sam Kernell, David Lake, Skip Lupia, Mat McCubbins, Andrew MacIntyre, Sam Popkin, Phil Roeder, Kaare Strom, and Tracy Strong have been tremendously generous in providing me with friendship, advice, and comments on different aspects of this project. Peter and David have been especially supportive, and their own work has been a continuing inspiration. At Princeton University Press I am deeply indebted to Chuck Myers for his encouragement and enthusiasm. For helpful comments on parts or all of this research in its later stages I am also very grateful to Mike Gilligan, Peter Katzenstein, Helen Milner, Eric Reinhardt, Cheryl Schonhardt-Bailey, and Daniel Verdier. I am especially indebted to Mike and Daniel since I drew very heavily from their own wonderful books on trade politics, *Empowering Exporters* and *Democracy and International Trade*, when recounting the histories of trade politics in France, Britain, and the United States and examining legislative voting on trade bills.

I owe very special thanks to Ron Rogowski. His year on leave at Harvard in 1995–1996, coinciding with the arrival of Jeff Frieden, was a great stroke of luck for me as I struggled with the early stages of this research. His masterful book, *Commerce and Coalitions*, was the principal source of inspiration for this project, and I remain deeply grateful for his generosity and friendship. In addition to allowing me to use him as a straw man in my written work, he also taught me to ski; both enduring gifts.

I owe my most profound debts to my late father, John Hiscox, my mother, Peg, and my sister, Anna, for all their support and encouragement. And finally, for keeping it all in proper perspective, my warmest thanks go to Verity and Molly.

Michael J. Hiscox
La Jolla, California

PART I

Trade Theory, Factor Mobility, and Political Conflict

CHAPTER ONE

Trade, Distribution, and Factor Mobility

The expansion of international trade has been a powerful engine driving economic growth in Western nations over the last two centuries. At the same time, since trade has had disparate effects on different sets of individuals within each economy, it has provoked an enormous amount of internal political conflict. Although such conflict between winners and losers has been a constant in trade politics over the years, the character of the political coalitions that have fought these battles—the nature of the societal cleavages that the trade issue has created—appears to have differed significantly across time and place. Most importantly, the extent to which conflict over trade policy has led to clashes between broad class-based coalitions has varied across historical settings.

As a consequence, the literature on the political economy of trade has developed something of a split personality. Many scholars following in the grand tradition of E. E. Schattschneider (1935) have focused on the political role of narrow industry groups, or "special interests," in the policymaking process. This approach, which emphasizes the competition between coalitions of business and labor groups positioned on both sides of the debate over trade, has been prominently adopted by Peter Gourevitch (1986) and Jeffry Frieden (1991) and is common to quantitative studies of trade barriers inspired by the endogenous policy literature in economics.[1] In contrast, Ronald Rogowski (1989) has examined broad factoral or class coalitions in a range of historical contexts, highlighting political conflicts between owners of land, labor, and capital over the direction of trade policy. Other analysts, drawing distinctions between owners of multinational and other types of capital or between skilled and unskilled labor, have made similar assumptions about the centrality of class cleavages in trade politics (Helleiner 1977; Midford 1993).

Empirical evidence suggests support for both approaches. The lobbying free-for-all among industry groups that led to the U.S. Smoot-Hawley Tariff Act in 1930 lives in infamy, and most accounts of contemporary U.S. trade politics indicate that such groups have played a prominent role in recent battles over the North American Free Trade Agreement (NAFTA) and the General Agreement on Tariffs and Trade (GATT). Historical accounts of trade politics in a variety of nations—particularly France during the nineteenth century—reveal that these kinds of industry-based cleavages have a

---

[1] For examples, see Anderson 1980, Lavergne 1983, and Baldwin 1985.

long and robust ancestry.[2] However, examples of broader class-based cleavages are also familiar. Perhaps most famously, workers in nineteenth-century Britain, taking on the ruling Tories and the landed elite, aligned with capitalists to provide mass support for freer trade and the Anti-Corn Law League. A similar contest developed in the United States after the Civil War—this time between pro-trade farmers and protectionist urban classes—and led to a Republican tariff in 1890 that was denounced by Democrats as the "culminating atrocity of class legislation."[3]

That both class and group approaches have found empirical support in a variety of contexts demonstrates the need for a way to bridge the gulf between them that would specify the conditions under which one is more appropriate than the other. This need is fundamental on both theoretical and substantive levels. Coalitions are the manifestation of conflicts of interests among individuals in society over the direction of policy. As such, they lie at the very heart of politics. Yet, in the past, scholars examining the political origins of trade and other forms of economic policy have been largely content to make opposing general assumptions about the nature of these conflicts of interest—assuming that individuals will take different positions in disputes over trade and other policies depending on their economic class or on the industry or sector of the economy in which they are employed.

These assumptions are the very building blocks of positive political economy, and their relative appropriateness, an issue rarely addressed directly, is a central concern for all engaged in explaining and predicting the evolution of economic policy. By better accounting for the types of coalitions generated by trade and other economic policy issues, analysts will also be better able to assess the degree to which these cleavages and other types of political divisions within a political system map onto one another and thus whether they are compounding or cross-cutting. For instance, class divisions over the trade issue appear to have complemented and thus intensified the broad conflict between urban and rural coalitions over electoral reform in Britain in the nineteenth century, and the conflict over remonetization of silver in the United States in the 1880s and 1890s. Narrower, industry-based divisions over trade, however, tend to cut across and thus mitigate class antagonisms over other policy issues.

In this book I apply the standard economic theory of trade to provide a solution to the problem by focusing on interindustry factor mobility—that is, the ease with which owners of factors of production (land, labor, and capital) can move between industries in the domestic economy. If factors are mobile between industries, the effects of trade on incomes divide individuals along class lines, setting owners of different factors (such as labor and capital) at odds with each other regardless of the industry in which they are employed. If factors are immobile between industries, the effects of trade divide individuals along industry lines, setting owners of the same factor in

---

[2] On the French case, see Smith 1980.
[3] See *Congressional Record*, September 15, 1949, 12902.

different industries (labor in the steel and aircraft industries, for example) at odds with each other over policy.

This book presents the first systematic evidence on levels of interindustry factor mobility, examining six Western economies (the United States, Britain, France, Sweden, Canada, and Australia) during the nineteenth and twentieth centuries.[4] The data indicate that substantial variation in factor mobility coincides with different stages of industrialization and different amounts of regulation in these economies. The patterns in this variation, and their anticipated effects, are shown to fit broadly with the development of trade politics in these nations during different historical eras. I examine trade cleavages in each nation since the 1820s, emphasizing the effects of such cleavages on the behavior of political parties and peak associations and the lobbying efforts of major industry groups. I also provide a detailed statistical analysis of the effects of changing cleavages on congressional voting on trade legislation in the United States between 1824 and 1994. The results indicate that broad class-based conflict is more likely when levels of factor mobility are relatively high, and narrow industry-based conflict is more likely when levels of mobility are relatively low.

The findings reported here have important implications for the analysis of trade politics and the politics of economic policy more generally. They suggest that the types of political coalitions that take shape in society and organize to influence economic policy making largely depend on one basic feature of the economic environment that may vary over time (and across nations): the extent to which factors of production are mobile between industries within the economy. Put simply, the stakes that individuals have in policies that affect the industry in which they are employed or invested will vary greatly depending on how easy it is for them to move their assets elsewhere. Thus, interindustry mobility is crucial for understanding the political-economic origins of a vast range of trade, monetary, industrial, and regulatory policies that affect the relative fortunes of different industries or mediate the effects of other exogenous changes upon them. The extent to which these policy issues generate class conflict, rather than industry-based rent-seeking, will hinge critically on levels of factor mobility in the economy.

Class conflict can be a tumultuous and disruptive force in politics, of course, producing sharp fluctuations in economic policy as first one side then another gains control of government. But broad-based class coalitions are also more encompassing of society as a whole, as Olson (1982) famously noted, and thus they are more likely than narrow industry groups to take an interest in expanding the size of the whole economic pie rather than just snatching the largest piece of it they can. If politics devolves into a free-for-all contest among industry-based lobby groups, a large portion of an

---

[4] These nations are particularly attractive candidates for close study since they have long histories of democratic government and the political disputes over trade in each have been well documented.

economy's resources may end up devoted to zero-sum distributive battles rather than to productive economic activities (Bhagwati 1982).[5] If a stable pattern of compromise can be established between broad class coalitions, providing for efficiency-enhancing types of economic policies and methods of compensation, class cleavages seem far more appealing (for reasons of efficiency quite apart from issues of equality). This is essentially the model crafted by the Swedish economists who shaped Social Democratic policies in the 1950s and 1960s, and they recognized that maintaining such a broad-based compromise required programs that discouraged industry rent-seeking by supporting and promoting high levels of interindustry mobility among owners of labor and capital. In the end, a very strong case emerges for extensive forms of adjustment assistance to workers and firms (allowances for retraining, relocation, and reinvestment) that would enable them to respond to changes in the international economy in more efficient, nonpolitical ways, while at the same time mitigating the costs imposed upon particular groups by such exogenous shocks.

1.1 THE EXISTING LITERATURE

Explaining differences in the types of cleavages that emerge in trade politics is a task that generally has been set aside in past research on the political economy of trade. The dominant tendency has been to assume one type of coalition exists, usually in order to explain particular policy outcomes, and ignore the problem entirely. Rogowski (1989) explicitly assumes class-based coalitions, for instance, while Gourevitch (1986) focuses on industries. Frieden (1991) adopts a sectoral or industry-based approach when outlining his theory but allows that class coalitions have actually emerged as more important political entities in some of the economies he examined.

When the coalition issue has been addressed in the broader political science literature, attention has focused primarily on the effects of electoral and policymaking institutions. Political organizations geared to representing broad types of coalitions are more likely when the franchise is extended more widely among society (see Duverger 1954; LaPalombara and Weiner 1966; Cox 1987). Some types of electoral systems that encourage intraparty competition and the development of a "personal vote" may be more conducive to group "rent-seeking" than alternative systems.[6] Along these lines, Rogowski (1998) has argued that whether proportional representation encourages politicians to appeal to broader or more particularistic interests actually depends on how attached voters are to the parties (that is, how easily they can be "bought").

Policymaking institutions may also have profound effects on coalitions,

[5] This is the portrait of political ossification usually painted of France in the late middle ages (North and Thomas 1973).

[6] The point has been made most clearly with reference to systems with multi-member districts and single, nontransferable voting. See Carey and Shugart 1992 and Katz 1986.

although since they are more malleable, the degree to which they can be considered exogenous to the coalitions themselves is more troublesome. James Alt and Michael Gilligan (1994) have suggested that rules under which policy is made by a small group of legislators and that allow more access and influence for lobbying groups (for example, during hearings by legislative committees) are less likely to encourage formation of broad class coalitions than more "majoritarian" alternatives. Daniel Verdier (1994) makes a similar argument, but attempts to endogenize such policymaking institutions by reference to the salience and divisiveness of the trade issue among voters.[7] Though wonderfully provocative, Verdier's study does not attempt to test this argument empirically and encounters some real problems. His argument treats voter preferences over trade policy as exogenous, for instance, ignoring their origins and treating them as separate from the preferences of firms and labor groups.[8]

These various institutional arguments warrant more empirical investigation aimed specifically at making sense of trade politics. It is highly unlikely, however, that they can explain all the variation we see in cleavages over trade policy. The broad urban-rural conflict that defined U.S. trade politics in the 1880s and 1890s, for instance (discussed in detail in chapter 4), developed within the same institutional structure that allowed the infamous lobbying free-for-all over the Smoot-Hawley bill in 1930. In Britain, intense Left-Right partisanship on trade in the 1920s gave way to internal bickering among groups and party factions at both ends of the spectrum by the 1960s, without a major change in institutions (see chapter 5).[9]

Electoral and policymaking rules undoubtedly have important effects on trade politics. But the evidence presented in this book suggests that cleavages are powerfully shaped by economic forces. The next step should be to specify just how cleavages and institutions interact to produce patterns in trade politics. That, however, is a topic for another book.

1.2 TRADE THEORY, COALITIONS, AND FACTOR MOBILITY

According to the Stolper-Samuelson theorem (1941), trade increases real returns for owners of the factor of production with which the economy is

---

[7] If the trade issue is salient and divisive among voters, Verdier claims, politicians will respond with rules that favor partisanship aimed at generating electoral support from broad class constituencies. If the issue is not salient politicians prefer to create a policymaking process that encourages group lobbying; and if the issue is salient but not divisive, he expects the delegation of policymaking authority to an executive agent and coalitions drop out of the political picture.

[8] For an alternative argument (focusing on the origins of the U.S. Reciprocal Trade Agreements Act of 1934) about how coalitions can shape policymaking institutions, see Hiscox 1999.

[9] See chapters 10 and 11 for detailed discussions of how several institutional arguments fare in explaining evidence from each of the six nations discussed above, and particularly for the U.S. case.

relatively abundantly endowed, while it reduces real returns for owners of the scarce factor of production. The result depends critically on the assumption that factors of production, though immobile internationally, are perfectly mobile within the domestic economy.[10] The logic is straightforward: increased trade lowers the price of the imported good, leading to a reduction in its domestic production and freeing up more of the factor it uses relatively intensively (the scarce factor) than is demanded elsewhere in the economy at existing prices. When factor prices adjust to maintain full employment, returns to the scarce factor fall even further than the price of the imported good. Meanwhile, returns to the abundant factor increase more than the price of the exported good. In this model, the perfect mobility of the factors assures that trade affects owners of each factor in the same way no matter where they are employed in the economy. The implication is that all owners of the same factor share the same preferences with respect to trade policy. It is this insight that encouraged Rogowski (1989) to argue that political coalitions form in the shape of factor-owning classes and to anticipate broad-based conflict among owners of land, labor, and capital in trade politics.[11]

Alternative models of the income effects of trade (often referred to as Ricardo-Viner models), in which one or more factors of production are regarded as completely "specific" or immobile between industries, generate very different results (see Jones 1971; Mussa 1974, 1982).[12] In these models, the returns to factors are tied closely to the fortunes of the industries in which they are employed. Factors specific to export industries receive a real increase in returns due to trade, whereas those employed in import-competing industries lose in real terms.[13] Under these conditions, factor specificity can drive a wedge between members of the same class employed in different

---

[10] Factors are identified as broad categories of productive inputs and include at least labor and capital. Traditional Heckscher-Ohlin studies of trade focus on land, labor, and capital, and I have relied on that basic framework in the following chapters. Leamer (1984), by contrast, has defined eleven separate factors: capital, three types of labor (professional, semiskilled, unskilled), four types of land (tropical, temperate, dry, and forested), coal, minerals, and oil. More complicated classifications of factors begin to blur the distinction between mobile and specific factors that is critical to the theory here, however, so I have generally maintained the simpler, traditional definitions.

[11] Classes are defined here simply in terms of factor ownership. Each class comprises those individuals well endowed with a factor relative to the economy as a whole, so that ownership of that factor accounts for the largest share of their income. This definition allows for the fact that individuals often own a mix of factors. See Mayer 1984.

[12] The original model was introduced independently by Jones (1971) and Samuelson (1971): the former christened it the "specific-factors" model, while the latter named it the "Ricardo-Viner" model.

[13] Again, the logic is straightforward: a decrease in the domestic production of an imported good releases any mobile factors for employment elsewhere in the economy and thus renders factors specific to the import-competing industry less productive, driving down their real returns. Returns to the mobile factor rise relative to the price of the imported good, but fall relative to the price of exports, so that the income effects of trade for owners of this factor depend on patterns of consumption.

industries since they can now be affected quite differently by trade. The implication is that political coalitions form along industry lines. This notion has guided work by Frieden (1991) and much of the empirical analysis in the endogenous trade policy literature, which relates variation in import barriers across industries to the incentives and capacities of industry groups to organize.[14]

1.3 THE ARGUMENT AND EVIDENCE

Both Stolper-Samuelson and Ricardo-Viner models examine extreme, or polar, cases in which productive factors are assumed to be either perfectly mobile or completely specific.[15] This is a modeling convenience, of course. Factor mobility is regarded more appropriately as a continuous variable affected by a range of economic, technological, and political conditions. Allowing that factors can have varying degrees of mobility, the simple prediction is that broad class-based political coalitions are more likely where factor mobility is high, whereas narrow industry-based coalitions are more likely where mobility is low. The trade issue should divide a society along very different lines when substantial variation exists in general levels of factor mobility.[16] (Appendix A develops this argument mathematically.)

To date, there have been no attempts made to measure general levels of interindustry factor mobility over any span of time or across countries. I have gathered data on interindustry differentials in wages and profits in the manufacturing sectors of six economies during the nineteenth and twentieth centuries (see chapter 2). These measures, along with other indicators of factor mobility, paint a compelling picture. Levels of interindustry mobility appear to be strongly related to industrialization. Early stages of develop-

---

[14] For example, see Anderson 1980, and Lavergne 1983.

[15] In the economics literature, the bifurcation is considered unproblematic since specific-factors effects are generally regarded as important in the short term but not the long term. See Mussa 1974, Caves, Frankel, and Jones 1990, 146–49, and Krugman and Obstfeld 1988, 81. It is simply assumed that, over time, all factors are perfectly mobile. The problem with this view lies in its neglect of politics: Factor owners not only choose between accepting lower returns in one industry or moving to another, they can also organize politically to influence policy and alter relative prices. When moving between industries is very costly, so that the time horizon for financing it is long, it is less likely that the discounted future benefits from such adjustment will exceed the gains immediately available via political action.

[16] This possibility was discussed briefly by Magee 1980. In a recent paper, Brawley (1997) has made a different type of argument, suggesting that factors might have both specific and nonspecific components that would complicate the cleavage patterns in trade politics. It is not exactly clear how these different components might be cleanly separated for analysis, however, and accurately predicting the preferences for each component may be problematic. (Brawley argues that nonspecific components of abundant factors would benefit unambiguously from free trade, but existing general equilibrium models would suggest otherwise.) Regardless, even in this type of framework, we can predict that class-based cleavages will be more important relative to industry-based cleavages when factor specificity is less prevalent. That is the basic argument I am advancing here.

ment have typically produced a sharp rise in interindustry mobility, as innovations in transportation lowered the costs of factor movement and innovations in production gave rise to the factory system and increased demand for unskilled workers and basic forms of physical capital. Later stages of development, however, have generally been associated with a decline in interindustry mobility, as new innovations have generated more specific forms of human and physical capital and far greater complementarity between technology and labor skills.

This analysis of mobility levels is combined with an extensive study of cleavages in trade politics in each of the six economies since the early 1800s. To date, discussions of coalitions and cleavages over trade policy have tended to ignore the question of how we should specify these phenomena in empirical terms. I address the problem by tracing the observable consequences of different coalition patterns in the behavior of political parties, peak associations, and industry groups. Specifically, I reason that class-based political parties and peak associations will be more internally unified on the trade issue when class coalitions are stronger, while lobby groups will take a more active, competitive role in policy making when industry coalitions are stronger. These linkages are mapped out in chapter 3.

The investigation of trade politics in each nation, presented in part 2, reveals a strong correlation between general levels of interindustry factor mobility and coalition formation. The analysis relies on qualitative evidence on the behavior of parties, peak associations, and groups, combined with quantitative measures of party unity in legislative votes taken on trade bills and measures of the activity of industry groups lobbying official committees deliberating on trade policy. The evidence reveals substantial variation, across nations and over time, in the cleavages that form over the trade issue. This variation corresponds in anticipated fashion with temporal and spatial variation in levels of interindustry factor mobility. In the United States and Britain, for instance, class conflict over trade appears to have peaked late in the nineteenth century, when major parties and peak associations were internally unified on the trade issue, pitting urban against rural coalitions. Since then, industry-based cleavages have grown in importance and lobbying by industry-based groups has increased markedly. Change has been less pronounced in France and Canada, by contrast, where the trade issue has rarely been the focus of broad-based class conflict and group lobbying has been more influential in shaping policy throughout most of the last two centuries. In Sweden and Australia, trade politics was rapidly transformed by sharp class cleavages early in the twentieth century, and these broad coalitions proved quite durable as parties and peak associations held fast to coherent positions on the trade issue at least until the 1980s. In Sweden, urban classes that favored trade openness dominated politics and shaped trade policy from the 1930s onward; in Australia, urban classes favored protectionism and held firm control of the direction of policy after 1919.

As an alternative way of testing the argument, in part 3 of this book I focus on trade policy making in the U.S. Congress since the 1820s. I present an analysis of congressional voting on 30 major pieces of trade legislation between 1824 and 1994. Using data on the importance of different factor classes and different industry groups in separate electoral districts, the statistical analysis tests for signs of change in coalition patterns (and the relative utility of class and group-based models) over time. The results indicate that voting decisions by members of Congress more clearly reflect class cleavages when levels of factor mobility are relatively high, but are more consistent with a group model when levels of mobility are relatively low.

1.4 THE ORGANIZATION OF THE BOOK

The following chapter discusses alternative measures of interindustry factor mobility, and presents detailed evidence on interindustry variation in wages and profits in the six selected economies over the last two centuries. Chapter 3 discusses ways to measure cleavages in trade politics, focusing on the major organizational channels through which political coalitions operate: political parties, peak associations, and industry groups.

Part 2 provides the historical core of the book. Chapters 4 through 9 survey evidence on trade cleavages and coalitions in each nation during different historical eras. I have arranged this analysis chronologically for each nation, rather than separating it into discussions of each historical period. Unlike other studies of similar scope that are structured by era,[17] the goal here is not to evaluate how each nation responded to common historical-economic shocks. The evidence indicates that levels of factor mobility actually vary considerably from nation to nation in each period. Although there are some common trends associated with the effects of industrialization, the timing of these shifts is not uniform across nations. Telling the story separately for each nation has the added benefit of preserving the flow of the historical narrative. Chapter 10 summarizes the findings from the case studies and shifts the focus from historical change within the nations to cross-national comparisons.

Part 3 focuses on quantitative evidence of cleavages and coalition patterns in the U.S. Congress. Chapter 11 describes trends over time in partisan positions on trade in congressional voting and examines trends in the lobbying activity of industry groups in hearings held by congressional committees. Chapter 12 presents the statistical analysis of congressional voting on major pieces of trade legislation. Chapter 13 concludes by discussing implications of the findings for the study of trade politics and the analysis of trade policy, and for the field of political economy more generally. I also consider qualifications and alternative hypotheses. At the end I suggest several possible avenues for future research.

---

[17] For examples, see Gourevitch 1986, and Rogowski 1989.

CHAPTER TWO

Historical Patterns in Mobility: Evidence from Six Nations

To test the plausibility of the argument, advanced in chapter 1, about the effects of variation in interindustry factor mobility on cleavages in trade politics, we need to establish some reliable indicator of mobility levels. Drawing heavily from previous studies of labor and capital market integration, in this chapter I discuss alternative methods for measuring interindustry factor mobility. For the basic indicators of factor mobility, I rely primarily on measures of interindustry variation in wage and profit rates using data on the major manufacturing industries in each economy that is available for extended periods of time over the last two centuries. The guiding assumption is that when factors are highly mobile, rate-of-return differentials between industries should be arbitraged away. The results are compared, wherever possible, with alternative indicators of interindustry mobility (such as labor turnover, job tenure, and firm spending on research and development) using data that is available for recent periods.

2.1 MEASURING LEVELS OF FACTOR MOBILITY

To date, no evidence on interindustry factor mobility has been compiled in systematic fashion for extended historical periods or for cross-national comparisons. The most direct measures of interindustry labor mobility have been provided in research on labor-market efficiency that examines interindustry wage differentials (e.g., Krueger and Summers 1988) and rates of labor turnover among workers in manufacturing industries (e.g., Ragan 1984). Indicators of interindustry capital mobility have been drawn from analysis of stock market returns (Grossman and Levinsohn 1989) and from prices in secondary markets for capital equipment (Ramey and Shapiro 1998). Indirect indicators of both labor and capital mobility have relied on revealed preferences of industry groups and voters in politics.[1] With the exception of some longitudinal work on labor turnover indicating a downward trend in mobility since the 1920s among U.S. manufacturing workers,

---

[1] The most frequently cited example is Magee's (1980) study of testimony by labor unions and management groups before the U.S. House Ways and Means Committee on the Trade Act of 1974. Irwin (1995) has examined county voting patterns in the British general election of 1923.

these studies have all aimed at examining characteristics of factor markets at a particular point in time—typically, at some point in the 1970s or 1980s. These studies all suggest significant factor specificity and sizeable industry "rents" in the U.S. manufacturing sector in recent years, but do not have a historical (or comparative) standard of reference with which to compare these findings.

By contrast, a great deal of empirical work has been done on the inter-*regional* mobility of labor and capital—especially in the U.S. economy— aimed explicitly at uncovering historical trends, with much of the attention focused on the geographic integration of the markets for labor and capital during the nineteenth century. A range of studies have indicated, for example, that the mobility of labor and capital across geographic locations increased in both the antebellum and postbellum periods in the United States, in line with improvements in transportation and communication.[2] Related work on the U.S. economy has examined the intersectoral mobility of labor between rural employment and manufacturing jobs in the nineteenth century (Lebergott 1964; Williamson and Lindert 1980).

Although levels of geographic factor mobility may well have a bearing on levels of interindustry factor mobility, since industries tend to be concentrated in different geographic locations, the two dimensions of factor market integration are very separate. Interindustry mobility is related not just to the costs of moving factors and information across geographic space but to the costs of moving them across product space. These costs are shaped by an array of variables that affect the specificity of human and physical assets to use in particular industries. Indeed, when historical accounts of industrialization touch generally on the issue of factor mobility, they suggest that it is profoundly affected not only by improvements in systems of transportation and communication but by technological changes in the methods of production that affect the value of specific skills and capital and by changes in regulations that impose costs on interindustry factor movement.

To compare levels of factor mobility in different periods and locations, I have relied principally on measurements of the difference between rates of return for factors employed in different industries; specifically, on the coefficient of variation for wage or profit rates across manufacturing industries. Interindustry factor mobility refers to the ability or propensity of owners of productive inputs to move them between different industries. This is best represented formally as the elasticity of substitution along the transformation curve that maps the conversion of a factor located in one industry for use in another industry at increasing opportunity costs.[3] This elasticity is not

---

[2] On the integration of regional labor markets in the antebellum period, see Lebergott 1964 and Margo and Villaflor 1987. On labor markets in the late nineteenth century, see Coelho and Shepherd 1976, Rosenbloom 1990, and Sundstrom and Rosenbloom 1993. On the integration of regional markets for financial capital, see Davis 1965, James 1976, and Odell 1989.

[3] See appendix A for the formal treatment of interindustry mobility, in a fully specified

directly observable. But when mobility is high, movement between industries (or even just the potential for it) should equalize returns to similar types of workers and capital across industries. This is simply an application of the "law of one price": If a factor is highly mobile, return differentials should be arbitraged away. Smaller differentials in wages and profits across industries are thus indicators of higher levels of mobility. The magnitude of the differentials will reflect the costs of moving factors between industries, costs that are influenced by a range of economic and political variables, including the firm and industry specificity of human and physical capital, factor-market regulations that affect firm entry and exit and hiring and firing, policies that assist relocation and retraining, the geographic dispersion of industries, and the costs of transportation and communication.

Different versions of this type of measure have been used previously in a wide range of studies of labor and capital mobility. Recent research on labor-market efficiency in the United States and elsewhere has examined interindustry wage differentials for evidence of industry rents that are not competed away in equilibrium.[4] Almost all of the major empirical work on the geographic integration of the U.S. labor and financial markets, meanwhile, has focused on interregional differences in wages and interest rates.[5] Research on the international mobility of financial capital has studied differences in returns earned by similar types of assets held in different national markets (see Frankel 1991).

There are, however, several reasons for exercising caution in using wage and profit differentials as measures of factor mobility. On a fundamental level, variation in wages and profits across industries might persist in equilibrium even at very high levels of mobility if economic actors have objectives other than maximizing real income (Rosenbloom 1989, 169). Differences in working conditions across industries, for instance, and in the locational attributes of industries that are concentrated in different regions or cities (for example, in climate, overcrowding, or sanitation) may lead to persistent variation in returns across industries in equilibrium. Return differentials may also reflect other features of factor markets besides underlying mobility levels, including regulations on wages and profits, and collective wage bargaining arrangements. In addition, measured differentials may be affected by short-run shocks to demand in particular industries, differences in the skill levels of workers whose wages are compared, and differences in the riskiness associated with employment and investment in each industry.

---

general equilibrium model of the economy. Similar formal specifications are applied by Jones 1971 and Hill and Mendez 1983.

    [4] See Krueger and Summers 1987, 1988, Katz and Summers 1989, Dickens and Katz 1987, and Gibbons and Katz 1992. A comparative study of wage differentials in the United States and in Sweden is provided by Edin and Zetterberg 1992. Older studies of interindustry wage differences are provided by Slichter 1950 and Glasser 1940.

    [5] See, for instance, Lebergott 1964, Coelho and Shepherd 1976, Rosenbloom 1990, Davis 1965, James 1976, and Odell 1989.

These problems, the most important of which I address in more detail later, do require that any inferences based on return differentials be made with great care and caution.[6]

Where possible, I have compared results based on these measures with other indicators of factor mobility, such as the rate of turnover in labor markets and spending by firms on research and development and worker training. These alternative indicators are less theoretically sound, however, and are limited in terms of the time period for which data are available. Measures of factor movement, such as labor turnover or rates of firm entry and exit, do not provide a reliable guide to interindustry factor mobility. The problem is that such measures cannot be interpreted without controls for the incentives for economic agents to move (which requires assessing return differentials). Factor owners may find movement between industries relatively inexpensive, but have little incentive to actually move if return differentials are low.[7] In such cases, evidence of low levels of factor movement is unreliable as an indicator of levels of factor mobility. Other indicators of asset specificity, such as amounts invested by firms in the generation of new physical and human capital via spending on research and development and training programs, address one important component of the costs of moving factors between industries but ignore others. Data on these variables is available for recent periods only.

Throughout, I am concerned with general measures of interindustry factor mobility in the manufacturing sector of each economy, rather than with measures of the particular ease with which factors can move into or out of individual industries. Some previous work has addressed the latter issue, using data on individual industries and firms and the specificity of their assets, judged typically by reference to levels of research and development spending, worker training, and industry concentration ratios (Alt et al. 1999; Frieden 1991).[8] Such measures are quite problematic, since it seems difficult to judge barriers to entry and exit in one industry in isolation from barriers to entry and exit in other industries from which and to which economic agents might move. In any case, my focus here is on gauging general levels of interindustry mobility across the manufacturing sector in each economy and how such levels change over time.

A limitation of the study is that it is very constrained in terms of what it can say about the mobility of owners of land and natural resources. Data on farm incomes are rare for the historical periods covered here, and the analysis must therefore be concentrated on the evidence available on wages and profits in manufacturing.

---

[6] On the related problems associated with interpreting regional wage differentials, see Rosenbloom 1990, 88.

[7] In the highly integrated international bond markets, for instance, returns on securities are equalized with minimal trading activity; see Frankel 1991.

[8] Both studies relate these measures of specificity to the energy with which industries or firms lobby for policy-induced rents.

2.2 INDUSTRY WAGES AND PROFITS

Overall, the evidence suggests that interindustry factor mobility has been affected powerfully by economic and technological changes associated with industrialization. Yet the impact and timing of those changes have varied substantially across nations. Figure 2.1 reports available data on interindustry variation in wage and profit rates for each nation.

For the first half of the nineteenth century, the only extensive data available is on wages and aggregated earnings for workers across major manufacturing industries and wage rates for different categories of skilled labor (artisans or tradesmen)—including carpenters, spinners, weavers, masons, smiths, and machinists—associated with different sets of industries (see appendix B for a comprehensive discussion of the available data and sources). In later years, we have data on wages for separate categories of skilled and unskilled workers in major manufacturing industries (at the two-digit level of the standard industrial classifications [SIC]) from which to calculate coefficients of variation.[9] Data on rates of return to capital in different industries are harder to come by for early periods than are data on wages. Prior to 1914, for example, there is very little direct data on firm revenues in the United States (Epstein and Gordon 1939, 122), and reliable data on corporation profits (as percentages of net worth and equity) are only available from the U.S. Securities and Exchange Commission from 1933, categorized according to their main activities into industry groups. Following Bateman and Weiss (1981), we can do somewhat better by using alternative data to estimate profits in different industries, calculated as value added minus wage costs as a percent of capital invested (or per man-hour or employee). Data for these calculations are available in some cases for part of the nineteenth century and in most cases from the 1940s.[10] For both wages and profit data,

---

[9] Only very basic controls can be applied to account for heterogeneity in labor skill levels across industries. A concern is that the results may reflect not so much changes in underlying factor mobility but changes in skill mixes or working conditions across industries. There is strong evidence, however, that controlling for skill variables in econometric wage equations (estimated using survey data available for recent decades) is not important for estimating the relative size of differentials over time. Comparing data on U.S. workers from the 1970s and 1980s, Krueger and Summers (1987) show that controlling for finely described skill differences at the individual level reduces the size of the estimated industry rents across-the-board, as one would expect, but does little to alter the relative size of measured differentials at different times. Hiscox (2002) replicates their technique, comparing the size of industry differentials in 1968 and 1992 using data on U.S. workers from the *Current Population Survey*. The results indicate a clear upward trend in industry rents over that period even when extensive controls are applied for skill, education, occupation, and other differences among workers.

[10] Again, some caution is warranted here since there are no controls for cross-industry differences in risk. Changes in profit dispersion might be reflecting changes in the relative riskiness of investment in different industries. However, I have found similar results using measures of profits disaggregated to the four-digit SIC level and estimating profit equations to

the industry definitions applied are the standard two-digit industry classifications employed by the United Nations or national reporting agencies, or the closest approximates to those classifications in earlier periods.

The temporal trends in the data are immediately apparent in all six economies. Recall that lower coefficients of variation indicate higher levels of interindustry mobility. Consider first the changes in the coefficients during the nineteenth century. In the first half of the century, wage differentials appear to be generally high (relative to those in later years) but falling. Although the data on profits are more scarce, a similar pattern is described by interindustry variation in profit rates. The trends indicate a general and steady rise in levels of interindustry factor mobility throughout most of the nineteenth century.

Just as interesting are the cross-national differences in this period. Much higher levels of both labor and capital mobility (that is, lower coefficients of variation) are evident in Britain, where industrialization proceeded most rapidly, than in France, where a heavier legacy of industrial regulation remained. In the early nineteenth century, wage differentials were much higher in the United States than in Britain, but fell much more dramatically over time. In the smaller nations of Sweden, Canada, and Australia, which lagged behind the others in industrialization, interindustry return differentials still remained relatively high in the 1860s, and changes are only clearly apparent late in the century.

By the turn of the century, interindustry wage and profit differentials had fallen to historically low levels for all six nations. Differentials reached the lowest levels in the United States and Britain, which were leading the other nations in industrial development, and wage variation was still twice as high in France as in Britain at century's end. Changes were most apparent around this time in Sweden and Australia, which actually had the lowest levels of wage variation in the sample by 1914. Higher differentials persisted in Canada, where factor markets were separated, notoriously, into distinct regional economies (although the data are scarce).

By about the 1920s, evidence indicates that the general long-term decline in interindustry wage and profit differentials had come to a halt. Wage and profit differentials had even begun to rise in some nations—most clearly, in the United States—although there was considerable turmoil in factor markets during the depression years. By the 1950s and 1960s, however, the turnaround in historical trends was more apparent; the data show that industry rents were clearly rising in all six economies.

Again, there are some marked cross-national differences. A particularly sharp rise in wage and profit differentials occurred in the United States and Britain after the 1940s. In Sweden and Australia, by contrast, the evidence indicates a much slower rise in interindustry wage and profit variation from

---

measure variation between the two-digit industries while controlling for risk (measured by variability in returns over time). See Hiscox 2002.

The United States

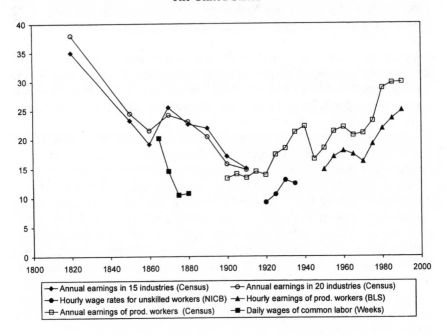

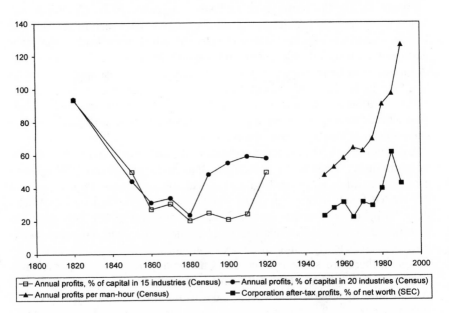

FIGURE 2.1 Interindustry variation in wages and profits (coefficient of variation)

Britain

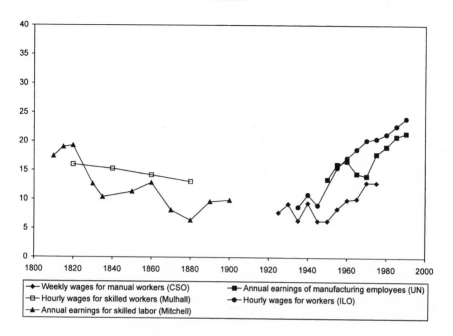

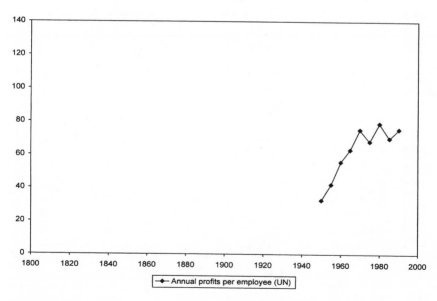

FIGURE 2.1 *Continued*

France

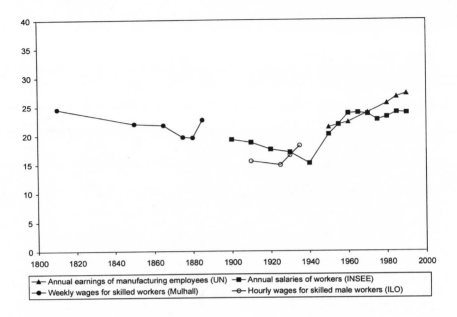

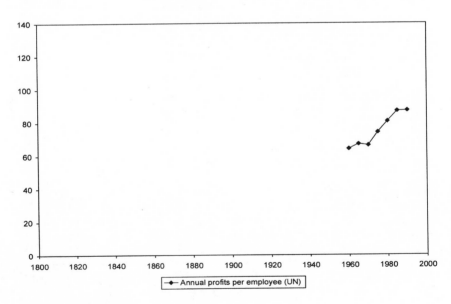

FIGURE 2.1 *Continued*

Sweden

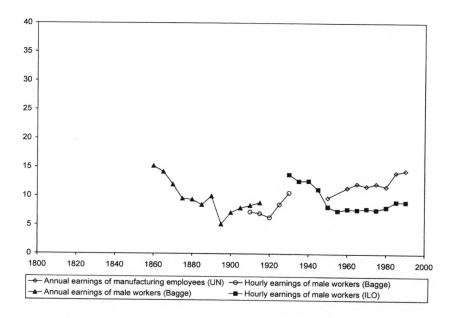

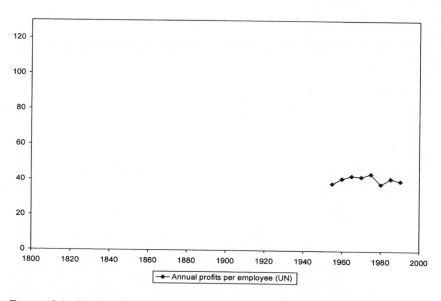

FIGURE 2.1 *Continued*

Canada

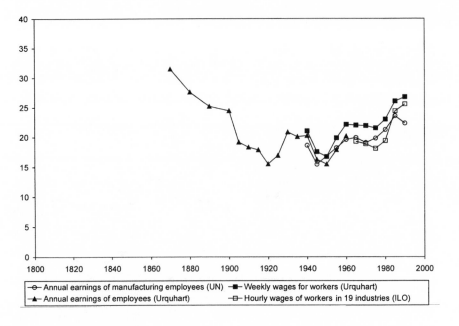

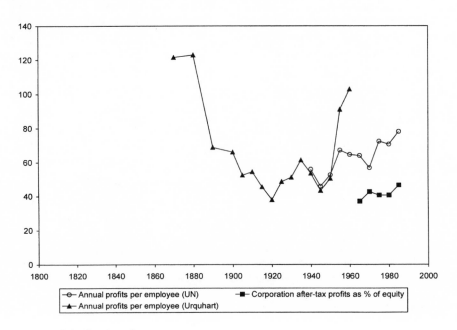

FIGURE 2.1 *Continued*

Australia

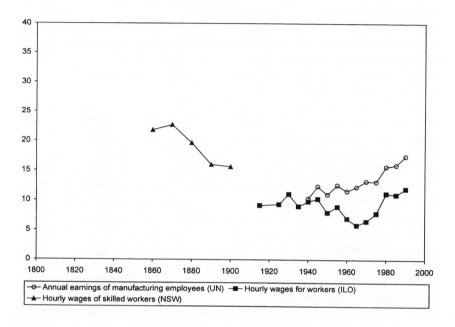

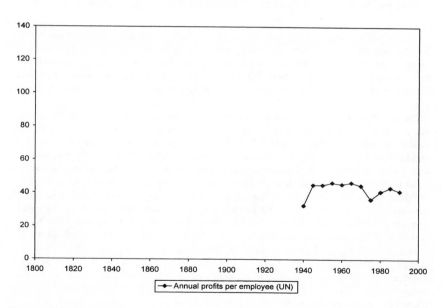

FIGURE 2.1 *Continued*

the very low levels measured early in the century. The lowest levels of wage variation in the postwar period are found in Sweden.[11] These no doubt reflect the solidarity wage policy that was the heart of the Rehn-Meidner approach to centralized wage negotiations during most of this period as well as Sweden's extensive adjustment assistance program (see Lundberg 1985).[12] The distinction, however, is not crucial for making predictions about preferences over trade policy.[13]

It is worth noting that the general correspondence between patterns in interindustry wage and profit differentials is broadly consistent with efficiency wage theories and rent sharing between capital and labor (Katz and Summers 1989), and it suggests, as I argue later, that factor markets have been shaped in broad ways by exogenous changes in methods of production. While the discovery of the long-term trends in these differentials is new, the evidence of sizeable differences in wages across industries in these economies during recent years appears quite consistent with recent work by labor economists. Using survey data on U.S. workers, for example, a variety of studies have revealed substantial, persistent dispersion in wages across manufacturing industries in the last two decades, even when controlling for a wide range of human capital variables and job characteristics (Dickens and Katz 1987; Krueger and Summers 1987, 1988; Katz and Summers 1989). Other studies also indicate substantial variation in returns to capital that suggests high levels of capital specificity or immobility across industries in recent years. Katz and Summers document substantial industry rents using

[11] Edin and Zetterberg (1992) use survey data to draw a similarly sharp contrast between Sweden and the United States, concluding that wage differentials were roughly three times larger in the United States than in Sweden in the 1980s. They find percentage standard deviations of 24.0 and 8.3 for the United States and Sweden, respectively. Introducing a multitude of skill-level controls using the survey data simply reduces these figures to 14.6 and 4.7 percent.

[12] One aim of wage compression was that inefficient firms and industries would be unable to survive by paying low wages appropriate to their low levels of productivity and profits, and active adjustment assistance would aid the flow of factors to more efficient uses (see Hibbs and Locking 1996). Mobility was made a major goal of policy; extensive retraining programs and a wide assortment of mobility subsidies were developed by Swedish policymakers in order to induce workers (and firms) to move into expanding sectors. See Lindbeck 1974.

[13] Factor mobility is important to the coalition story precisely because it plays a key role in determining the generation of industry rents, and rate-of-return differentials are the clearest measure of whether such rents actually exist. The bottom line is that, for most of the postwar period, as Rivlin points out, Swedish workers in high-wage industries like steel did not face reductions in living standards comparable to those faced by steel workers in the United States if they were laid off since the wages of U.S. steelworkers were much higher compared to average U.S. wages than were the Swedish steelworkers' wages compared to average Swedish wages (Rivlin 1987, 13–14). It is worth noting that centralized wage bargaining that compresses the wage structure in an economy is unlikely to be politically sustainable if labor is actually immobile between sectors and so there are significant rents being passed up by workers with skills specific to growing industries. In fact, the breakdown of the Swedish bargaining arrangement came in 1983 when unions in the high-wage engineering and metals industries broke ranks to bargain separately with employers (see Hibbs and Locking 1996).

data on U.S. corporation profits in the 1980s, and Grossman and Levinsohn (1989) reach a similar conclusion based on a study of stock market returns in several U.S. industries during the 1970s and 1980s and how they responded to unanticipated shocks in import prices. Interestingly, the larger set of data I have examined indicates that the size of these types of rents appears to have varied substantially over time (trending downward during earlier stages of industrialization and upward more recently) and across nations in different historical periods.

2.3 Alternative Indicators of Interindustry Factor Mobility

The findings drawn from the study of wage differentials are strongly supported, at least in the twentieth century, by the available data on labor turnover. It was the postwar decline in turnover among U.S. manufacturing workers, in fact, that prompted early concern among economists about a "new industrial feudalism" in the 1950s. The issue was raised by Ross (1958) and dismissed as a temporary development. However, Ragan's (1984) analysis of the quit rate in manufacturing industries (the number of quits, or voluntary separations, per 100 employees) revealed a persistent downward trend between 1957 and 1979. Extending the analysis using all the available data on quits for the period 1919 to 1981 confirms that result, as shown in Table 2.1. The results indicate a significant downward time trend in the quit rate. When we control for business-cycle effects, as in column 1, the time trend is negative and significant at the .001 level. When we also control for demographic changes in the work force (female workers are more likely to quit than males, and younger workers are more likely to quit than older ones), the magnitude of the estimated time trend increases, as shown by the results in column 2.

Conducting a similar analysis for the other nations is difficult because most official statistics do not report quits separately from layoffs. Holmlund (1984) has examined quits reported for workers in Swedish manufacturing industries and suggested that labor mobility has also fallen in Sweden, albeit at a much slower rate than in the United States. I have used his data for the period 1916 to 1982 to replicate the statistical analysis performed above for the United States. The results, shown in Table 2.2, indicate that there is indeed a downward time trend in the Swedish quit rate, although it is smaller than the effect estimated using similar data on U.S. manufacturing industries. Moreover, if we control for differences in unemployment rates during the period for which data are available for both nations (1919–1981), the average rate of quits in Sweden is almost twice as high as the rate for U.S. manufacturing workers.

Evidence of a general long-term increase in the job tenure among manufacturing workers in the U.S. economy is consistent with these findings. Studies indicate that the length of time workers stay in jobs with particular

TABLE 2.1
Regression Results for U.S. Quit Rate, 1919–1981*

Independent Variables	1	2
Constant	2.30	−1.18
	(7.87)	(−1.90)
% Unemployment	−0.26	−0.39
	(−6.24)	(−9.67)
% Female employees		0.14
		(1.41)
% Employees aged 16–24 years		0.21
		(3.23)
Time	−0.06	−0.08
	(−3.25)	(−2.25)
N	63	42
Adjusted R^2	0.40	0.82
SER	0.92	0.34
ρ	0.64	0.58

Sources: Data on quits, unemployment, and the gender and age components of the labor force, are from Department of Commerce, *Historical Statistics*, and Department of Labor, *Employment and Earnings*. Gender and age data are available from 1940.

*Estimated coefficients and *t* statistics in parentheses. Both equations were adjusted for first-order autocorrelation. Time = 1 for the first observation.

firms has risen significantly since the 1890s (Carter and Savocca 1990; Jacoby and Sharna 1992). The proportion of workers holding jobs for over twenty years almost tripled between the 1890s and the 1970s. Survey data on job tenure reveal that the number of years spent on the same job by the average worker, in all age groups, rose substantially between 1950 and 1990. Workers aged fifty-five to sixty-four were in their jobs an average of 16 years in 1991 compared with 9.5 years in 1951; those aged forty-five to fifty-four had been in their jobs an average of 12.2 years in 1991, up from 7.9 years in 1951; and for those in the thirty-five to forty-four age bracket, average tenure rose to 7.9 years in 1991 from 4.3 years in 1951.[14]

As far as the interindustry mobility of capital is concerned, the findings from the examination of profit differentials in the previous section are also consistent with alternative types of evidence. Research and development spending by manufacturing firms is a popular indicator of asset specificity

[14] Data are from the Employee Benefit Research Institute; see *The Economist*, January 28, 1995. Note that research on wage differentials has shown that the relationship between industry wage premiums and job tenure is positive and significant, strongly supporting the notion that workers in high-wage industries do receive economic rents. See Krueger and Summers 1988, Pencavel 1970, and Freeman 1980.

TABLE 2.2
Regression Results for Swedish Quit Rate, 1916–1982*

Independent Variables	
Constant	3.88
	(8.01)
% Unemployment	−0.31
	(−6.85)
Time	−0.04
	(−3.01)
N	67
Adjusted R^2	0.48
SER	0.88
ρ	0.60

Source: Holmlund 1984.
*Estimated coefficients and t statistics in parentheses. Both equations were adjusted for first-order autocorrelation. Time = 1 for the first observation.

among analysts of industrial organization since it captures the emphasis placed by firms on developing their own production technologies and products (Acs and Isberg 1991). Owners of more specialized capital, by definition, find it more difficult to adapt their equipment to alternative production and find it more costly to sell their equipment following a decline in the fortunes of the industry to which it is tied. Figure 2.2 charts the available data on research and development spending by U.S. manufacturing companies (as a percentage of sales) between 1950 and 1990.[15] Spending on research and development rose from approximately 0.5 percent in 1950 to more than 3 percent in 1990.

The more specialized the physical characteristics of capital equipment, the less value it will hold for manufacturers in other industries when it is sold to them. Ramey and Shapiro (1998) have examined this issue very directly using data available for recent years from aerospace industry auctions. They track the flow of used capital across industries and the discounts at which that capital sells. Their results suggest that capital is indeed very specialized by industry in recent years in U.S. manufacturing and that reallocating capital across sectors entails high costs for owners. In particular, they find that capital flowing out of the aerospace sector in the 1990s sold for only one-third of its estimated replacement costs.

Comparative studies of evidence on interindustry capital mobility are more rare. Lawrence and Bosworth (1987), however, have measured rates of

[15] The data are from the Department of Commerce, *Historical Statistics of the United States* and *Statistical Abstract of the United States*, various years.

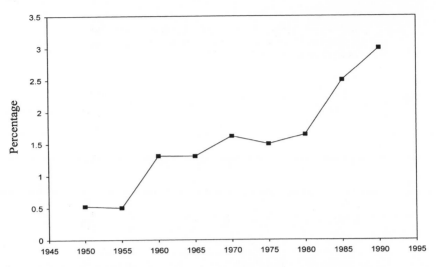

FIGURE 2.2 Company research and development spending in the United States as a percentage of sales

structural adjustment to economic shocks in several nations in the 1970s and 1980s by examining changes in industry shares of output and employment. They were particularly concerned with testing the notion that the Swedish economy might have had trouble adjusting to economic shocks due to wage solidarity and generous welfare policies, which, some critics argued, may have reduced incentives for the efficient reallocation of resources. On the contrary, the study by Lawrence and Bosworth found that the pace of resource allocation in recent decades was much more rapid in Sweden than in the United States, Germany, and Japan.

Two more general and closely linked developments also fit with the observed increase in interindustry profit differentials in recent years. The first is the impressive deepening of equity markets in the last century, which has made it far easier to trade ownership of capital assets in different industries. The second is the apparent trend toward portfolio diversification among owners of equities; the rise of the professional fund management industry and mutual funds is perhaps the clearest signal of this change. That the first development should be related to increasing capital specificity is suggested by Williamson's (1985) analysis. When capital is less mobile between uses, we should expect greater reliance on equity financing rather than borrowing, since lenders are more reluctant to invest in more specific assets and charge premiums for the added risks. Regarding the second development, as Mussa (1974) pointed out, when capital is less mobile—so that returns in different industries are more varied—investors have a greater incentive to diversify their portfolios.

2.4 Explaining Variation in Factor Mobility

The general correspondence between changes in interindustry wage and profit differentials over time in each of the six economies is consistent with the notion that broad, exogenous technological and regulatory changes have powerfully shaped factor markets. The patterns that emerge in the evidence appear to make considerable sense in the light of regulatory changes that occurred in various nations and the technological transformations associated with different stages of industrialization. Economic historians, for instance, have frequently discussed the lifting of legal restrictions on factor movement that was a common, though by no means uniform, concomitant of early industrialization in Europe, and they widely cite England's head start in deregulation—traceable as far back as the Statute of Artificers in 1563 (see Landes 1969, 62; North and Thomas 1973; and Olson 1982). The legal restrictions on business and labor that supported the old guild system had largely vanished in England by the beginning of the eighteenth century, and were abolished entirely in 1814, but they lived on well into the nineteenth century in France and were only fully removed in Sweden in 1864 (Landes 1969, 62, 131; Rustow 1955, 15).[16]

Historical accounts of Western economic development have emphasized a range of technological changes that combined to make these economies more fluid during the early stages of industrialization in the nineteenth century (Sokoloff and Villaflor 1992). Major innovations in systems of water, rail, and road transportation drastically lowered the costs of factor movement and diminished the importance of geography to economy (see Taylor 1949; Davis, Hughes, and McDougall 1961, 276–96; and North 1965). Again, England led the pack with its efficient canal system and turnpike roads and the first railway mania (Pratt 1912; Clapham 1927, 94).[17] Change was more gradual elsewhere. In France, railway construction only accelerated in the 1850s when new lines connected Lille to Bordeaux and Le Havre to Strasbourg. In the sprawling United States, inland freight rates began to fall along roads and rivers beginning in the 1820s, along canals beginning in the 1830s, and along the new railroads from the 1850s (North 1965).[18] In Sweden, Canada, and Australia, rapid extension of railroads took place much later in the century.[19] Table 2.3 indicates the pace of railroad expansion in each of the six nations.

---

[16] While the *Loi Le Chapelier* officially abolished guilds in France in 1791, business associations were immediately exempted from its provisions, and it had little effect on the activities of craft and labor associations. See Lorwin 1954.

[17] Parliament passed 37 railway acts in 1843, 248 in 1844, and over 700 in 1845.

[18] The first transcontinental line began operation in 1869.

[19] In Sweden, provinces were still quite isolated from one another as late as the 1860s yet, by 1890, a national rail network was in place (Heckscher 1954, 213). In Canada, a transcontinental network was not established until the 1880s with the completion of the Intercolonial Railway, linking the Maritimes with the central provinces, and the Canadian Pacific Railway.

Table 2.3
Length of Rail Line in Operation (in Miles)

Year	United States	Britain	France	Sweden	Canada	Australia
1830	23	94	19			
1840	2,818	1,434	246		15	
1850	9,021	5,878	1,749		64	
1860	30,626	8,762	5,500	316	1,994	
1870	52,922	12,935	9,326	1,036	2,572	917
1885	128,363	16,032	17,903	4,134	9,919	6,163
1895	174,443	17,392	21,744	5,854	15,427	11,202
1905	210,600	18,874	23,764	7,588	19,782	14,285
1915	245,060	19,574	21,840	8,737	33,682	21,498

Sources: Mitchell 1980 and 1984.

The general effect was that production became less concentrated by region and more subject to integrated commodity and input markets (O'Brien 1983; Rosenbloom 1990). In particular, land owners could put farms to a wider range of alternative uses as distance from markets became less important (Rogowski 1989, 19). Although we have no detailed data on farm incomes with which to measure the flexibility of agricultural producers, it seems likely that they were affected profoundly. Production of meat and perishable farm goods, for example, could be extended to areas much farther from urban markets after the arrival of the railway; innovations in refrigerated transportation reinforced this trend. General improvements in irrigation and artificial fertilizers, most apparent in the late 1800s, also helped to make agricultural production more flexible (Heckscher 1954, 176). Notice, too, that farmers can effectively move between industries not only by switching their land to alternative uses but by moving themselves to take up new land suited to alternative production. In the United States, Canada, and Australia, vast areas of different types of land were being taken over in the late nineteenth century by large numbers of settlers flexible about what they would cultivate.

Technological innovations in methods of production in the nineteenth century also had profound implications for interindustry factor mobility. The very heart of the industrial revolution, of course, was the interrelated succession of technological changes that substituted machine manufacture for handicraft production and revolutionized the manufacture of textiles, iron and steel, and steam power, first in England and then elsewhere (Landes 1969). New mills and factories replaced craft shops and home manufacture, most rapidly in the West Riding of England but also in the industrial centers of continental Europe and North America, and the old skills of the artisan class were rendered increasingly obsolete (Sokoloff and Villaflor 1992, 32–33).[20]

[20] As Marx and Engels dramatically observed in 1848: "All fixed, fast-frozen relations, with their train of ancient and venerable prejudices and opinions, are swept away, all new-formed ones become antiquated before they can ossify" (Tucker 1978, 476).

A second cluster of innovations in the manufacture of electric power, electrical machinery, and internal combustion engines brought assembly-line production and precision manufacturing, and the great shift from nodal to linear-flow manufacturing that swept through industry in the last two decades of the nineteenth century (Landes 1969, 305–7; Sawyer 1954). Much of the new technology provided new ways to pipe, pump, lift, convey, shape, press, heat, and measure raw materials and was readily adaptable to use in alternative industries (Landes 1969, 293–94). Meanwhile, the introduction of labor-saving technology on a massive scale and the advent of the production line created a vast demand for unskilled workers and increased the ease with which industrial workers could shift between manufacturing industries (Sokoloff 1986; Goldin 1990, 115).[21]

Later stages of industrialization had a very different impact on levels of factor mobility in the twentieth century. The apparent decline in interindustry mobility in these economies beginning around the 1920s (the timing varies by nation) was most likely due to the growing complementarity between labor skills and technology.[22] Whereas the key technological advances of the nineteenth century had substituted new physical capital, raw materials, and unskilled labor for skilled workers, later advances began to demand specialized forms of human capital to go with the new forms of physical capital (Cain and Patterson 1986; James and Skinner 1985; Sokoloff 1984). Goldin and Katz (1996) argue that the key change in U.S. industry took place in the 1910s and 1920s and involved moving from assembly-line to continuous-process technology—the latter requiring more skilled workers in the management and operation of highly complex tasks. In particular, dramatic technological advances in the fields of microelectronics, robotics, telecommunications, chemical engineering, and microbiology made specialized human and physical capital vastly more important in almost all areas of industrial production. Growth in the demand for human capital, or knowledge and skills, has been concomitant with continued technological improvements since that time (see Goldin and Katz 1996 and Mincer 1984).[23]

Studies have revealed a clear inverse relationship between investments in industry and firm-specific human capital and labor mobility (Bloch 1979;

[21] Goldin argues that, by the turn of the century, the market for labor in the U.S. manufacturing sector was essentially a spot market with most jobs easily handled by the average worker (1990, 115). Gordon, Edwards, and Reich make a similar point, arguing that a single class of "semi-skilled factory operatives" came to share very similar jobs across the manufacturing sector (1982, 112–28). This period witnessed the birth of "scientific management," aimed at standardizing tasks and minimizing worker autonomy. See Aitken 1960.

[22] See Griliches 1969, Hammermesh 1993, Bartel and Lichtenberg 1987, and Fallon and Layard 1975.

[23] One crude indicator of the trend is the ratio of "professional and technical" employees to "production workers and laborers" in manufacturing, as measured by the International Labour Organization. Between 1960 and 1990, that ratio rose from 0.30 to 0.64 in the United States, from 0.31 to 1.19 in Sweden, from 0.30 to 0.69 in Canada, and from 0.22 to 0.31 in Australia; see International Labor Office, *Yearbook of Labor Statistics*, various years.

Parsons 1972; Ragan 1984). Since the cost of quitting has increased for employers with greater emphasis on worker training, the rational response for firms has been to encourage longer tenure among employees. The general expansion in the use of fringe benefits tied to seniority and its negative impact on mobility have been well documented (Oi 1962; Block 1978; Mitchell 1982). Viewed in this light, the recent downward trend in interindustry worker mobility and the upward trend in wage differentials make considerable sense.[24]

Concurrent with the growing emphasis on specialized human capital in these economies since the turn of the century has been the increasing importance placed on specialized physical capital and knowledge. There has been a general and substantial rise in the importance placed by firms on private research and development spending aimed at creating new products and production processes. Caves and Porter (1979) have argued that barriers to exit and entry rose in the twentieth century because of the growing importance of specialized equipment in manufacturing and as a function of higher start-up costs and increased investments in physical capital associated with the general growth in the scale of production.[25] The available evidence does indicate a dramatic rise in average plant output in the economies under study in recent decades.[26] Data on the total value of equipment and structures per establishment owned by U.S. manufacturing firms, reported in Figure 2.3, reveal a similar marked change.[27]

Whereas the evidence is not strong that scale economies alone act as powerful barriers to entry (Scherer 1980),[28] there is more evidence that larger capital requirements result in fewer individuals or groups being able to secure the funding needed for entry, or that they can obtain such funding only at interest rates that place them at a cost disadvantage due to unequal access to credit (Hay and Morris 1984; Geroski and Jacquemin 1985). Marcus (1967) has shown that the heavier a firm's weight of fixed invest-

---

[24] Apart from the technological forces at work, several other changes have been identified as having had a negative effect on labor mobility in the postwar era, including the growing number of two-income families, unionization, and the introduction of sick-leave and maternity policies. See Holmlund 1984 and Freeman 1976 and 1980.

[25] The first industry laboratory in the United States was established by General Electric in 1900; by 1931, some 1,600 U.S. companies reported research labs. See Reich 1985, 2 and Galambos 1979.

[26] Between 1960 and 1986, real value-added per establishment in the United States rose from $1.91 to $3.35 million (in 1986 U.S. dollars); in Canada, it grew from $1.13 to $1.9 million; and in Australia from $0.27 to $1.06 million. Data on the number of establishments was unavailable for the other economies over this time period. See United Nations, *Industrial Statistics Yearbook*, various years.

[27] The data are from Department of Commerce, *Statistical Abstract of the United States*, various years.

[28] Scale economies feature prominently in Bain's classic (1956) discussion of barriers to entry, but much debate has centered on whether firms in an industry can credibly deter new entrants to protect monopoly rents.

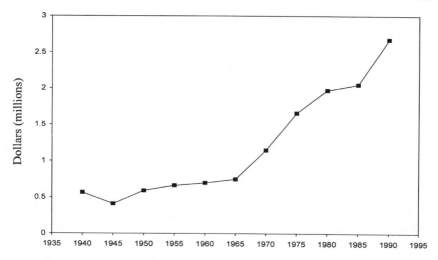

FIGURE 2.3 Value of equipment and structures in U.S. manufacturing industries in constant 1982 dollars

ment, the less likely it is to exit from an industry. Strategic considerations clearly play a role here. Since exit by one firm can increase the profitability of others when scale economies are large, each firm has an incentive to "out wait" the other, even in the face of persistently low returns (Ghemawat and Nalebuff 1990).

Most of these recent trends, it should be noted, were actually identified very clearly by the economists at Sweden's Landsorganisationen in the 1950s and 1960s. The report they prepared for the labor union confederation's sixteenth congress in 1961 expressed grave concerns about growing barriers to structural adjustment in the Swedish economy. They noted explicitly that the increased knowledge required of most trades, and the growing importance of specialized worker training as a result, created greater obstructions to what they called the "functional mobility" of workers between different industries (Johnston 1963, 42). For owners of capital, the report argued that more durable and specialized machinery meant that firms were increasingly equipped for only a small range of tasks, and this made reorganization for other activities far more costly. For these reasons the report strongly advocated expanding policies aimed at increasing the adaptability of workers and firms in the Swedish economy. The report is a remarkable document.

2.5 CONCLUSIONS

The evidence presented in this chapter indicates that levels of interindustry factor mobility have varied substantially both across nations and within each economy over time. The data indicate that the early stages of industrialization in these six economies typically produced a sharp rise in labor and capital mobility (with falling interindustry wage and profit differentials), as major innovations in systems of transportation drastically lowered the costs of factor movement and as a cluster of innovations brought with it assembly-line production and precision manufacturing that increased demand for unskilled workers. However, the data also confirm recent suggestions that a major shift occurred in the first years of the twentieth century when new innovations began to involve far greater complementarity between technology and skills and larger investments in specific assets by owners of capital and labor. Interindustry variation in wage and profit rates, falling throughout most of the nineteenth century, began to climb in all these economies early in the twentieth century with greater reliance on specialized physical and human capital in production. This recent downward trend in interindustry labor and capital mobility in manufacturing is reflected in a variety of alternative indicators, including measures of labor turnover, job tenure, and firm spending on research and development.

In light of this evidence of historical changes and cross-national differences in levels of factor mobility, the question remains whether or not this variation has produced observable changes in cleavages in trade politics that are consistent with expectations. I begin answering that question in the next chapter.

CHAPTER THREE

Coalitions in Trade Politics:
Parties, Peak Associations, and Groups

Evidence indicates that levels of interindustry factor mobility have varied substantially both across nations and over time during the last two centuries in the six economies under study here. According to the argument advanced in chapter 1, the formation of broad factor-owning class coalitions should have been more likely when factor mobility was high, while narrow industry-based coalitions should have been more likely when mobility was low. How exactly would we recognize such differences in coalition patterns? What are their observable implications? These are questions that must be addressed prior to any empirical investigation of cleavages in trade politics, and I focus on them in this chapter.

The term *coalition* implies more than just a set of individuals with shared policy preferences; it implies some form of political activity (such as voting, lobbying, protesting, or threatening to do any of these) that is aimed at influencing policy. In democratic systems the primary organizational channels through which coalitions of individuals influence policy are political parties, peak associations, and lobbying groups. These are the logical places to look for inferences about coalition patterns.

3.1 PARTIES

What can we infer from the behavior of political parties in trade politics? The clearest signals will be broadcast when parties are closely associated with particular factor-owning classes—broad categories of workers, capitalists, or farmers. This has often been the case for the major parties in Western democracies.[1] The British Labour and Australian Labor parties are prime examples of parties tied closely to workers and the trade union movement, as are the French Socialists and Communists. The old Agrarian Party in Sweden, and the Country Party (now National Party) in Australia, are good

---

[1] Indeed, traditional theories of party systems locate the origins of modern parties in the national and industrial revolutions that created sharp divisions between urban and rural interests and between capitalists and workers (see Lipset and Rokkan 1967). Much recent work in comparative political economy, in fact, has revealed a firm link between major parties and distinctive class constituencies in the formulation of economic policy. See Hibbs 1977, Lange and Garrett 1985, Alesina 1989, and Alesina and Rosenthal 1995.

examples of parties with re-election constituencies consisting mainly of rural interests.

In such cases, linking party behavior in trade politics to coalition patterns is a relatively simple matter. We can map the class preferences over trade (derived from the Stolper-Samuelson theorem) onto a model of partisan politics. All else constant, the stronger the class cleavages over trade, the more unified will be the parties representing factor-owning classes on either a protectionist platform (when representing scarce factors) or a free-trade platform (when representing abundant factors). Variation in levels of factor mobility, in such cases, should have clear effects on intraparty unity on the trade issue. At high levels of factor mobility, Stolper-Samuelson effects should ensure that whole factor classes have more unified views on trade and this should favor party unity. At low levels of mobility, however, Ricardo-Viner effects will create divisions between owners of the same factor in export and import-competing industries, dividing party constituencies and party representatives in legislatures—these representatives will have very different calculations of the net utility associated with supporting a policy change depending on which industries assume the greatest importance in their particular electoral districts.[2]

For parties that are not so clearly aligned with particular factor-owning classes and instead have diverse economic constituencies centered around religious, ethnic, or regional groupings, we can make few, if any, inferences about trade coalitions by examining party behavior.[3] There is also the possibility that parties may have core constituencies that include more than one factor-owning class. This will pose a problem if the included classes comprise owners of both abundant and scarce factors engaged in both exporting and import-competing industries. We would then expect that the party would always be divided internally over trade by a class cleavage when levels of mobility are high and by industry cleavages when mobility is low.[4]

The presumption here, it should be noted, is that the trade issue itself, and the cleavages it generates, is not sufficient to transform the existing party system. If trade were the only political issue, we could expect that two parties would always take up unified and opposing platforms; they might reflect class-based coalitions when mobility levels were high or industry-based coalitions when mobility was low. Changes in levels of mobility would simply induce partisan realignment around the new cleavage. Although trade has often been a highly salient partisan issue, it has seldom (if

---

[2] Note that the extent to which the trade issue divides legislative parties under these conditions should be an increasing function of the degree to which production is concentrated geographically.

[3] The Bonapartists and Clericalists in the French Third Republic are good examples, along with the Ministerials in Sweden after the reform of the Riksdag in 1866. The Parti quebecois, in modern Canada is a more familiar example of a regional party.

[4] The best (perhaps only) example is the anti-labor Liberal Party in Australia, formed in 1909 by a merger between the Free Trade Party (representing rural interests) and the Protectionists (representing urban business).

ever) generated new party systems or partisan realignments itself.[5] The working assumption here is that party systems are the exogenous product of deeper-seated urban-rural, Left-Right, church-state, ethnic, or regional cleavages, in combination with electoral institutions.[6]

3.2 PEAK ASSOCIATIONS

We face fewer problems in interpreting evidence about the behavior of encompassing or peak associations. The class affiliations of confederations of labor unions, business associations, and farm organizations are clearly delineated.[7] We can simply map onto these associations the class preferences derived from trade theory. All else constant, we expect such associations to be more unified in support of coherent protectionist (scarce factors) or free-trade (abundant factors) policies the stronger the class cleavages over trade; that is, according to the theory advanced in chapter 1, the more mobile are factors of production. We should expect, for instance, that national federations of labor unions, such as the Trades Union Congress (TUC) in Britain or the AFL-CIO in the United States, will express firmer, more cohesive positions on the trade issue when labor is more mobile between industries: When levels of factor mobility are low, the gap between the preferred trade policies of unions in different industries will be wide, creating internal disagreement.

3.3 GROUPS

Finally, what inferences about coalitions can be made based on the behavior of lobbying groups? Industry-based labor unions and management associations are the logical modern conduits for industry pressures in trade politics, and we should expect that lobbying by such groups will be shaped by industry preferences (as derived in the Ricardo-Viner model).[8] All else constant, the stronger the industry cleavages over trade, the more active will be industry groups in lobbying for protection (in import-competing industries) or for

[5] Again, the Australian case provides one example: national Free Trade and Protectionist parties competed (along with Labor) after federation in 1901. As noted, however, the trade issue was quickly overwhelmed by more rudimentary class issues (taxation, welfare, nationalization, labor regulation) and the two parties joined forces to confront Labor.

[6] For a discussion of the debate about the relationship between cleavage structures and party systems, see Cox 1997, 19–27. Cox argues forcefully that electoral institutions have powerful effects, in interaction with cleavages, in determining party structures.

[7] There is often more than one peak association for each factor-owning class, of course. In France, for instance, the non-communist labor union confederation, the Confédération française démocratique du travail (CFDT) still competes with the older, more radical Confédération générale du travail (CGT).

[8] Industry groups, like parties, are here assumed to exist for exogenous reasons (or to be readily formed ad hoc if factor owners in an industry have an incentive to lobby)—that is, collective action problems are in the "ceteris" considered "paribus."

freer trade (in export industries). At low levels of mobility, Ricardo-Viner effects tie factor returns more closely to the fortunes of each industry, giving labor unions and management associations an incentive to lobby for trade policies that will confer rents by either limiting import-competition or boosting exports. At high levels of mobility, industry rents are eliminated and Stolper-Samuelson effects mean that any benefits to be had from lobbying will be dispersed among all owners of the same factor (that is, they have the nonexcludable quality of a public good).

It might be noted here that this last point exposes a grave bias in Magee's famous "test" of the Stolper-Samuelson theorem. In that test, Magee (1980) assessed whether labor unions and management associations, when lobbying on trade legislation before Congress in 1974, lined up according to factor or industry interests. Yet, if industry groups are active lobbyists in trade policy making, ipso facto it is almost certain that they will be lobbying according to their industry's position. Magee's test improbably requires that industry groups are equally likely to lobby on behalf of their factor class when mobility levels are high as they are to lobby when mobility is low and they can win industry-specific rents. The pattern of group alignments that Magee observed in 1974 should be the same no matter what the underlying levels of factor mobility; it is the general prevalence and intensity of group lobbying efforts that should vary more substantially with levels of factor mobility.

3.4 SUMMARY AND MEASUREMENT ISSUES

Table 3.1 provides a summary of the anticipated effects of variation in levels of mobility and coalition patterns on the behavior of class-affiliated political parties and peak associations and on group lobbying. For simplicity, variability in levels of factor mobility is rather crudely categorized here; in practice, categorizing an economy in absolute terms (as either closer to the Stolper-Samuelson or to the Ricardo-Viner extreme at any particular time) may be very difficult. Relative assessments of mobility levels are much more feasible when considering the changes in an economy over time or, perhaps more problematically given the data limitations, when comparing one economy with another.[9]

We can use these simple relationships to assess whether coalition patterns in trade politics appear to have been shaped by changes in levels of factor mobility. Chapters 4 through 9 present the evidence. To provide for easy comparisons over time, the analysis for each nation is divided into four parts dealing with four reasonably distinct historical periods: 1815–1869, 1870–1914, 1919–1939, and 1945–1994. The available evidence on parties,

---

[9] Note also that, for simplicity, levels of mobility are treated as general to all factors here. We might prefer to distinguish variation in levels of mobility for each separate factor, and so anticipate separate effects for class-based organizations and industry groups representing owners of each factor. But the evidence presented in chapter 2 strongly suggests that broad exogenous forces have shaped levels of mobility among factors in a very general fashion.

TABLE 3.1
Anticipated Effects of Variation in Levels of Factor Mobility

Level of Factor Mobility	Coalitions	Effect on Class-based Parties and Peak Associations	Effect on Industry Groups
Low	Industry coalitions	Internally divided over trade issue and adopt ambiguous policy positions	Lobby actively for protection in import-competing industries and for freer trade in export industries
High	Class coalitions	Internally unified on the trade issue and adopt coherent pro-tectionist (when representing scarce factors) or free-trade (abundant factors) positions	Inactive

peak associations, and industry groups for each of these periods will be considered.

The analysis presents quantitative data on party unity on the trade issue, measured by cohesion indexes calculated using legislative votes cast by party members on major trade bills in each period. I examined the most votes for the U.S. case, where the data are more easily gathered, and those votes are used again later in the book in a more rigorous statistical analysis (see chapter 12). Sweden was the only nation for which I could not examine votes due to the unavailability of historical records of roll call voting. Votes on key trade legislation were examined for each of the other nations under study. These indexes are compared to general levels of party discipline in each case, measured by cohesion scores for all other votes taken in the legislative chamber.[10] The latter is a basic control for exogenously deter-

[10] I use the standard Rice index, which is simply the absolute difference between the percentage of party members voting yea and nay and thus ranges from zero to one hundred. The recommended method for calculating a Rice index for multiple votes, applied here for measuring general levels of cohesion, involves dividing the total number of party members voting in the majority by the total number of votes cast by party members, then converting this to the 0–100 scale (by subtracting 50 and multiplying by 2). This method provides a result that is not sensitive to variations in absenteeism or abstentions across votes (unlike a simple average of indexes calculated for each vote). A limitation of the Rice index is that it may overstate party unity by failing to distinguish partisan from bipartisan votes—what Turner and Schneier (1970) call "hurrah" votes. A popular alternative measure of general cohesion is the percentage of votes that are "party" votes (votes in which a majority of one party votes against a majority of another). This measure has problems of its own, however, since it tends to understate party strength when major parties vote together against minority-sponsored legislation, the cut-off points for defining party votes are arbitrary, and it is useless outside a two-party

mined shifts in party discipline. For the United States, it is a simple matter to calculate these general cohesion scores using the available data on all congressional votes and the party affiliations of members of Congress (Rosenthal and Poole 1991). It is a more difficult task for the other nations, for which the data must be gathered separately. I have followed the approach used by Cox (1987, 23) and calculated cohesion scores based on 10 percent random samples of votes taken in each legislature for the years in question.[11]

As a basic measure of group lobbying activity, I also report data on the number and type of industry groups volunteering testimony to legislative and executive committees deliberating on trade policy. Although it is clear that much group lobbying is conducted in less public fora, the committee data provide a blunt, general indicator of group activity that can be compiled for more than one nation in several historical periods.[12] Again, I have concentrated my efforts on the U.S. case, where there is an enormous amount of data available on congressional committees over a long historical period. In the other cases, legislative and executive committees have been convened much less frequently to hear testimony from private groups and have typically exercised far more control over the groups granted access. Where possible, I have made use of evidence from those cases in which official committees did hold open hearings on the tariff issue in the various nations.

This data on legislative votes and group activity is often threadbare, but there are no clear alternatives. Irwin (1995) uses election data to investigate trade cleavages, examining county voting patterns in the 1923 election in Britain, which was fought largely on the tariff issue. He examines the relationships between the class and industry characteristics of the counties and votes for the Conservatives, who campaigned on a protectionist platform. He finds evidence that industry cleavages were stronger than class cleavages. But, since elections are rarely ever fought on the trade issue alone, this approach is limited. In chapter 12, however, I have adapted the approach in order to draw inferences about cleavage patterns in the United States from congressional votes on trade legislation over a broad span of time.

Another possibility involves the use of data from public opinion surveys on the trade issue. In recent work, Scheve and Slaughter (1998, 2001) have

---

context (see Turner and Schneier 1970, 16–20; Cox and McCubbins 1993, 141–42). I have favored the Rice index as the simplest and most direct measure of party cohesion and since it has the great advantage of allowing straightforward comparisons between cohesion on single votes and all other votes in the same session of a legislature.

[11] Sources for the data in each case are cited in the specific chapters. All data are available from the author and from the web page for this book (http://www.pup.org).

[12] As Schattschneider argued, in assessing committee evidence for his classic study of the Smoot-Hawley Tariff of 1930: "it is probably safe enough to assume that an overwhelming majority of the groups which were active participants in the controversies so far registered their opinions that they became a matter of record" (1935, 106).

examined responses to a question included in National Election Studies surveys in 1992 and 1996 about the desirability of new limits on imported goods, relating them to the occupational characteristics of individuals. In a similar fashion, Gabel (1998) has employed data from recent Eurobarometer surveys on public support for European Union membership. Scheve and Slaughter address the issue of cleavages most directly and conclude that a basic class characteristic of respondents (their skill level as measured by the level of education or their wage) was a better predictor of their opinions on trade policy than the competitive position of the industry in which they were employed. However, the results from these types of analyses are far from clear, and they are limited to recent events by the absence of survey data in past eras.[13]

In the following chapters, the quantitative data are embedded in historical descriptions of politics in each nation that focus on the major political parties, their leaders, factions, and constituencies, and the debates over principal pieces of trade legislation. I describe the positions taken in these debates by peak associations representing business, labor, and agricultural interests, and I discuss the various demands made on policymakers by industry groups. The descriptions tell a story for each case that helps to place the quantitative data in their particular historical context. Parsing the evidence in these political histories is by no means simple. Often, there are signs that seem counterpoised. I try not to distort the picture in such cases, but some level of fuzziness and uncertainty is unavoidable. I do not suppose that there will be no signs at all of class-based divisions in trade politics when levels of factor mobility are relatively low or that there will be no signs of industry-group pressures when mobility is relatively high. Cleavages patterns, I imagine, do not often approach the absolute extremes. My task in the next six chapters is to present the key evidence on the behavior of parties, peak associations, and industry groups, and to draw whatever inferences seem possible about the extent to which trade policy in each case is shaped more fundamentally by conflict between broad-based class coalitions or by competition between a multitude of narrower, industry-based groups.

---

[13] Much depends on the wording of the particular survey question and the context in which it is asked. In 1992, for example, survey responses are likely to have hinged on attitudes toward NAFTA. This becomes critical when measuring the competitive position of particular industries in which respondents are employed. Since skill levels are likely to be correlated with industry employment (as there are more skilled workers in more competitive industries), it is difficult to disentangle class from industry effects. Much depends on the accuracy of the alternative measures of industry competitiveness. Scheve and Slaughter (1998, 2001) use measures of each industry's net export share and tariff level, both of which may be significantly distorted by nontariff barriers to trade. Interestingly, they have also found that respondents in counties in which import-competing industries account for larger shares of employment tend to have more protectionist views. This seems like a reasonable confirmation of industry-based preferences, although they argue that it reflects calculations the respondents are making about the effects of international trade on housing values in their counties.

PART II

Political Conflict in Six Nations over Trade

The following chapters present detailed accounts of the cleavages that have appeared in trade politics in the United States, Britain, France, Sweden, Canada, and Australia over the last two centuries. Readers well versed in tariff history will recognize much familiar terrain here, especially in the accounts of trade politics in the United States, Britain, and France since 1870. The discussions of events in the first half of the nineteenth century, however, and the accounts of the Swedish, Canadian, and Australian experiences, will likely be less familiar to most. The argument advanced in chapter 1 provides insights into the new cases, fresh interpretations of the previously studied cases, and solutions to some old historical controversies.

The analysis presents a blend of qualitative and quantitative evidence on trade cleavages and coalitions in each nation during each historical era. To preserve the flow of the historical narrative, the discussion is arranged chronologically by nation. The focus in chapters 4 through 9 is on changes in coalition patterns occurring within each nation over time and how well these changes fit with expectations derived from the theory. Chapter 10 summarizes the findings from all the case studies and shifts the focus to cross-national comparisons.

CHAPTER FOUR

The United States

According to the argument advanced in chapter 1, the formation of broad factor-owning class coalitions in U.S. trade politics was more likely to form during periods of relatively high factor mobility—roughly, the late nineteenth and early twentieth centuries, as evidenced in Figure 2.1. In periods of lower mobility—the early nineteenth and late twentieth centuries—narrow industry-based coalitions were more likely to form.

These anticipated effects are summarized in Table 4.1. The table includes the classifications for factor endowments (abundance or scarcity) for each case from Rogowski's (1989) study, which overlaps for almost the entire period covered here.[1] The data on rate-of-return differentials reported in chapter 2 are used here (and in subsequent chapters) to distinguish relative levels of mobility in each case. To facilitate comparisons across cases, I have used a very simple rule of thumb: Mobility levels were designated as high when the mean coefficient of wage variation was less than twelve, low when the mean was greater than sixteen, and intermediate otherwise.[2]

Table 4.1 also reports a brief summary of the observed outcomes for each case, stated in terms of levels of cohesion over the trade issue among political parties and peak associations and levels of industry-group lobbying. Summarized in this rudimentary fashion, the effects anticipated by the theory, based on levels of interindustry factor mobility, fit rather well with the observed changes in U.S. trade politics. Overall, in periods when levels of factor mobility were relatively high, the trade issue generated deeper class cleavages in the U.S. polity, and the major parties and peak associations were more internally united. When factor mobility sank to lower levels, narrower, industry-based coalitions were more apparent, more internal divisions emerged within parties and peak associations, and lobbying by industry groups became more intense. These changes are described in some detail in the following sections.

---

[1] Rogowski used data on industrialization, population, and land area to classify nations according to their relative factor endowments. For the 1945 to 1994 cases I have also referred to recent, more sophisticated empirical work on measuring factor endowments—specifically, the study by Bowen, Leamer, and Sveikauskas (1987).

[2] Since the median of the mean coefficients for these cases (that is, for the set of country periods) lies between 12.4 and 16.1, this was the simplest rule that suggested itself. Wage data were used since they are available for most cases.

TABLE 4.1
Anticipated and Observed Outcomes in the United States

Period	Factor Endowments	Mobility	Prediction[a]	Outcomes	
				Class-based Parties and Associations	Industry Groups
1815–1869	Abundant land; scarce capital and labor	Low	Industry coalitions	Parties split along regional lines; more unified in 1850s with Democrats opposing Republican protectionism	Very active; vast number of petitions from groups to Congress
1870–1914	Abundant land; scarce capital and labor	High	Class coalitions	Republicans strongly favored high tariff; Democrats championed cuts in tariffs; voting almost unanimous	Sharp decline in groups lobbying congressional committees up to turn of century
1919–1939	Abundant land and capital; scarce labor	Intermediate; falling	Mixed	Parties adhered to old platforms; some division among Democrats with realignment of labor	Increased lobbying activity leading to Smoot-Hawley Act in 1930
1945–1994	Abundant land and capital; scarce labor[b]	Low	Industry coalitions	Parties and peak associations internally divided since 1950s and took ambiguous positions	Active lobbying; number of groups testifying rose swiftly despite delegation from Congress to executive

[a]Class coalitions are expected to imply that class-based organizations are internally unified on trade and adopt coherent platforms while groups are inactive. Industry coalitions imply that class-based organizations are internally divided on trade and adopt ambiguous positions (see Table 3.1).
[b]Using 1966 data, Bowen, Leamer, and Sveikauskas (1987) find the United States to be most abundant in arable land and agricultural workers, and very abundant in capital; while abundant in professional and technical workers, it is very scarce in all other categories of labor.

4.1 ANTEBELLUM TRADE POLITICS

The tariff debate was a predominantly local group-based affair in the United States at the beginning of the nineteenth century (see Stanwood 1903, and Pincus 1977). In the years after 1815, as trade with Europe was rejuvenated in the aftermath of the Napoleonic wars, "memorials" from groups poured in to Congress, alternately "praying for" or "remonstrating against" a change in the tariff. New textile and iron manufacturing industries, which had grown rapidly under the protection provided by wartime embargoes, were quick to appeal to Congress for higher tariffs. The lobbying came almost exclusively from groups based in particular cities and towns, often representing more than one industry and an assortment of farmers, manufacturers, and workers ("mechanics"). The high costs associated with communications meant that it was still far easier to raise a petition on a range of products within a city than to organize producers of one product in several cities (Pincus 1977, 58).

The first major victory for protectionists was the Tariff Act of 1824, which substantially raised import duties. Some fifty-eight memorials were referred to the House Committee on Manufactures in 1824 as it deliberated on the new legislation. (Table 4.2 reports tallies of industry-group petitions and testimony referred to the Committee during this period.) Remonstrances against new duties came mostly from agricultural societies and communities in the southern states, which expressed fear at losing export markets and being burdened with higher prices on clothing, and from commercial groups and related manufacturers in the major port cities. The strongest pleas for higher duties came from the new industrial interests of the northeast, organized at meetings of iron producers in Philadelphia and cottons and woolens

TABLE 4.2
Group Lobbying and the Committee on Manufactures, 1824–1842

| | Legislation | Form of Lobbying | Number of Industry Groups by Position | | | |
			Free Trade	Protectionist	Ambiguous	Total
1824	Tariff Act	Memorials	24	32	13	58
1828	Tariff of Abominations	Memorials	32	29	0	61
1842	Tariff Act	Memorials and Witnesses	3	43	0	46

Source: See appendix C.

manufacturers in Rhode Island and Massachusetts.[3] These groups carried their campaigns to the press as well, with *Niles' Weekly Register* championing their cause, and they sent representatives to Washington to lobby policymakers more directly.[4] In the House, James Hamilton of South Carolina complained that there had been "more outdoor than indoor legislation in regard to the bill" and described how "all sorts of pilgrims had travelled to the room of the Committee on Manufactures, from the sturdy ironmaster down to the poor manufacturer of whetstones, all equally clamorous for protection."[5]

A similar process was repeated in 1827 and 1828, when Congress was again forced to deal with all the "petitions and memorials that have crowded in upon us without mercy."[6] The most important of these originated from the convention sponsored by the Pennsylvania Society for the Encouragement of American Manufactures, held at Harrisburg in 1827 to discuss "the present state of the wool-growing and wool-manufacturing interests and such other manufactures as may require encouragement" (Stanwood 1903, 264–66). One hundred delegates from thirteen states adopted a memorial that advocated new protection for wool and woolens, as well as for iron, glass, hemp, and flax.[7] Another meeting of merchants and manufacturers in Boston produced a competing free-trade memorial authored by Henry Lee.

What is very clear from the pattern of lobbying is that among factor-owning classes there was a range of contrasting positions. Different groups of farmers, manufacturers, and workers lobbied both sides of the debate. Southern farmers, particularly the cotton and tobacco growers reliant on export markets, were strong opponents of protection, but farmers growing wool and hemp in the northern and border states advocated higher tariffs. The iron and textile industries in the Northeast were staunch protectionists, but the commercial, shipping, and railroad interests along the Atlantic coast and manufacturers of products like cotton bagging in the South were strong supporters of free trade.[8]

---

[3] The memorial from textile manufacturers in Rhode Island was authored by Samuel Slater, already famous for bringing to the United States the design for Arkwright's spinning frame in 1790 and establishing the first successful spinning works in Pawtucket.

[4] Hezekiah Niles published his "Register" from Baltimore and took up the cause of protection in 1815 in the name of manufacturers. Other publishers and pamphleteers became prominent in these years, including Mathew Carey, who late in his career would suggest that he should be reimbursed by the manufacturers for all his efforts on their behalf (see Stanwood 1903, 248n). On the lobbyists who were sent in person to Washington, see Stanwood 1903, 237.

[5] Quoted in Stanwood 1903, 237.

[6] *Annals of Congress*, 5 March, 1828.

[7] Taussig (1931, 82–83) points out that this convention did not represent a broad coalition of manufacturers, but was organized solely by wool growers and wool manufacturers who only tried to elicit support from other protectionist industries after the defeat of the Woollens Bill in 1827.

[8] Several industries relying on imported inputs came out in favor of free trade. These in-

These divisions cut across party lines and were reflected in the congressional votes on trade legislation that split the parties internally (Taussig
1931, 25–36; Stanwood 1903, 240–43). Average party cohesion indexes for
votes on major trade bills in the House (on a 0–100 scale) were only 2.8 in
1824, and 20.6 in 1928. (Table 4.3 shows the record of congressional voting
on trade legislation in this period.)[9] It was an attempt to manipulate these
divisions that led to the infamous Tariff of Abominations in 1828. Martin
van Buren's purported plan was to use the protectionist bill to split the
Adams Party between its free-trade and protectionist constituencies, allowing Jackson supporters in the North and West to be seen as championing
tariffs (especially for wool and hemp growers), while supporters in the
South could take a firm stand against the bill and ensure its defeat.[10] Southern Jacksonians were persuaded to withhold amendments and assured, mis-
takenly—and deceptively, according to their later protestations—that such a
bill would be defeated at the vote (Taussig 1931, 88–98).

Jackson so carefully worded his own statements that he was regarded as a
supporter of the tariff in the North and as a free-trade advocate in the South
(Stanwood 1903, 367). Once elected, however, his affinity with the southern
wing of the party became more apparent, and by 1831, as government revenues swelled and the South raised the specter of nullification, he was urging
a downward revision of duties. The 1832 Adams Compromise Act reduced
revenue duties and ended the much-vilified minimums system, but left the
1828 protective duties untouched. The political crisis was averted in the
following year by a new compromise act authored by Henry Clay and John
Calhoun. Their agreement provided for incremental reductions in duties between 1834 and 1840, followed by two sharp cuts in 1842 (Taussig 1931,
110–11). In effect, they had agreed to resume the political struggle over the
tariff in 1842.

When the Democrats announced the first official party platform in 1839,
they were deliberately vague on the tariff. They resolved "that justice and
sound policy forbid the federal government to foster one branch of industry

---

cluded the Union of Hardware Manufacturers and the various railroad companies that lobbied
for reduced iron duties or remissions, and apparel manufacturers who complained about the
high costs of protected cloth. See *American State Papers: Finance* V, 968, 1036, 1040.

[9] While elections still turned mostly on personal contests in the "first" party system, when
the Federalists squared off against Jefferson's Republicans, the development of distinctive
national parties with predominantly urban (Adams' Republicans/Whigs) and agrarian (Jackson's Democrats) bases of support was clearer by the late 1820s; see Stanwood 1903, 240–43.

[10] The Committee drew up a bill with very high duties on several items (including wool and
hemp), but denied higher duties to woolens manufacturers, the group responsible for most of
the protectionist agitation in 1827 and 1828, and a core support base for Adams in the North.
The Committee requested and received, over the protests from Adams men, the authority to
select the witnesses it would hear testimony from in 1828 (seven of these were actually
Jacksonian members of the House). See Stanwood 1903, 269. A smiling Van Buren was
reported to be continually "lurking" outside the committee room, repeatedly calling out members for private discussions (Remini 1958, 907).

TABLE 4.3
Congressional Votes on Trade Bills, 1815–1869

	Legislation	Party	Senate					House				
			Yeas	Nays	Cohesion[a]	Average Cohesion[b]	General Cohesion[c]	Yeas	Nays	Cohesion[a]	Average Cohesion[b]	General Cohesion[c]
1824	Tariff Act	Democratic	21	10	35.5	43.6	37.9	55	51	3.8	2.8	22.7
		Federalist	1	7	75			19	19	0		
1828	Tariff of Abominations	Jacksonian	17	17	0	11.6	35.2	44	59	14.6	20.6	35.3
		Adams	7	2	55.6			61	35	27.1		
1832	Adams Compromise	Democratic	19	11	26.7	41.5	48.7	89	35	43.6	35.7	39.9
		National Republican	10	1	81.8			27	20	14.9		
1833	Clay Compromise	Democratic	14	12	7.7	18.9	48.7	92	34	46	43.5	39.9
		National Republican	8	3	45.5			16	35	37.3		
1842	Tariff Act	Democratic	6	15	42.9	37.8	77.6	21	65	51.2	44.1	61.9
		Whig	16	8	33.3			82	36	39.0		
1846	Walker Tariff Act	Democratic	25	6	61.3	66.0	64	111	25	63.2	73.3	60.3
		Whig	3	19	72.7			2	64	93.9		
1857	Tariff Act	Democratic	28	3	80.7	67.4	46.4	9	53	71	59.6	60.3
		Republican	4	8	33.3			70	26	45.8		
		American						31	4	77.1		
1861	Morrill Tariff Act	Democratic	2	13	73.3	84.2	66.7	7	61	79.4	86.9	62.5
		Republican	22	1	91.3			90	3	93.6		
		American						6	1	71.4		

Sources: Annals of Congress, Gales and Seaton's Register, Congressional Globe, and Rosenthal and Poole (2000).
[a]Rice cohesion score for each party.
[b]Weighted average of party cohesion scores.
[c]Weighted average of party cohesion scores for all votes in the chamber in the same session of Congress.

in detriment to another, or to cherish the interest of one portion to the injury of another portion of our common country."[11] The language was skillful enough to sooth protectionists in the party (who believed protection was of benefit to all industries and all regions) while appealing to free traders at the same time (Stanwood 1903, 38). The Whigs were no more unified, although they included in their number the leaders of the protectionist cause. When they took control of Congress in 1841 and prepared legislation to increase duties (abolishing the Clay compromise), their chief difficulty lay in winning the approval of their own president, John Tyler.[12]

Only in the late 1840s did majorities of the two parties assume clearly opposing positions and begin to appeal to broader class coalitions. In 1845, southern Democrats, led by Calhoun, held a convention in Memphis aimed at solidifying an alliance between agriculturalists of the South and West; meanwhile, Treasury secretary Robert Walker issued a lengthy report arguing that the tariff provided solely for the profits of manufacturers at the expense of agriculture and explicitly linked the interests of "farmer and planter." It was this coalition of western grain growers and southern planters that pushed through the liberalizing Tariff Act in 1846.[13] The Whigs, meanwhile, appealed directly to the labor vote, with the argument linking the tariff to high wages artfully made in numerous articles by Horace Greeley.[14] Partisanship over trade was propelled to new heights in Congress. At the same time, the intensity of group lobbying appears to have declined. Memorials and petitions continued to flow into Congress but in nothing like the torrent that occurred in 1824 and 1828. Only forty-six groups lobbied the Committee on Manufactures in the deliberations on the trade bill in 1842.[15]

In 1856, the Democratic platform finally called for "progressive free trade throughout the world," and in the following year the Republicans openly endorsed protectionism—a position they tied neatly to a defense of the rights of workers and the rejection of the slave labor of the South (Foner 1970). In 1857, forced to reform the tariff to deal with the surplus revenues that were flooding the government's coffers, Republicans in the House drew up legislation (known later as the "manufacturers bill") cutting duties only on raw materials and thereby raising rates of effective protection for manu-

[11] Quoted in Stanwood 1903, 302.

[12] Tyler had supported a proviso in the Distribution Act of 1841 ensuring distributions of proceeds of sales of public land to the states would be halted if tariffs were raised, so that revenue needs caused by distributions could not be used to justify future protectionist legislation. He vetoed two successive tariff bills in 1842 that overrode that proviso; see Stanwood 1903, 1–25.

[13] As James and Lake (1989) have noted, the prior repeal of the Corn Laws in Britain in 1846 undoubtedly played a role in the conversion of the western agriculturalists to free trade in the United States since the potential market for grain exports expanded enormously.

[14] Commons 1909, 487.

[15] One remarkable petition in favor of protection came from a group of boys in York County, Pennsylvania, who requested a high duty on all imports so that "when they are grown they may not see such times as now" (*Congressional Globe*, 21 April 1842).

factures. The Democratic majority in the Senate substituted a bill of their own that substantially reduced protective duties. An untidy compromise was ultimately reached and passed with bipartisan support in the waning hours of the session.

The Republicans won a majority in the House in the election of 1858 and set about designing a new protectionist bill in 1859, despite Democratic control of the Senate and White House. The bill, authored by Justin Morrill, raised duties substantially on manufactured goods and substituted specific for ad valorem rates (Taussig 1931, 158–59). It was passed by the House in May of 1860. When Congress reassembled in December, South Carolina had already seceded, and after the subsequent withdrawal by the senators of Georgia, Alabama, Florida, Mississippi, and Louisiana, the bill was passed by the Senate. The votes on the bill were, up to that time, the most partisan taken on the trade issue in Congress.

4.2 FROM RECONSTRUCTION TO WORLD WAR I

In the years following the Civil War, the tariff rapidly became the issue at the center of partisan debates. The Republicans appealed to urban classes, particularly in the Northeast and Midwest, who had long favored protection, and every one of its platforms after 1860 emphasized the value of a high tariff (Rogowski 1989, 44; Stewart 1991, 218).[16] The Democrats' support base was largely agricultural and southern, and from 1876 on, their platforms advocated a tariff levied for revenue purposes only.[17]

By the late 1860s, the high Civil War tariffs began generating massive amounts of redundant government revenue. However, the postwar dominance of the northern Republicans ensured that cuts in protective tariffs were largely avoided. In 1870 and 1872 they passed legislation lowering or removing duties and taxes levied for revenue purposes, leaving in place very high protective duties (see Taussig 1931, 178–89). When the financial panic of 1873 gave way to depression, and revenues fell more rapidly than expected, the Republicans took the opportunity to raise duties again in 1875. When the Democrats won a majority in the House in 1876, they supported the Mills resolution, which again championed the notion of a tariff levied only for revenue purposes, but Republican control of the Senate and White House ensured that any real efforts to cut duties came to nothing.

---

[16] Maintaining support in the West among farmers not engaged in the protected wool-growing industry, however, was a nagging concern for the Republicans (see Stanwood 1903, 151–53). The party tried various ways to pacify Westerners in these years, including reciprocity provisions in trade bills aimed at expanding exports of certain farm products and direct subsidies to western farmers.

[17] *Congressional Record*, 15 August 1949, 12902. An unexpected obstacle for the Democratic tariff reformers in the early 1880s was a strong northern component of the party, led by Samuel Randall of Pennsylvania (see Verdier 1994, 73).

TABLE 4.4
Group Lobbying and the Committee on Ways and Means, 1870–1914

	Legislation	Number of Industry Groups by Position			
		Free Trade	Protectionist	Ambiguous	Total
1884	Morrison Bill	4	17	0	21
1890	McKinley Tariff Act	6	20	2	28
1894	Gorman Tariff Act	2	21	1	24
1897	Dingley Tariff Act	2	12	0	14
1909	Payne-Aldrich Tariff Act	1	20	0	21
1913	Underwood Tariff Act	6	24	0	30

Sources: See appendix C.

The Democrats tried in vain to reform tariffs again in 1883, launching a major review of the tariff under the leadership of William Morrison, chairman of the House Ways and Means Committee. Their attempt was ultimately stymied by Republicans in the Senate. Very few industry groups—twenty-one in total—actually volunteered testimony to the Committee when hearings were held by Morrison. The level of group lobbying activity in these years was significantly lower than in earlier times. Table 4.4 reports the numbers of industry groups lobbying the Committee during deliberations over various pieces of legislation between the 1880s and 1910s. Group lobbying appears to have played a very limited role in a policy process dominated by conflict between broader-based coalitions.[18]

One especially interesting feature of the testimony given to the Ways and Means Committee by these groups, in view of the argument advanced in chapter 1, was the high degree of class solidarity among owners of capital in various industries. Not only did all these groups support continued or increased protection, they supported protection for each other. No matter how much Democratic committee members prodded and cajoled, manufacturers refused to accept that they would benefit from lower duties on products other than their own.[19] Prominent examples included textile manufacturers,

[18] In fact, Verdier (1994) has compared the duties granted in the 1894 Tariff Act against specific requests made by trade associations before the Ways and Means Committee and found that industry-based lobbying had no significant effects for either protectionists or free traders (114).

[19] One exchange between S. D. Phelps, representing producers of fine cotton yarns, and Hilary Herbert, a Democrat on the Committee in 1883, is particularly noteworthy in this regard. Phelps disclosed that most of the textile machinery in use was not imported but came instead from the Lowell machine shops:

Mr. Herbert: Then what was the use of raising in the last tariff the duty on machinery from 35 per cent up to 45 per cent?

who would not concede that high duties on textile machinery had hurt them, and iron manufacturers who actually testified in union with producers of iron ore.[20]

The long depression intensified rural demands for tariff reform and re-monetization of silver and sparked the Greenback and Granger movements and the Farmers' Alliance. Cleveland fanned the flame of class conflict in 1887 by devoting his entire address to Congress to an attack on Republican protectionism. In 1888, House Democrats introduced a bill (authored by Roger Mills) providing for major tariff reductions. They were blocked again by the Republicans in the Senate, who then transformed the bill into a protectionist measure. The votes in each chamber reveal that party unity on the trade issue had reached unprecedented levels: The average party cohesion score in the House was 94.2 compared to a general cohesion score of 67.8 (see Table 4.5). Thereafter, large partisan swings in policy coincided with each change in control of Congress, and votes on trade legislation displayed extremely high levels of party cohesion.

The Republican party won control of both the House and Senate in 1888 and, led by William McKinley in the House, crafted legislation providing for a substantial general increase in protection.[21] The Democrats, having

---

Mr. Phelps: That I cannot say.

Mr. Herbert: Was not the direct effect of that to injure the rising industries in the West and South engaged in the manufacture of textile fabrics?

Mr. Phelps: That is a pretty broad question.

Mr. Herbert: I would like to have your answer to it.

Mr. Phelps: We paid more for machinery a number of years ago than we are paying now.

Mr. Herbert: But do we not pay more for machinery under the 45 per cent period than we paid under the 25 percent period?

Mr. Phelps: I doubt it.

Mr. Herbert: You do not think we do?

Mr. Phelps: No, sir. . . .

Mr. Herbert: If the effect of [the increase to 45 percent] is to give them control of the market, and if they have control of the market, have they not the power to make persons pay for their machinery right up to the line of the 45 per cent tariff? Can they not charge higher than they would under the 35 per cent tariff?

Mr. Phelps: No.

Mr. Herbert: Please explain why.

Mr. Phelps: I have found, in my own experience, that where an industry has been as protected in this country as that the persons engaged in it have made money, their neighbors have seen that they were making money and have gone into the same business; and the sharp competition between the home manufacturers has not only kept the price at where it was before they commenced manufacturing in this country, but has reduced it very materially. I do not know of an exception to that rule (U.S. House, Committee on Ways and Means 1884, 173).

[20] Meanwhile, cooperation between manufacturers and those farmers who actually supported protection broke down; the clearest case was the unraveling of the agreement between woolens manufacturers and wool growers. See Verdier 1994, 77.

[21] The act also included two measures aimed at helping solve the party's western problem:

vilified the McKinley tariff as "the culminating atrocity of class legislation," took control in 1892 and moved quickly to reduce duties.[22] But Cleveland's commitment to the gold standard inspired a mini-revolt among Democrats from the Midwest and West who defected to the side of the pro-silver Populists (formed out of the Farmers' Alliance) and held up passage of the tariff reform bill (Taussig 1931, 287–91).[23] The Democratic insurgents voted against the bill in the House and delayed and amended it in the Senate.[24] Accusing them of "party perfidy and party dishonor," Cleveland eventually allowed the diluted reform to become law without signing it. The dispute over silver was finally resolved by "Fusion" in 1896, which severed the party's ties to pro-gold supporters in the East, and placed the urban-rural cleavage at the center of U.S. politics.

The Republicans nominated McKinley for president that year and campaigned on a platform of high tariffs and the gold standard. The American Federation of Labor (AFL) and the National Association of Manufacturers, created in 1895, both strongly endorsed the Republican tariff.[25] The party won a resounding victory, and in 1897 passed the Dingley Tariff, mandating another general increase in import duties. Only one party member voted against the bill in both the House and Senate. By 1904, the Republican platform stated that "the measure of protection should always at least equal the difference of cost of production at home and abroad," and this was

---

subsidies for domestic producers of beet sugar and provisions for reciprocity treaties with Latin American nations, which held the promise of expanding grain exports. The latter turned out to be an impracticable complement to protection since any useful treaty would have imposed significant costs on major domestic industries. See Stanwood 1903, 280.

[22] Quoted in Johnson and Porter 1973, 87.

[23] Cleveland supported the repeal of the Sherman Silver Purchase Act in 1893. That act, passed in 1890, had provided for Treasury purchases of silver and new issues of Treasury notes backed by silver as well as gold. The Republicans hoped that the move would help them maintain support in the West. They held similar hopes for the Sherman Antitrust Act, passed the same year. See Tarbell 1911, 201.

[24] An amendment to the House bill provided for an income tax (as a sop to Populists) and created much dissent. In the Senate, protection was restored to the sugar, coal and iron ore industries (Stanwood 1903, 326–27). Democrats from Louisiana took the opportunity to push for the sugar amendment; others from West Virginia and Maryland, pushed for the exceptions for mining. Worse than these defections, Matthew Quay, a Republican from Pennsylvania, filibustered for twelve days until he received assurances that duties on a range of products in the bill would be raised. See Tarbell 1911, 228–29.

[25] The major unions were vehemently protectionist and Republican. Officers of the Amalgamated Association of Iron and Steel Workers, for instance, regularly took up jobs in the Republican Party upon retiring (see Ware 1935, 268). One president of the union, John Jarret, was actually supplied with money from the American Iron and Steel Association when he retired in 1886 and was sent to Illinois to campaign for the Republicans against Morrison, the Democrats' eloquent trade policy leader in the House and author of Cleveland's reform bills in 1884 and 1886. Jarret employed a small army of men and enlisted the support of local unions to organize boycotts and protests, and Morrison was ousted.

TABLE 4.5
Congressional Votes on Trade Bills, 1870–1914

			Senate					House				
	Legislation	Party	Yeas	Nays	Cohesion[a]	Average Cohesion[b]	General Cohesion[c]	Yeas	Nays	Cohesion[a]	Average Cohesion[b]	General Cohesion[c]
1875	Tariff Act	Democratic	0	20	100			2	76	94.9		
		Republican	32	11	48.8	65.1	51.6	125	39	52.4	66.1	61
1884	Morrison Bill	Democratic	0	36	100			43	153	56.1		
		Republican	37	0	100			113	4	93.2	70	61.5
1888	Mills Bill	Democratic	0	31	100			157	5	93.8		
		Republican	40	0	100	100	78.4	4	145	94.6	94.2	67.8
1890	McKinley Tariff Act	Democratic	0	31	100			1	139	98.6		
		Republican	40	0	100	100	74.8	163	1	98.8	98.7	78.5
1894	Gorman Tariff Act	Democratic	40	1	95.1			196	17	84		
		Republican	0	35	100	94.9	75.6	0	126	100	90.2	73.1
		Populist	1	1	0			8	0	100		
1897	Dingley Tariff Act	Democratic	1	26	92.6			5	115	91.7		
		Republican	37	1	94.7	93.9	71.3	199	0	100	98.9	80.8
		Populist	0	1	100			1	7	75		
1909	Payne-Aldrich Tariff Act	Democratic	1	30	93.5			4	160	95.1		
		Republican	50	10	66.7	75.8	67.8	213	1	99.1	97.4	72.3
1913	Underwood Tariff Act	Democratic	46	2	91.7			276	6	95.7		
		Republican	1	38	94.9	93.1	66.8	4	128	93.9	94.3	65.9
		Progressive						2	6	50		

Sources: Congressional Record and Rosenthal and Poole (2000).
[a] Rice cohesion score for each party.
[b] Weighted average of party cohesion scores.
[c] Weighted average of party cohesion scores for all votes in the chamber in the same session of Congress.

amended to include that protection should provide "a reasonable profit to American industries."[26]

The Republican hold on trade policy only relaxed in 1910. The party had faced growing problems with its western wing, always an uneasy rural ally for a largely urban Republican constituency. By 1908 this group had originated the "Iowa Idea" of cutting protection for highly concentrated industries (Hechter 1940, 86–105). The idea, and the antimonopoly sentiment behind it, resonated among midwestern grain farmers who were increasingly reliant on export markets.[27] Taft made overtones about tariff reductions in the 1908 election campaign, but helped House Republicans push the protectionist Payne-Aldrich bill through the Senate in 1909. The factional dispute escalated in the Senate, with ten party members from the Midwest and West voting against the bill. The dissenting senators threw their support to the Progressive movement and split the party (Taussig 1931, 374–75).

In 1910 the Democrats won a majority in the House, and in 1912 Wilson campaigned on the principle of a "competitive tariff," stressing the unhealthy relationship between protection and domestic monopolies.[28] They won sweeping victories in both chambers. Wilson supervised passage of new trade legislation, taking the unprecedented step of appearing on Capitol Hill himself to speak in favor of the bill. As a scholar, Wilson had argued that the absence of party discipline was a major weakness in the U.S. system, and he now made support for tariff reform a test of party loyalty. Only six Democrats in the House, and two in the Senate, voted against his reform bill.[29]

4.3 THE INTERWAR YEARS

By the 1920s, significant rifts had emerged within both parties over the tariff issue. With agricultural prices falling, Democrats in Louisiana and Texas were lured away from the party's free-trade position by proposals for new agricultural duties on sugar and meat. Republicans in the Midwest and East,

---

[26] Quoted in Schattschneider 1935, 8n.

[27] Ironically, in several of the most concentrated industries, firms were expressing more favorable views toward trade. Prominent among them were producers of iron and steel. See Terrill 1973, ch. 8. The American Iron and Steel Association actually broke apart in 1908, with the most prominent firms (including U.S. Steel, Bethlehem, and Cambria) founding the new American Iron and Steel Institute and rejecting protectionism.

[28] The Democratic platform called for an immediate downward revision of duties and for placing on the free list all imports in competition with "trust-controlled products" (*Congressional Record*, 15 August 1949, 12902).

[29] The act greatly expanded the duty-free list and made large reductions in tariffs. It also provided for a federal income tax to replace customs duties as a source of government revenue.

TABLE 4.6
Congressional Votes on Trade Bills, 1919–1939

	Legislation	Party	Senate					House				
			Yeas	Nays	Cohesion[a]	Average Cohesion[b]	General Cohesion[c]	Yeas	Nays	Cohesion[a]	Average Cohesion[b]	General Cohesion[c]
1922	Fordney-McCumber Tariff Act	Democratic	3	33	83.3	81.3	71.6	7	88	85.3	84.4	74.5
		Republican	54	6	80			220	19	84.1		
1930	Smoot-Hawley Tariff Act	Democratic	5	34	74.4	62.5	52.1	17	148	79.4	79	67.9
		Republican	44	13	54.4			228	27	78.8		
1934	Reciprocal Trade Agreements Act	Democratic	51	5	82.1	74.2	55.1	279	12	91.8	92.1	68.8
		Republican	7	30	62.2			4	111	93		
1937	RTAA Extension	Democratic	56	8	75	77.5	47.9	286	11	92.6	92.8	59.2
		Republican	1	15	87.5			3	87	93.3		

Sources: Congressional Record and Rosenthal and Poole (2000).

[a]Rice cohesion score for each party.

[b]Weighted average of party cohesion scores.

[c]Weighted average of party cohesion scores for all votes in the chamber in the same session of Congress.

influenced by demands from financial interests and export industries, broke ranks and opposed new protectionist bills.

The Republican party increased its majorities in the election of 1920, and Harding, a staunch advocate of protection, moved to "make the tariff work for agriculture," supporting the Emergency Tariff Act of 1921, which imposed duties on a range of farm products including wheat, corn, meat, wool, and sugar.[30] In 1922, the Republicans passed legislation, the Fordney-McCumber Act, making the new agricultural duties permanent and raising duties on a wide range of manufactured goods. The votes on passage of the bill show that party unity on the tariff issue had already fallen sharply (to scores of 81.3 in the House and 84.4 in the Senate) from the high levels of earlier years (see Table 4.6).

Republican dissenters emerged not only in the grain states of the Midwest but also in the industrial and financial centers in the East, where several concentrated, capital-intensive industries producing automobiles, farm machinery, and specialized steel products supported freer trade.[31] The 1922 act did provide authorization for the president to negotiate trade agreements based on the principle of reciprocity as a way to appease these interests, but only a handful of limited agreements were actually signed in the 1920s (Verdier 1994, 194).[32]

By 1928, as prices of farm goods continued to plummet, it was clear that the crisis in agriculture had not been avoided. Traditional export staples— grain, cotton, and tobacco—met with stiffer foreign competition, and imports of many farm goods, including wool, rose to the point that the United States ran an overall agricultural trade deficit for the first time ever in 1923 and again between 1925 and 1939.[33] In the 1928 campaign, Hoover promised to solve the problems of agriculture with new tariffs, and the Republican platform was amended to include the claim that "a protective tariff is as vital to American agriculture as it is to American manufacturing."[34]

The tariff now had broader appeal to farmers, and this posed a real prob-

---

[30] Harding had emphasized the tariff issue in his campaign speeches and the American Protective Tariff League had actually paid his hotel bill at the Republican National Convention (Lake 1988, 173n).

[31] These industries had formed the National Foreign Trade Council in 1914, that lobbied for export promotion and a flexible bargaining tariff, and were a force behind the creation of the Tariff Commission in 1916. See Dobson 1976, 83–93.

[32] The act also authorized the president to raise or lower duties by as much as 50 percent on the recommendation of the Tariff Commission. But the Commission was given strict instructions that tariffs could only be altered so as to equalize costs of production, and Harding appointed three new commissioners who were all known protectionists; see Dobson 1976, 87. Commission investigations in the 1920s produced thirty-three recommendations for tariff increases and only five for tariff cuts; see Lake 1988, 169.

[33] Eichengreen (1989) points out that northern farmers were the most threatened by imports of high-grade milling wheat, potatoes, eggs, and dairy products from neighboring Canada, while most farmers in the interior and South were unaffected by foreign competition.

[34] Quoted in *Congressional Record*, 15 August 1949, 12899.

lem for the Democrats. The shifting labor vote also placed them in a difficult position. The AFL, although taking a neutral position on the campaign, strongly supported protection. At the 1928 AFL convention, a powerful caucus of pro-tariff unions (calling itself the "Wage Earners' Protective Conference") took a leading role (Eichengreen 1989, 44). The Democratic candidate, Alfred Smith, had established a base of support among ethnic, urban labor in New York, as had many members of the party in cities where labor issues were a growing source of political tension (Key 1964, 530–31). Yet the party's free-trade tradition, still supported by a vast section of its rural constituency in the West and South, stood as an obstacle to expanding this urban electoral base. In the end, the party adopted an ambiguous position.[35]

The Republicans retained the White House in 1928 and increased their majorities in the House and Senate. Upon taking office, they made good on Hoover's promise to address the problems of agriculture with new trade legislation. The new tariff bill was quickly expanded, however, to include increased duties for a broad range of manufacturing industries. Divisions over trade protection were exacerbated within both parties: Average party cohesion indexes for votes in 1930 were 79.0 in the House and only 62.5 in the Senate (see Table 4.6). As in 1922, the main insurgents among the Republicans were those representing the midwestern farm states. On the Democratic side, party members linked to import-competing sugar and meat producers, and those who, like Smith, had forged ties to urban interests in the Northeast, crossed the floor to vote for higher tariffs.

The most indelible impression left by the passage of the Smoot-Hawley Tariff Act, however, was created by industry groups. A record number of groups appeared before Congress attempting to influence the shape of policy. More industry groups testified before the House Ways and Means Committee in hearings on the 1930 bill than on any trade legislation since the Civil War (see Table 4.7).

The Smoot-Hawley Act had already been labeled the "worst tariff bill in the nation's history" before it was passed.[36] Retaliation from trading partners was swift and substantial. Within months, tariffs on American imports had been raised by Canada, France, Italy, Spain, Australia, New Zealand, Mexico, and Cuba; within a year, a total of twenty-six nations had enacted new quantitative restrictions on American imports (Pastor 1980, 79). The worsening economic crisis accelerated the political realignment already taking

---

[35] Smith himself endorsed protection for manufactures, and the party platform stated that the "actual difference of cost of production at home and abroad, with adequate safeguard for the wage of the American laborer, must be the extreme measure of every tariff rate." Yet the platform also voiced support for a policy that would "permit effective competition, insure against monopoly, and at the same time produce a fair revenue," and linked monopolies explicitly to "special tariff favors." See Schattschneider 1935, 8.

[36] The declaration was made by Progressive senator Robert La Follette of Wisconsin (*New York Times*, 25 March 1930).

TABLE 4.7
Group Lobbying and the Committee on Ways and Means, 1919–1939

| | Legislation | Number of Industry Groups by Position | | |
		Free Trade	Protectionist	Total
1922	Fordney-McCumber Tariff Act	5	43	48
1930	Smoot-Hawley Tariff Act	9	69	78
1934	Reciprocal Trade Agreements Act	1	3	4
1937	RTAA Extension	1	4	5

Sources: See appendix C.

place in the 1920s, as workers deserted a Republican party that proved incapable of improving their plight (Burnham 1970, 55–58). In 1932, promising an activist program of job creation and social insurance for workers and a system of price supports for farmers, the Democrats won massive majorities.

In the 1932 campaign, Roosevelt refused to stake out a clear position for the Democrats on trade. He supported the plank in the platform, coauthored by Cordell Hull, that returned the party to Wilson's idea of a competitive tariff and advocated reciprocal trade treaties (Cole 1983, 96). But he also endorsed a cost-equalizing approach that he admitted was "not widely different from that preached by Republican statesmen and politicians."[37] Once elected Roosevelt did appoint Hull as his secretary of state. Having reluctantly accepted that unilateral tariff reductions were politically impractical in the midst of recession, Hull began to champion bilateral agreements with trading partners as "the next best method" of reform (Hull 1948, 356). In 1933 he drafted a bill authorizing the president to negotiate such treaties. That bill became the basis for the Reciprocal Trade Agreements Act (RTAA) passed in 1934, granting the president authority (for three years) to negotiate alterations of up to 50 percent in the existing import duties.

Between 1934 and 1939, twenty-two separate agreements were negotiated under the authority of the RTAA (Tasca 1938). However, only a very limited range of products was actually included in the agreements, and products were often reclassified on the tariff schedule or subjected to new import quotas so that the unwanted effects of the agreements could be avoided (Haggard 1988, 92). The Jones-Costigan Act, also passed in 1934, provided for quotas on imports of sugar, wheat, rye, barley, dairy products, cotton, oats, and a range of other farm goods. In 1937, quotas were introduced on dairy products, beef, potatoes, and lumber, which effectively offset negotiated tariff reductions on Canadian imports of these goods. New quotas on tobacco, cotton, and crude oil were adopted in following years and, by 1939,

[37] Quoted in Haggard 1988, 106.

a full quarter of dutiable imports were subject to quantitative limits (Diebold 1941, 19).

The ambiguity makes considerable sense given the Democrats' shifting support base and the divisions within the party over trade policy. While still shaped by traditional ties to rural voters in the South and West, in 1932 the Democrats had actually gained a majority of congressional seats from metropolitan areas. In the 1936 election the party took more than 70 percent of metropolitan districts (Turner and Schneier 1970, 119). The party was torn by new disagreements among its rural base over trade policy and by its need to cement support among its new labor constituency. The Democratic compromise stressed the ability to increase exports without raising the threat of import competition.[38] New cleavages over trade, and electoral realignment, had begun to transform trade politics.

In 1934 and 1937 only a handful of industry groups testified before the House Ways and Means Committee on the trade agreements legislation (see Table 4.7). It would be wrong to conclude from this, however, that group lobbying activity had fallen dramatically. These hearings only addressed the question of passage of the RTAA and its extension, unlike previous hearings in which tariffs on specific products were discussed individually by the committee. Against Hull's wishes, the RTAA was actually amended to provide for public notice of impending trade negotiations and for separate hearings to be held in which interested groups could voice their concerns; an interdepartmental "Committee for Reciprocity Information" fulfilled these functions. In the 1930s this committee came under intense lobbying pressure from import-competing and export-oriented groups whenever a set of trade negotiations was about to begin (Kottman 1968, 222).[39]

4.4 TRADE POLITICS IN POSTWAR AMERICA

World War II and the ensuing Cold War invested the trade issue with security implications and helped to embed it within a new framework of cooper-

---

[38] Existing explanations for the RTAA typically suggest that the delegation of authority it entailed was the result of "learning" by Congressional legislators who realized that logrolling in tariff bills produced suboptimal policy results (see Baldwin 1985; Goldstein 1986; Lohmann and O'Halloran 1994). A major weakness with this view, as Schnietz (1994) has pointed out, is that the voting records indicate precious little learning by legislators: Almost all those who voted for Smoot-Hawley in 1930 voted against the RTAA in 1934. An alternative view suggests that, favoring liberal policy, the Democrats made an institutional change that was intended to lock in tariff reductions by tying them to reciprocal reductions made by trading partners (see Bailey, Goldstein, and Weingast 1997). A shortcoming with this interpretation is that it does not do justice to the ambiguity in the positions taken, and in the policies adopted, by the party leadership at the time. See Hiscox 1999 for a full discussion of competing views.

[39] When plans to negotiate with Belgium were announced in late 1934, for example, the committee received eighty-six communications: forty-eight argued against granting concessions on various products, twenty-one sought Belgian concessions, and eleven just urged U.S. tariff reductions (Haggard 1988, 116).

ation among Western allies. In one of his last messages to Congress in 1945, Roosevelt made a request for new authority to negotiate trade treaties that stressed the nation's new responsibilities as a prosperous and powerful world leader. He requested a "workable kit of tools for the new world of international cooperation to which we look forward."[40] Although voting on the legislation was quite partisan (see Table 4.8), its passage paved the way for U.S. leadership in the new multilateral trade negotiations that produced the General Agreement on Tariffs and Trade (GATT) in 1947.

The Republicans had regained control of both the House and Senate in the 1946 elections and in 1947 pressured the Truman administration into demanding an "escape clause" in the new trade agreements, allowing for their suspension in the event they caused serious injury to domestic producers (Pastor 1980, 99–100).[41] In 1948, the party altered its platform, removing the pledge to end the reciprocal trade agreements program and promising, "while safeguarding our own industry and agriculture," to "support the system of reciprocal trade and encourage international commerce."[42] In the bill extending the presidential negotiating authority that year, however, the Republicans inserted a "peril point" provision requiring that the Tariff Commission advise the administration on the permissible concessions that could be granted without causing or threatening serious injury to the domestic industry. In 1951 they passed new provisions for escape clause relief for industries harmed by trade agreements.

A more significant shift occurred in 1953 when Eisenhower, in his State of the Union message, called for the extension of the negotiating authority and championed trade liberalization as a key component of U.S. foreign policy. Congress granted him one-year extensions in 1953 and 1954, and in 1955, with the Democrats back in control, a bipartisan majority approved a three-year extension.[43] Party positions on the trade issue, and votes in Congress, were thrown into flux. Average party cohesion indexes for votes on trade bills in the House were only 43.9 in 1955, 43.3 in 1962, and 36.3 in 1974.[44]

The Republican Party was increasingly split by allegiances to capital-

---

[40] Quoted in Ratner 1972, 155.

[41] The administration also ensured that U.S. agricultural programs, and specifically import quotas on farm commodities, were unaffected by the agreements.

[42] Quoted in *Congressional Record*, 15 August 1949, 12901.

[43] To help gain Republican support in 1953, Eisenhower established a special commission made up of ten congressional Republicans and seven presidential appointees to consider the trade agreements issue. Despite deep divisions, the commission ultimately endorsed an internationalist approach; see Pastor 1980, 102.

[44] Voting in the Senate in 1974 indicated more bipartisan support for granting authority to the president, perhaps as a function of greater concern for foreign policy considerations. As a check, I included an earlier vote in the Senate in 1974 on a very general protectionist amendment to the Trade Act (proposed by Thomas McIntyre) that would have precluded the president from cutting protection on manufactured goods for which imports exceeded 33.3 percent of domestic consumption during three of the five previous years. Senate votes on this bill look much like the House votes on passage of the general bill in 1974.

TABLE 4.8
Congressional Votes on Trade Bills, 1945–1994

	Legislation	Party	Senate					House				
			Yeas	Nays	Cohesion[a]	Average Cohesion[b]	General Cohesion[c]	Yeas	Nays	Cohesion[a]	Average Cohesion[b]	General Cohesion[c]
1945	RTAA Extension	Democratic	44	7	72.5			216	13	88.6		
		Republican	15	21	16.7	49.4	54.8	33	159	65.6	78.1	66.6
1955	RTAA Extension	Democratic	40	6	73.9			190	38	66.7		
		Republican	40	8	66.7	70.2	62.5	113	80	17.1	43.9	65.2
1962	Trade Expansion Act	Democratic	61	0	100			215	36	71.3		
		Republican	23	14	24.3	71.4	57.1	85	91	3.4	43.3	69.7
1970	Mills Bill	Democratic						143	90	22.7		
		Republican						85	88	1.7	13.8	64.6
1974	Trade Reform Act	Democratic	47	3	88			115	124	3.8		
		Republican	38	1	94.9	91	58.9	163	19	79.1	36.3	62.2
1974	McIntyre Amendment	Democratic	26	23	6.1							
		Republican	9	26	48.6	58.9	58.9					
1984	Trade Remedies Reform Act	Democratic						194	25	77.2		
		Republican						66	72	4.3	49	68.4
1991	Disapproval of Fast-Track	Democratic	32	25	12.3			172	91	30.8		
		Republican	6	37	72.1	38	59.8	21	143	74.4	47.5	53.4
1993	North American Free Trade	Democratic	27	28	1.8			102	156	20.9		
		Republican	34	10	54.5	25.3	59.8	132	43	50.9	33	53.4
1994	Uruguay Round Agreement	Democratic	41	14	49.1			167	89	30.5		
		Republican	35	10	55.6	52	65.2	121	56	36.7	33	57

Sources: Congressional Record and Rosenthal and Poole (2000).
[a]Rice cohesion score for each party.
[b]Weighted average of party cohesion scores.
[c]Weighted average of party cohesion scores for all votes in the chamber in the same session of Congress.

intensive export-oriented sectors and to those industries, such as textiles and steel, that began to meet stiff import competition in the 1950s and 1960s. The two general business associations, the National Association of Manufacturers (NAM) and the Chamber of Commerce, provided only cautious support for multilateral trade negotiations and, constrained by internal conflicts of interests, took few positions on more controversial trade issues or legislation (Friman 1990, 65–66; Bauer, de Sola Pool, and Dexter 1972, 334–36).[45]

The Democrats faced their own problems. The AFL-CIO voiced lukewarm support for the trade agreements program during the postwar boom, but when cheap imports began to pose a serious threat to wages and jobs in several major industries, withdrew their support (Rogowski 1989, 120). Led by the powerful steel and textile unions, the organization began advocating protection for those industries in the late 1960s and then endorsed the protectionist Mills and Burke-Hartke bills in 1970 and 1971, driving a wedge through the Democratic Party (Hughes 1979, 23). Meanwhile, the party's rural support base grew increasingly divided over the trade issue along commodity lines. The American Farm Bureau took positions on some broad trade measures, generally supporting GATT negotiations—from which agricultural trade barriers had been excluded—while opposing preferences for imports from developing nations. But, it left the most important lobbying up to commodity-specific farm groups (Destler and Odell 1987, 42).

Growing pressure from industry groups exacerbated the problem for the parties.[46] Large numbers of groups began appearing before congressional committees lobbying for and against new trade agreements: Forty-two groups appeared before the House Ways and Means Committee in 1955 to testify about the new legislation extending bargaining authority to the president, sixty-three groups testified about the Trade Expansion Act in 1962, and forty-six groups appeared to state their position on the Trade Reform bill in 1974.[47] Table 4.9 reports the statistics for lobbying activity in these years.

The lobbying resulted in a spate of special legislation in Congress and a new array of nontariff barriers aimed at protecting faltering industries. In 1956, for instance, in response to an intense lobbying effort begun by the textile industry the previous year, the White House negotiated voluntary

---

[45] The NAM remained neutral, for instance, on the Trade Expansion Act in 1962. Based on interviews with members of these associations, Destler and Odell (1987) reported that beginning in the 1960s, they became increasingly divided over trade and less effective in taking concerted political action.

[46] On the rise of lobbying, both for and against trade liberalization, see Destler and Odell 1987.

[47] These numbers are especially remarkable since the hearings only concerned the issue of whether the president should be given authority to negotiate trade agreements, whereas prior to 1934, the committee was concerned with setting the duties to be levied on specific items of interest.

TABLE 4.9
Group Lobbying and the Committee on Ways and Means, 1945–1994

| | Legislation | Number of Industry Groups by Position | | |
		Free Trade	Protectionist	Total
1945	RTAA Extension	1	9	10
1955	RTAA Extension	9	33	42
1962	Trade Expansion Act	18	45	63
1974	Trade Reform Act	12	44	56
1984	Trade Remedies Reform Act	7	33	40
1991	Disapproval of Fast-Track	9	33	42
1993	North American Free Trade	7	32	39
1994	Uruguay Round Agreement	16	38	54

Sources: See appendix C.

export restraints to limit cheap textile imports from Japan (see Bauer et al. 1972, 60). These were replaced in 1961 by the Short Term Agreement on Cotton Textiles and, a year later, the Long Term Arrangement Regarding International Trade in Cotton Textiles, setting up a framework for international agreements on quantitative controls. Voluntary export restraints (VERs) were established in 1969 to limit European and Japanese steel imports, and the administration negotiated a set of such restraints for all textile imports in the 1973 Multi-Fiber Arrangement. Between 1968 and 1970, almost 300 members of the House introduced separate quota legislation of one sort or another.[48] The Mills bill of 1970 proposed quotas on textile and footwear imports and a mechanism (the "Byrnes basket") for triggering protection for other products, and the 1971 Burke-Hartke bill proposed a system of import quotas covering a range of products, along with measures aimed at discouraging foreign direct investment. Both bills garnered significant support from Democrats and Republicans.

In response to pressures from powerful groups, Congress also began attaching more strings to the legislation authorizing the president to negotiate internationally. The 1974 legislation created a framework of advisory committees so that concerned manufacturers and labor groups had a forum for pressing industry concerns, and it granted special exceptions for a wide range of industries including steel, textiles, ceramics, footwear, televisions, radios, and petroleum (Baldwin 1985, 143). Legislation was also amended under Section 301 of the act making it easier for domestic industries to win protection on the grounds of unfair foreign trade practices. In 1977, in the

[48] In this period (the 90th Congress), the Ways and Means Committee considered fifty-nine bills related to steel imports, forty-seven on textiles, forty on milk and dairy products, twenty-four on footwear, and fifty-five bills directing the president to impose quantitative restrictions generally to assist troubled industries; Pastor 1980, 125.

wake of complaints by steel producers about dumping by competitors, the Carter administration established a "Trigger Price Mechanism" that actually provided for automatic antidumping investigations if import prices fell below acceptable levels. In 1979, while passing legislation that implemented the Tokyo Round agreements, Congress passed new protective measures for the textile, footwear, dairy, and television industries, and further tightened the unfair trade laws.

The trade issue was sidestepped by both parties in the 1980 campaign. Reagan stated a general preference for trade openness while making vague campaign promises to provide relief from import competition to large industries, including the auto industry (Goldstein 1993, 231–32). Republican leaders in the Senate were divided on the issue. John Danforth, who wielded particular influence as the new chair of the Senate Finance Subcommittee on Trade, and in whose home state of Missouri both the ailing auto and footwear industries were concentrated, introduced a bill in 1981 applying quotas on Japanese auto imports. Under pressure, the White House negotiated export restraints with Japan the same year. The auto issue resurfaced in 1982 and 1983 when the powerful United Auto Workers union was able to push domestic content legislation before Congress.[49] Meanwhile, John Heinz, a Republican from Pennsylvania on the Senate Finance Committee, helped create bipartisan caucuses of members representing steel districts in both the Senate and the House and began moving quota legislation through Congress. The steel industry itself began swamping the International Trade Commission (ITC) with antidumping and countervailing petitions, and Reagan moved quickly to negotiate new restraints on steel imports from Europe. Steel again became an issue in the 1984 campaign, when the ITC ruled in favor of domestic producers under antidumping laws and recommended that the White House impose tariffs or quotas. The Democratic presidential candidate, Walter Mondale, quickly declared his support for tight steel quotas.[50]

Fueled in part by the appreciation of the dollar and its effect on import-competing and export industries, a range of trade bills were making their way through Congress around the same time. The most important of these, the Trade Remedies Reform Act, which was passed by the House in July, greatly expanded the range of unfair trade practices eligible for retaliation.

[49] Supporters of the legislation (from both parties) succeeded in having the bill referred to the House Energy and Commerce Committee, which was chaired by John Dingell, a Democrat from Michigan, who was a strong advocate for the auto industry. See McGillivray and Schiller 1996, 17. The chair of the House Ways and Means Trade Subcommittee was Bill Frenzel of Minnesota, a devout advocate of freer trade.

[50] Mondale, who had been a consistent spokesmen for openness until the 1980s, also endorsed the auto domestic content legislation in response to pressure from the UAW and attacked the Reagan administration for failing to get tough with the Japanese. When he met with criticism from internationalist Democrats, Mondale backed away from his early hard-line approach in the campaign, placing less emphasis on trade and more emphasis on the macroeconomic causes of U.S. economic problems. See Destler 1992, 47.

The bill was ultimately written into the omnibus Trade and Tariff Act of 1984, along with a mix of other measures passed in the House and Senate, including an extension of the president's authority to grant preferences to developing nations and a new grant of authority to negotiate free-trade agreements with Israel and Canada, a commitment to new steel export restraints, and over one hundred commodity-specific provisions (see Destler 1992, 86–88). In July 1985, Democrats in Congress, led by Richard Gephardt, introduced a bill proposing a 25 percent import surcharge on products from Japan, Taiwan, Korea, and Brazil, unless those nations reformed their trade policies. In the same year, Congress passed new quotas on textile imports. Reagan vetoed the bill, but the congressional vote on overriding the veto was delayed to put added pressure on the White House as it negotiated the extension of the Multi-Fiber Arrangement.

While the Reagan administration negotiated new VERs on textiles, machine tools, and semiconductors, Congress set about passing another omnibus trade bill in 1986. It was a mixture of measures that included authorization for trade negotiations, enhanced assistance for workers and firms harmed by imports, and increased spending on education. The bill was most notable, however, for the amendment proposed by Gephardt providing for the imposition of mandatory sanctions on nations running large trade surpluses with the United States. The bill was defeated in the Senate but garnered significant support among Senate Republicans. When the Democrats won back control of the Senate in 1986, they pushed through the same omnibus legislation with some additions, most controversially, a provision that employers give workers sixty days notice of any plant closings or layoffs. Reagan vetoed the bill, and the override attempt failed by just five votes in the Senate. A retooled compromise finally became law in 1988 as the Omnibus Trade and Competitiveness Act: The employer-worker provisions were dropped and the Gephardt amendment was replaced with a more ambiguous grant of authority to the president to take action against nations found to be employing unfair practices (the so-called "Super 301" provision). In the end, both parties appear to have been happy with this centrist position going into the 1988 election, and the legislation passed with bipartisan support.[51]

The new Republican administration continued to support openness in principle, while using strong threats to force trading partners to restrain exports to the United States or expand their U.S. imports in key sectors. In 1989, the U.S. Trade Representative, Carla Hills, named Brazil, India, and Japan under the Super 301 provision as nations with unfair trade practices

---

[51] The U.S.-Canada Free Trade Agreement passed with bipartisan support in the same session. The final version of the agreement included enough compensations and exemptions to assuage any real opposition. The industries that were most likely to be disadvantaged (the grain, timber, oil, and fishing industries) were all covered by exemptions, delays, or new forms of protection. Plywood, for instance, was exempted, the windfall profits tax on oil was repealed in the Omnibus bill, export enhancement programs for grain were expanded, and unfair trade investigations were initiated for a range of products.

and outlined a plan for a "Structural Impediments Initiative" to negotiate reductions in Japanese import barriers. In 1990, deals were struck on super-computers, satellites, wood products, and telecommunications. Bush made his own market-opening mission to Tokyo in 1992, taking along twenty-one business leaders, including executives from automobile and computer indus-tries. All the while, the Republican administration pushed on with multi-lateral negotiations in the GATT's Uruguay Round and with trilateral nego-tiations on the North American Free Trade Agreement (NAFTA). In 1991, Bush requested an extension of his authority to continue at both negotiating tables. As the voting on the legislation (reported in Table 4.8) makes appar-ent, while Republicans rallied somewhat to support Bush, the Democrats were deeply divided.[52]

By the 1990s, the old class coalitions were in disarray over the trade issue, and the two parties were rent by internal divisions over major trade legislation. In the 1992 election, the two candidates took virtually identical middle-of-the-road positions. In 1993, the new Clinton administration pushed ahead with the NAFTA and GATT negotiations, but adopted a self-styled results-oriented ap-proach to dealings with major trading partners—an approach little different from that adopted previously by Reagan and Bush aimed at forcing other nations to limit exports to the United States while expanding imports. A new framework agreement was negotiated with Japan on opening specific markets to American exports, and talks began on automobiles and auto parts, telecom-munications, medical technology, insurance, and construction.

In the fall of 1993, Clinton took on the challenge of steering the NAFTA through Congress, knowing that a large number of congressional Democrats, along with the AFL-CIO, were openly opposed. The administration at-tempted to build support by framing it as a bipartisan effort, and former Presidents Reagan and Bush appeared with Clinton at the White House to endorse the treaty. But many members of Congress, influenced by industry lobbies within their electorates, held off announcing their intended vote until the administration had offered them some satisfactory quid pro quo. Florida representatives in the House, for example, withheld their support until spe-cial protection was provided for citrus and vegetable growers. Similar ex-ceptions or delays in the removal of trade barriers were made for producers of textiles, beef, peanut butter, wheat, wine, sugar, corn sweeteners, bed frames, washing machines, and flat glass. The final result was a much-compromised treaty.[53] Nevertheless, the congressional votes indicate just how much division had been generated in each party: Average party cohe-sion scores were only 25.3 in the Senate and 33 in the House.

In 1994, the administration prepared for another uphill battle to secure

[52] As Destler (1992, 178) notes, the ambivalence among the Democrats on the trade issue was reflected in the behavior of Gephardt in his new role as House Majority Leader. He voted in favor of extending fast-track authority in the spring, but then rebalanced his position by introducing a new protectionist measure targeting Japan in the fall.

[53] For a description of these provisions see reports in *New York Times*, 11 and 17 November 1993.

passage of the agreements that had finally been reached in the Uruguay Round of the GATT. In October, Democratic Senator Ernest Hollings, chair of the Commerce Committee to which the bill had been referred, forced a delay in the vote until after the November elections.[54] Hollings, whose home state of South Carolina was heavily reliant on the textile industry, was a strong opponent and hoped the elections (which produced new Republican majorities in both the House and Senate) might disrupt support. Senator Jesse Helms of North Carolina, the incoming chair of the Foreign Relations Committee and another opponent of the bill tied closely to the textile industry, sent a letter to Clinton in which he threatened not to cooperate with the White House on foreign policy matters in the future if the vote was not delayed again until the new Congress was convened in January.[55] To placate opposition, the administration changed the customs rules on apparel to limit cheap imports from Asia (clothing made in Asia was deemed to originate in the country where it was assembled rather than where it was cut), changed antidumping rules along lines suggested by Hollings to make decisions in favor of domestic industries more likely, and renewed the Super 301 provisions. The legislation passed, but the final votes showed how deeply the two parties were divided over the trade issue. The contrast between trade politics in the 1990s and trade politics in the 1890s could hardly be more striking.

4.5 CONCLUSIONS

In light of the evidence that levels of factor mobility have varied substantially in the U.S. economy over time, the anticipated political effects fit rather well with the evolution of trade politics. The tariff issue was a predominantly local, group-based affair at the beginning of the nineteenth century. The emerging political parties were split over the tariff issue along regional lines and trade legislation reflected the competing pressures placed on Congress by a vast array of locally organized groups. In the years following the Civil War, however, trade became the partisan issue in U.S. politics as Republicans, drawing broad support from business and labor, supported protectionist tariffs over the vehement opposition of Democrats and their largely rural constituency. More recently, at least since the 1950s, growing rifts have been apparent in both parties and peak associations over the trade issue, and industry groups have exercised a powerful role in shaping policy outcomes.

---

[54] The GATT bill faced the hurdle of requiring a waiving of new budget rules that any tax cut must be fully financed. The administration lighted on the idea of extracting license fees from operators of new broad spectrum radio wave bands to be allocated under GATT as a source of new revenue. Unfortunately, this move placed the bill under the jurisdiction of the Commerce rather than the Finance Committee.

[55] See *New York Times*, 16 November 1994.

CHAPTER FIVE

Britain

According to the theory advanced in chapter 1 and the data on changes in levels of factor mobility reported in chapter 2, one would expect a rather different historical pattern in the cleavages over trade in Britain than in the United States over the last two centuries. Most importantly, the evidence reported in Figure 2.1 indicates that levels of factor mobility were far higher in Britain than in any of the other economies in the early part of the nineteenth century. We should thus expect that, other things equal, the development of class coalitions was likely to have occurred much earlier in Britain than elsewhere. We can also anticipate change: Class lines of cleavage should have been replaced by stronger industry coalitions in trade politics when levels of interindustry factor mobility declined rapidly from around the 1920s. While it is common to talk about British trade politics in terms of class conflict, especially when characterizing the debates over policy in the nineteenth century (see Rogowski 1989 and Verdier 1994), the theory advanced here anticipates significant change over time in the coalition patterns.

Table 5.1 summarizes the expectations for the British cases, making simple distinctions between them based on general levels of factor mobility and factor abundance.[1] The table also reports a brief summary of observed outcomes for each case, again in terms of levels of cohesion over the trade issue among class-based political parties and peak associations, and levels of industry-group lobbying. The match between the effects anticipated by the theory and the observed changes in British trade politics is quite close. Britain was characterized by high levels of factor mobility from very early in the nineteenth century until early in the twentieth century, and trade politics was clearly defined by stable class cleavages. Beginning in the 1920s, however, as measured levels of mobility began to fall, these broad coalitions appear to have splintered along industry lines, with deep divisions over trade growing within the political parties and peak associations.

5.1 From the Napoleonic Wars to the Cobden-Chevalier Treaty

With the revival of trade after the Napoleonic Wars, debates in Britain centered on the protectionist Corn Laws, which restricted importation of var-

---

[1] As described in the previous chapter, the same rule is applied throughout to distinguish "high" cases (coefficients of variation on wages below 12) from "low" (coefficients above 16). Rogowski (1989) is again the primary source for the classifications of factor endowments.

TABLE 5.1
Anticipated and Observed Outcomes in Britain

				Outcomes	
Period	Factor Endowments	Mobility	Prediction[a]	Class-based Parties and Associations	Industry Groups
1815–1869	Abundant labor and capital; scarce land	High	Class coalitions	Liberals strongly supported free trade; Tories protectionist, but split by Peelite faction in 1846	Little independent activity; combined in Anti-Corn Law League
1870–1914	Abundant labor and capital; scarce land	High	Class coalitions	Liberals and Labour gave strong, unified support for free trade; Tory leaders censored protectionist members	Few groups gave testimony to commissions
1919–1939	Abundant labor and capital; scarce land	Intermediate; falling	Mixed	Tories advocated tariffs under Baldwin but were divided; Labour and TUC supported free trade until Depression	Activity increased after onset of Depression
1945–1994	Abundant labor and capital; scarce land[b]	Low	Industry coalitions	Tories and Labour split in votes over entrance to EC and GATT rounds; CBI and TUC also internally divided	Very active in pressuring planning agencies for assistance

[a] Class coalitions are expected to imply that class-based organizations are internally unified on trade and adopt coherent platforms while groups are inactive. Industry coalitions imply that class-based organizations are internally divided on trade and adopt ambiguous positions (see Table 3.1).

[b] Using 1966 data, Bowen, Leamer, and Sveikauskas (1987) find Britain to be very abundant in all categories of labor (except agricultural workers) and very scarce in all types of land. In contrast to Rogowski's findings, however, they find Britain to be relatively scarce in capital.

ious grains (wheat, rye, barley, and oats, as well as peas and beans). The laws were defended resolutely by the landowning elite (Toynbee [1884] 1958, 5). Pressure for reform came most strongly from manufacturers, especially textile producers in Leicester and Manchester, anxious to reduce labor costs (McCord 1958, 16). It was these manufacturers who formed the leadership of the Anti-Corn Law League in 1838, and a cotton manufacturer, Richard Cobden, became the League's most famous advocate. But the push for reform soon drew a mass following among both the urban middle and working classes and attracted support from the working-class Chartist reform movement that organized the "bigger loaf" campaign in the 1840s (Magnus 1964, 65–66).[2]

The effects were quickly apparent in Parliament, where politics had been transformed by the Great Reform Act of 1832.[3] Liberals and Radicals backed the League wholeheartedly and Tories voted strongly against liberalizing bills (McCord 1958, 17). Average party cohesion indexes on votes to abolish the laws were quite high: 78.6 in 1834 and 84.1 in 1842, compared with cohesion indexes of just 67.9 and 58.4 on all other votes in the corresponding sessions of Parliament (see Table 5.2).[4] Cobden himself entered Parliament in 1841, campaigning with the cry "You must untax the people's bread!" The League stepped up its campaign with a storm of pamphlets, petition drives, public meetings and addresses to labor unions, and the launching of a weekly newspaper.

By the 1840s, widespread economic distress was having a great impact on the Tory leader Robert Peel. His statements on trade policy revealed a flagging faith in protection (McCord 1958, 189–92). Peel introduced a sliding scale for grain duties in 1842 and in an attempt to ease the food crisis, reduced those rates slightly in 1844, arousing fierce opposition from landed interests and from within Conservative ranks.[5] Tory supporters were increasingly divided, however, between those whose interests were bound up exclusively in agriculture and those who had diversified by investing in manu-

---

[2] There was a good deal of competition between Chartist leaders and the League organizers, since the former were very worried that the League would distract supporters from the broader goal of electoral reform. See Longmate 1984, 81–95. The more radical elements of the Chartist movement were deeply distrustful of the manufacturers.

[3] The Reform Act abolished the small and rotten boroughs, extended new county divisions to include the large industrial cities of the West Riding, and increased the electorate by an estimated 50 to 80 percent; see Cox 1987, 10. The enlargement of the electorate was the prime impetus for the consolidation of the political parties and Chartism and the Anti-Corn Law League were the precursors of mass-based parties in Britain. See McKenzie 1963, 13.

[4] Data on votes and party affiliations are from the *Hansard Parliamentary Debates* (1834–1971), *McCalmont's Parliamentary Poll Book of All Elections 1832–1895* (1895), and the *Parliamentary Companion* (Dod 1834–1860). General cohesion indexes are calculated from 10 percent random samples drawn by the author from all votes in the given year.

[5] The sliding scale mandated high duties when domestic grain prices were low but allowed for lower duty rates when domestic prices climbed above set levels. The adjustment lowered the rates slightly and also set a maximum tariff on manufactured items at 20 percent.

TABLE 5.2
Divisions on Trade Bills in the House of Commons, 1815–1869

	Legislation	Party	Yeas	Nays	Cohesion	Average Cohesion	General Cohesion
1834	Hume Motion on the Corn Laws	Conservatives	29	221	76.8	78.6	67.9
		Liberals (Reformers)	126	45	47.4		
1842	Villiers Motion to abolish Corn Laws	Conservatives	10	209	90.9	84.1	58.4
		Liberals (Reformers)	33	184	69.6		
1846	Peel Motion to repeal Corn Laws	Conservatives	84	222	45.1	82.5	58.4
		Liberals (Reformers)	223	4	96.4		
1860	Address approving Treaty with France	Conservatives	22	44	33.3	88.9	58.5
		Liberals	260	12	91.2		

Sources: Hansard Parliamentary Debates, McCalmont (1895), and Dod (1834–1860).

facturing and railways (Schonhardt-Bailey 1991; Aydelotte 1962, 290–307). Peel himself had interests in cotton spinning, and Leaguers noted wryly that he had "commercial blood in him."[6] In 1844, the League organized a new petition against the Corn Laws with over two million signatures and conducted a series of mass meetings in Covent Garden; a new weekly journal, *The Economist*, added to pressure for reform.[7]

In March of 1845, Cobden made a historic speech to the House that appears to have been the decisive moment for Peel.[8] The failure of the potato crop in 1845, and the ensuing food crisis, gave Peel the pretext to act. Amid reports of widespread starvation, the prime minister called an emergency session of his cabinet in October and recommended suspension of restrictions on imports. When they refused to support him, he resigned. The leader of the opposition, Lord John Russell, had announced his support for abolition of the Corn Laws but was unable to form a government, so Peel assumed the leadership again and summoned Parliament to consider his repeal bill.

The voting patterns among party members in the Commons reflect the coalitions that had formed on the trade issue. The average cohesion score for the vote on repeal was 82.5. The Liberals were highly unified, while there was a division among Tories between the Peelites and those opposed to any reform (the old guard landed elite). The conflict over the repeal of the Corn Laws split the Conservatives irrevocably. Peel's rival, Benjamin Disraeli, charged him with a betrayal of party, and the expelled Peelite faction (which included the young Gladstone) eventually gravitated to the Liberal fold (Bradford 1984, 159).

The new shape of British party politics had profound effects for the international trading system in the second half of the nineteenth century. The "purified" Tories (known for years as the Protectionists) were increasingly isolated on the trade issue, drastically so with later extensions of the franchise. Drawing on an immense base of support among owners of capital and labor, the Liberals and their free-trade platform enjoyed a considerable advantage. Gladstone formally entered the Liberal Party in 1859 and became prime minister in 1860. His first budget included the Anglo-French (Cobden-Chevalier) Commercial Treaty, which eliminated all remaining protectionist duties in Britain.

---

[6] Quoted in McCord 1958, 194.

[7] Industry groups, it should be noted, played little or no discernible role in these great policy debates. The majority of extant groups were still locally based trade associations whose role was limited to contributing funds to the League and circulating League petitions in the 1830s and 1840s; see Kirby 1977, 11.

[8] According to one account:

> The Prime Minister had followed every sentence with earnest attention; his face grew more and more solemn as the argument proceeded. At length he crumpled up the notes which he had been taking, and was heard by an onlooker who was close by, to say to Mr. Sidney Herbert, who sat next to him on the bench, "You must answer this, for I cannot." (Morley 1881, 318)

5.2 YEARS OF FREE TRADE AND EMPIRE

In 1867 the second Reform Act nearly doubled the size of the electorate and, by enfranchising more members of the urban working and middle classes, created a massive base of support for free trade (see Cox 1987, 10). By tying their party to the free-trade cause, Gladstone's Liberals forged a huge electoral support base. The Tories could not ignore demands from rural supporters for protection, but to openly endorse tariffs would be electoral suicide. Agricultural producers in Britain, unlike farmers elsewhere, were simply too few in number to be a force at the polls.[9] In addition, the Tories began to draw more support from the expanding Victorian middle class, which grew defensive on labor and social issues but favored trade openness (Ostrogorski 1902, 267–68).

Tory leaders responded by cultivating an ambiguous position on the tariff. After victory in the 1885 election, Lord Salisbury continued to be evasive on the issue, only very tentatively supporting retaliation against unfair foreign trade practices (Zebel 1940, 173). After 1886 the party had an added incentive for shelving the trade issue when they were joined by a faction of the Liberal Party, the Liberal Unionists, who had split with Gladstone on Irish home rule and held strong free-trade views (Lubenow 1988). Party leaders censured backbenchers from speaking out on the issue and avoided any discussion of a change in policy (Brown 1943, 65). Voting on trade legislation in the House of Commons, limited to divisions over proposals for minor policy adjustments, produced high cohesion indexes: 91.1 in 1881, 94.6 in 1894, 95.2 in 1897, and 92.6 in 1906 (see Table 5.3).

Although there were some demands for "fair trade," the parties came under little pressure from industry lobbies (Verdier 1994, 84–85; Zebel 1940, 161–85).[10] Only eleven trade associations responded to inquiries from a Royal Commission on trade and industry in 1886, and four of these expressed no particular opinion (Verdier 1994, 84–88). But the Tories could not shelve the trade issue and paper over the divisions within their ranks indefinitely. In 1903, twenty-seven Unionist backbenchers challenged the party leadership on the trade issue by supporting Baldwin's Tariff Reform program. The program tapped into agrarian dissent but was driven by growing concerns among Unionists about imperial ties and the need for preferen-

---

[9] As Lord Derby put it at the time, the working class "can, if it chooses, outvote all other classes put together" (quoted in McKenzie 1963, 147).

[10] The sugar industry was a lonely leader in the fair trade campaign: Hurt by foreign subsidies to beet sugar production, the British Sugar Refiners Association (which relied on cane sugar from the West Indies) and their workers (who formed the Workingmen's National Association for the Abolition of Foreign Sugar Bounties) pushed for countervailing duties in the 1880s. Though the Tories introduced an anti-bounty bill when in power, they ultimately withdrew it when it risked turning trade into a campaign issue. See Brown 1943, 29–57.

TABLE 5.3
Divisions on Trade Bills in the House of Commons, 1870–1914

	Legislation	Party	Yeas	Nays	Cohesion	Average Cohesion	General Cohesion
1881	Ritchie Motion	Conservative (Unionist)	6	69	84.3	91.1	82.5
		Liberal (Labour)	142	7	90.9		
1894	Foreign Goods (Mark of Origin) Bill	Conservative (Unionist)	154	5	93.9	94.6	90.3
		Liberal (Labour)	3	178	96.3		
1897	Foreign Prison-Made Goods Bill	Conservative	219	5	95.8	95.2	91.2
		Liberal (Labour)	2	78	95		
1906	Kitson Motion	Conservative	6	84	86.5	92.6	88.9
		Liberal (Labour)	462	14	94.1		
1911	Tariff Reform Amendment	Conservative	209	8	92.7	94.2	88.5
		Liberal-Labour	5	305	96.9		

Sources: Hansard Parliamentary Debates, and McCalmont (1895).

tial trade policy (Verdier 1994, 140).[11] The bickering in Balfour's cabinet reopened old wounds within the party and split the leadership.

Balfour hedged and delayed. In the 1906 election campaign he finally committed to some unspecified reform that would raise agricultural import duties. The Tories lost decisively that year and twice again in the elections prior to World War I. Led by David Lloyd George, and drawing strength from their relationship with the newly formed Labour Party, the Liberals dominated the scene. They made good on their platform of free trade and social reforms, introducing old-age pensions, sickness insurance, and unemployment benefits.[12]

In opposition after 1906, Balfour kept equivocating on Tariff Reform. He edged toward a more protectionist position, while still refusing to formulate a policy program in opposition, and even promised (in the 1910 campaign) that any tariff on food imports would be put to a referendum. In 1911 he resigned as leader and was replaced by Bonar Law, a prominent tariff reformer. While there still remained a division between the two factions (the "free fooders" and "wholehoggers" as they were called), his 1912 declaration in favor of Tariff Reform reportedly received an ovation from the 12,000 assembled delegates at the national conference (Peel 1913, 165).

5.3 INTERWAR TRADE POLITICS

After the dissolution of the wartime coalition under Lloyd George in 1922, the tariff became grist for open partisan competition, pitting the Liberal-Labour alliance against the Conservatives. In 1923, Baldwin made the Tories' commitment to protection the focus of the election campaign. Although he took pains to promise that no new duties would be levied on food imports (to avoid the stigma of a "stomach tax"), the platform was disastrous and Ramsay MacDonald led Labour to victory.[13]

---

[11] On the minimal role played by industry demands in the Tariff Reform movement, see Marrison's (1983) response to Semmel (1960) and Rempel (1972). When supporters of the Reform program set up an unofficial, privately financed Commission to discuss tariff changes in 1904, the lack of group response was striking. Only nine trade associations and eight agricultural groups testified at the Commission's request, and of the thirteen manufacturing industries selected for study by the Commission, eight were not represented at all in the hearings by their trade associations; see Verdier 1994, 140.

[12] The social reforms, financed by increased taxes on property and income, accelerated the shift among capitalists away from the Liberal Party and toward the Conservatives. Although favoring free trade, industrialists objected to increased taxes and feared the growth of socialism. As the Duke of Northumberland stated famously at the time: "Protectionism cannot be worse than Socialism . . . And as . . . Tariff Reform or Socialism are the only possible alternatives at the moment, I am quite prepared to swallow the former" (quoted in Blewett 1968). On the realignment in party constituencies that began in these years, see Blewett 1972.

[13] In 1921, in fact, as part of the old coalition government, the Conservatives had actually helped repeal farm price guarantees even as world agricultural prices began falling; see

In 1924 the new government removed the imperial preferences put in place by the Tories, repealed the wartime McKenna duties (levied on revenue items), and allowed many of the safeguarding duties applied to defense-related items to expire (Verdier 1994, 175n). The Labour-Liberal alliance remained solidly committed to free trade, as did the Trades Union Congress (Lowe 1942, 82–83). Stung by the defeat, the Tories backed away from protection again and limited its support in the next few years to only minor adjustments to trade policy. When they returned to power in 1925, the initial moves the Tories made were to reinstate the McKenna duties, to add some items to the safeguarding duties list, and to apply imperial preferences to those duties. Baldwin was drawn to the tariff issue again in the election of 1929 and committed the party to support the old Tariff Reform program, promising to impose new duties on manufactures and strengthen imperial preferences. MacDonald led the alliance to another decisive win.

The onset of depression discredited MacDonald's policies, however, and broke apart the Liberal-Labour alliance over the issue of nationalization. Middle-class voters flocked to the Tories, who were swept into office in 1931. Among business interests, the old consensus began to dissolve and more industries began concerted lobbying efforts aimed at securing rents (Turner 1984, 48; Verdier 1994, 176). A divided Federation of British Industry came out in favor of tariffs. On the left there had been little dissent from the TUC's support for free trade (Carr and Taplin 1962, 341; Boyce 1987, 124–25). But after 1930, key unions in the woolens and iron and steel industries began demanding special protection (Verdier 1994, 174).

In 1932 the new Tory government passed the Import Duty Act, which set duties of 33.3 percent on a long list of key commodities and a 10 percent duty on all other imports, with only a few exceptions. The parliamentary votes on the 1932 bill, like other votes on trade legislation in this period, reveal a substantial decline in party cohesion from previous periods: Average cohesion indexes fell to 66.3 in 1921, 58.0 in 1924, and 67.8 in 1932 (see Table 5.4).

5.4 THE POSTWAR ERA

By the 1960s, the Tories and Labour had both committed themselves to a program of planning that included subsidies targeted to major trade-affected industries as a counterweight to GATT-mandated tariff reductions (Blank 1978; Verdier 1994, 265). This approach helped to paper over deep rifts in each party's core class constituency, while responding to lobbying pressure from individual industries. In fact, trade associations and labor unions from

---

Whetham 1974, 36–49. By 1923, the National Farmers Union had switched from demanding tariffs to pushing Conservatives to support a subsidy program for agricultural production.

TABLE 5.4
Divisions on Trade Bills in the House of Commons, 1919–1939

	Legislation	*Party*	*Yeas*	*Nays*	*Cohesion*	*Average Cohesion*	*General Cohesion*
1921	Safeguarding of	Conservative	221	87	43.7		
	Industries Act	Liberal-Labour	91	5	89.8	66.3	87.2
1924	McKenna Duties	Conservative	68	180	45.6		
	Amendment	Liberal-Labour	210	41	67.5	58	88.6
1932	Import Duties	Conservative	341	12	93.6		
	Bill	Liberal-Labour	101	50	33.8	67.8	90
1937	Anglo-American	Conservative	30	184	72		
	Trade Agreement	Liberal-Labour	88	41	36.2	56.5	88.1

Sources: Hansard Parliamentary Debates.

major industries were granted special access to planning agencies to help ensure that their demands were met.[14]

After winning power from the Tories in 1964 under Harold Wilson, Labour poured money into the major British industries in selective subsidies. They located planning authority in Whitehall in a new Department of Economic Affairs, which usurped the role of the independent National Economic Development Council (or "Neddy") set up by the Tories in 1961. The Industrial Development Act of 1966 substituted industry subsidies for investment tax incentives and introduced a greater degree of ministerial discretion in the allocation of government favor (Ganz 1977, 25–36). At the same time, Labour created the Industrial Reorganization Corporation (IRC), aimed at encouraging mergers in industry via state equity participation and consultation (Hayward 1974, 142).

A growing division separated Labour moderates from the Bevanite left wing of the party that, linked to powerful unions in the mining, steel, and textile industries, supported unilateral tariff increases in violation of the GATT and vehemently opposed British entry into the European Community. The TUC itself was deeply divided along industry lines and vacillated on trade issues (Rose 1980, 233; Hall 1986, 60). Wilson applied for EC entry in 1967 but opposed the same move by the Heath government in 1971 after the left wing gained strength within the party (Nairn 1972). In the one vote on EC entry in the House of Commons in 1971 (shown in Table 5.5), the cohesion index for Labour was only 46.5 (69 for, 189 against). The cohesion index for the Tories was 75.7 (282 for, 39 against).

On the right, tensions over trade policy also grew among Conservatives. When the Heath government reacted to the recession in the early 1970s by providing selective protection for major industries (Ganz 1977, 40; Young

[14] See Hall 1986, 56; Grant 1980; Shonfield 1965, 151–52; Hayward 1974, 401. This was a major feature of what Beer (1965) labeled the "new group politics" in Britain.

TABLE 5.5
The Division in the House of Commons over British Entry into the European
Community, 1971

	Legislation	Party	Yeas	Nays	Cohesion	Average Cohesion	General Cohesion
1971	European	Conservative	282	39	75.7		
	Community	Labour	69	189	46.5	66.5	91.3
	entry						

Sources: Hansard Parliamentary Debates.

and Lowe 1974), it drew intense criticism (especially from small business) at party conferences (Gamble and Walkland 1974, 78–81; Grant 1980). While supported by party members comfortable with the import barriers and industrial intervention sought by many of the large industries that dominated the Confederation of British Industry (CBI), those Tories aligned more closely with export interests and small business were openly opposed to such selective protection. In 1973, a group of Tory backbenchers created the Small Business Bureau within the party to campaign for reduced intervention.

Wilson led Labour back to power in 1974 and was only able to resolve the internal dispute over EC entry by holding a referendum on the issue. After the vote (67 percent favored membership), Labour stepped up its dirigiste approach. It created the National Enterprise Board, a new version of the IRC, which quickly rescued British Leyland, Rolls Royce, Ferranti, and Alfred Herbert from bankruptcy (Young 1978) and set about creating planning agreements between the state and individual firms in which commitments to government objectives were given in exchange for subsidies and tax allowances (Wilks 1981). Under Callaghan's "new industrial strategy," the TUC and the CBI were charged with organizing working parties in each major industry consisting of trade associations, trade unions, and government representatives. This provided industry groups a direct channel for lobbying for nontariff forms of protection. New quotas on imports were swiftly applied to consumer electronics, knitted products, textiles, and footwear.

When the Conservatives returned to power under Thatcher in 1979, it was on a laissez-faire platform favored by the small-business faction of the party. They did begin a program of privatization, reduced regional subsidies, and dismantled the sponsoring divisions responsible for planning within the Department of Trade and Industry (Shepherd 1987, 169–74). Yet, at the same time, they increased selective subsidies to targeted high-technology industries, directed government procurement policy toward favoring such industries, and negotiated voluntary export restraints for automobiles and electronic equipment. A new minister for Information Technology was appointed to aid export growth in the areas of microelectronics, fibre optics, and satellites (Hall 1986, 113).[15] All the while, divisions among Tories over European integration widened further as the right wing of the party became increasingly vocal in its opposition. In 1994, Lord Howe founded a pro-Europe group within the party to counter growing anti-European sentiment.[16]

Among Labour supporters, the rift over trade policy continued to widen. When the left wing succeeded in radicalizing the party platform in the 1980s, it reinserted a pledge to withdraw from the EC and impose import barriers (see King 1977). The left wing was gradually reined in during the late 1980s, and the party retreated from its more extreme position under the leadership of a moderate, Neil Kinnock. Nevertheless, deep divisions remained and resurfaced in the midst of leadership tussles in the 1990s, with party leaders split between right-wing "modernizers" enthusiastic about further European and international integration and left-wing "traditionalists."

5.5 CONCLUSIONS

The study of changes in British trade politics over time reveals considerable evidence consistent with the expected political effects of changing levels of factor mobility. The battle over repeal of the Corn Laws in the 1830s and 1840s helped to reshape politics around factoral cleavages early in the nineteenth century, and the trade debate in the latter half of the century (lasting until 1914) was characterized by highly unified parties and peak associations—with the one complication that the Tories were divided not by loyalties to different constituencies but by whether to make the tariff a campaign issue when doing so would almost certainly lead to electoral defeat.

After the realignments of the 1920s and 1930s, there were growing internal divisions over the trade issue within the Conservative and Labour parties, and both weathered disputes between internal factions over European integration. The CBI and the TUC were equally splintered. Industry groups became increasingly influential in the "new group politics," and rival party leaders gravitated toward similarly ambiguous approaches to trade policy that favored selective intervention and nontariff instruments.

---

[15] The Minister for Trade and Industry, Michael Heseltine, split his department into sections charged with assisting individual industries and created a new industrial competitiveness division. At the 1992 party conference he actually promised to "intervene before breakfast, lunch, tea and dinner" (quoted in *The Economist*, 30 January 1993).

[16] See *Financial Times*, 5 December 1994.

CHAPTER SIX

France

The theory anticipates a very different pattern of trade cleavages in France over the last two centuries. The evidence reported in chapter 2 indicates that levels of interindustry factor mobility have been far lower in France than in any of the other economies during almost the entire period under study. According to the theory then, all else constant, strong industry-based cleavages over trade should have been much more likely in France than elsewhere, and it would be surprising to find any evidence of robust class coalitions in trade politics. Perhaps only in the interwar years, when the evidence indicates a slight increase in levels of interindustry mobility, should we expect to see any evidence of class cleavages in French trade politics. For the most part, however, the French economy stands apart from the others as especially fertile ground for the formation of narrow industry-based coalitions.

This French "exceptionalism" fits well with previous accounts of French trade politics that emphasize the role of pressure groups in different historical eras (Smith 1980; Milner 1988; Verdier 1994). Table 6.1 summarizes the anticipated effects and the observed outcomes for each case, again focusing on levels of cohesion over the trade issue among class-based political parties and peak associations and levels of industry group lobbying. Summarized in this simple way, the evidence does appear to fit quite well with the expectations based on the theory. Overall, relatively low levels of factor mobility have corresponded with strong and active industry-based coalitions in French trade politics. Even when parties appealed to distinct class constituencies, they have generally been divided internally over the trade issue. Peak associations representing business, labor, and rural interests have been similarly riven.

6.1 FROM 1815 TO LOUIS NAPOLEON

The absence of democratic institutions and party competition in the turbulent years after 1815 makes testing the theory against French politics of the first part of the nineteenth century difficult. It does seem clear, however, that no matter how the political institutions changed in these years, active lobbying by industry groups was a constant feature. Under Louis XVIII, grain interests won higher tariffs even as an array of agrarian interests (led by wine makers and silk growers) pushed for freer trade (Caron 1979, 95–97; Brogan 1967, 405). Capitalists were also divided over trade. Particularly

TABLE 6.1
Anticipated and Observed Outcomes in France

Period	Factor Endowments	Mobility	Prediction[a]	Outcomes		
				Class-based Parties and Associations	Industry Groups	
1815–1869	Abundant labor and capital; Scarce land	Low	Industry coalitions	n/a	High activity; great number of petitions from groups to Assembly	
1870–1914	Abundant labor and capital; scarce land	Low	Industry coalitions	Republicans, Bonapartists, monarchists, and Radicals divided; Socialists supported free trade	High activity; industry lobbies mounted major efforts to alter outcomes of Chamber hearings on tariff	
1919–1939	Abundant labor and capital; scarce land	Intermediate	Mixed	Increase in partisanship; Socialists favored liberal reform; Radicals opposed, and ended Front Populaire	Group lobbies active in pressuring committees for tariff alterations and in treaty bargaining	
1945–1994	Abundant labor and capital; scarce land[b]	Low	Industry coalitions	Gaullists and Socialists divided over trade and EC, as were FNSEA and CNPF; CGT more protectionist than CFDT	Planning process dominated by intense industry lobbying	

[a]Class coalitions are expected to imply that class-based organizations are internally unified on trade and adopt coherent platforms while groups are inactive. Industry coalitions imply that class-based organizations are internally divided on trade and adopt ambiguous positions (see Table 3.1).
[b]Using 1966 data, Bowen, Leamer, and Sveikauskas (1987) find France to be abundant in all types of labor (though least abundant in agricultural workers) and scarce in arable land. In contrast to Rogowski's findings, they find France to be relatively scarce in capital.

strong lobbying for protection came from the Chambre consultative des arts et manufactures of Saint-Etienne, which was composed chiefly of iron and steel producers (Caron 1979, 94). The silk industry in Lyon, on the other hand, and the merchants of Bordeaux and Le Havre were vocal proponents of trade liberalization (Smith 1980, 18). Although Louis XVIII favored lower tariffs, between 1814 and 1826 the Assembly voted for prohibitions on manufactured imports and for duties on grain and other foodstuffs (Clough 1939, 60).

Under the July Monarchy, industries flooded the Assembly with petitions and sent leaders to represent them in Paris (Gille 1964, 209–49; Verdier 1994, 98). An 1834 national survey on trade found that many chambers of commerce held very protectionist views (including those representing cotton weavers and iron producers), but in commercial circles and export industries (such as fine fabrics and metal goods) there was firm support for freer trade (Caron 1979, 96; Smith 1980, 90). Manufacturers in the provincial cities, in general, were far less supportive of reform than industrialists in the major cosmopolitan centers of Paris, Lyons, and Marseilles (Ratcliffe 1978, 65).

In the wake of the dramatic reform in Britain in 1846, the wine makers of Bordeaux took the initiative in forming a free-trade association. A Paris-based association soon followed under the devoted leadership of the economist Frédéric Bastiat, who had authored a succession of brilliant essays advocating trade liberalization in the *Journal des économistes* beginning in 1844.[1] The association set about following the model of the Anti-Corn Law League: sponsoring petitions, holding public meetings, circulating pamphlets and a newspaper (*Le libre échange*). But, unlike the League, it never mobilized a class base of support (Russell 1969, 97–98).[2]

Enough pressure for change had mounted by early 1847 that a bill to reduce duties was introduced in the Assembly by the Guizot ministry. The committee that reviewed the bill, however, was headed by Adolphe Thiers, a noted protectionist, and the exceedingly hostile committee report scuttled the reform.[3] It was only under the authoritarian rule of Louis Napoleon that significant trade policy reform was achieved. Until 1860, the emperor made some attempt to involve the elected Corps législatif in his reforms, but protectionists there (particularly those representing textiles, coal and iron inter-

---

[1] Bastiat was a master of the reductio ad absurdum and is best remembered for his satirical "Petition on behalf of the candle-makers and allied industries" for protection against the unfair competition from the sun. The petition carefully laid out a protectionist logic for a law requiring the covering of all windows and skylights and other openings through which sunlight freely entered houses.

[2] Keenly aware of the very different political context in France, Cobden had advised his friend Bastiat that "the free trade movement, which was formed on a broad base in England and forced upon the legislature, must in France start with the legislators and be imposed on the people" (quoted in Russell 1969, 84).

[3] The economist Michel Chevalier dubbed the report "a soliloquy by the private interests meditating among themselves"; see Dunham 1930, 10.

ests, and owners of large wooded estates) rejected his major proposals (Dunham 1930, 18–38). He resorted instead, under the advice of Chevalier, to negotiating a series of bilateral trade treaties in the 1860s, beginning with the landmark treaty with Britain in 1860.[4] Protests ultimately forced the government to adopt a range of measures aiding particular interests harmed by the treaties, including programs that subsidized landowners and made loans to industry (Fohlen 1956, 293; Dunham 1930, 150).

6.2 Trade Politics in the Third Republic

After the collapse of the Second Empire, a complex multiparty system began to take shape in the 1870s. By 1872 there were eight major parties contesting elections. On the tariff issue, positions were poorly delineated and the parties were internally split in votes in the Chamber of Deputies (Gourevitch 1986, 104; Elwitt 1975, 270–72). On the right, most Bonapartists remained loyal to the Emperor's pro-trade legacy, while monarchists of various stripes tended to favor agricultural tariffs or were divided according to how trade affected different landed interests. On the left, Socialists generally supported freer trade, but Radicals were less clearly positioned (Verdier 1994, 101). The Republicans, who emerged as the dominant centrists in parliament with strong support among urban business interests and the middle class, were especially divided. Average party cohesion indexes on trade votes were only 24.5 in 1872, 29.7 in 1878, and 47.1 in 1892 (see Table 6.2).[5]

The divisions widened when the trade treaties with Britain and Belgium came up for renewal in 1878. When the Chamber began hearings it was swamped by lobbyists.[6] Protectionist industries lobbied independently and also combined forces in the Association de l'industrie française (AIF). The largest contingent in the AIF came from among the textile manufacturers: specifically, the cotton and flax spinners and the makers of jute and burlap. Iron and steel producers and the coal mining industry were also prominent participants.[7] Support for free trade, on the other hand, emanated predomi-

---

[4] The agreement removed French prohibitions on imports and sharply reduced tariffs. By 1868 the emperor had signed similar bilateral treaties with Belgium, the German states, Italy, Switzerland, Sweden, Norway, the Hanse towns, Spain, the Netherlands, Austria, and Portugal; see Dunham 1930.

[5] Data on votes are from Verdier 1994, and the Assemblee nationale, *Annales de la chambre des députés* 1871–1910. Party affiliations are from the *Dictionnaire des Parliamentaires français* (Jolly 1977). General cohesion indexes are calculated from 10 percent random samples drawn by the author from all votes in the given year.

[6] See Smith 1980, 90–140 for a wonderfully detailed account.

[7] Groups were represented by their own associations, such as the Comité des houilleres du nord et du Pas-de-Calais (whose officers were leaders in the AIF) and the Comité des forges, and by the chambers of commerce in the cities where the industries were concentrated— chambers from centers of the cottons industry, including those from Rouen, Lille, and Roubaix, were prominent lobbying forces and members of the AIF.

nantly from the major centers of trade, finance, and transport: Paris, Lyons, Marseilles, Bordeaux, Le Havre, and Nantes. Major sections of industry joined them—including the woolens and silk industries and the wine producers—and helped to form a Free Trade Association (the Association pour la défense de la liberté commerciale) in 1878 as a counterweight to the AIF.[8] Some seventy-three separate industry groups offered testimony, including almost every member group of both the AIF and FTA.

When the Commission submitted its bill in 1879, the lobbying began again. The AIF, FTA, and the major industry groups organized rallies aimed at pressuring ministers and deputies preparing to vote. The major industries formed committees of managers and workers to contact deputies and circulate petitions (Smith 1980, 160–63). FTA delegations from Lyons, Bordeaux, and Saint-Etienne took up residence in Paris for the length of the deliberations, and textile representatives met with iron masters at the AIF's Paris headquarters each day. The *Echo du Nord* reported that "All who have an interest in [this] grave deliberation . . . are now represented in Paris . . . on all sides arms are being furbished."[9] The urban protectionists in the Chamber sought a deal with the agricultural bloc by pledging support for higher duties on foodstuffs in return for support for industrial protection. But free traders were able to derail the plan and force a compromise law, eventually passed in 1882, that altered tariffs in moderate fashion and allowed the treaty negotiations to go ahead.[10]

By the late 1880s, with the treaties set to expire again, protracted agricultural recession had pushed more farmers and the agrarian peak association, the Société des agriculteurs de France (SAF), toward protectionism (Golob 1944, 43). In 1888 the AIF and SAF agreed to cooperate in earnest as the 1889 Chamber elections approached. The Republicans, locked in battle with the monarchists and clericalists, drew rural support away from the conservative right by courting this new urban-rural coalition. The key political challenge was to patch together a sizable electoral support base from the variety of different groups, each favoring protection for their own industry but not for others. After the election of 1889, the new Republican government headed by Méline engineered a compromise that assured major industries duty-free imports of key raw materials while providing new assistance for a range of agricultural producers and manufacturers (Verdier 1994, 126;

[8] Prominent support for the FTA came from chambers of commerce in cities where the woolens industry thrived (including Reims, Mazamet, and Carcassone) and from the centers of the silk industry in the Rhône and the Loire, and especially from Lyons (the Association de la fabrique lyonnaise was particularly vocal). The other great center of free-trade agitation was among the wine producers of Bordeaux. Manufacturers of some chemicals, refined sugar, and luxury items—typically based in the port cities and Paris—joined in lobbying for the free trade.

[9] Quoted in Smith 1980, 171.

[10] They managed this by dividing the vote on the bill into four votes on separate sections. This meant that the protectionists could not retaliate if the agricultural bloc did not support them in the votes on industrial duties; the protectionists betrayed their partners first and voted against food duties: See Smith 1980, 174.

TABLE 6.2
Voting on Trade Legislation in the Chamber of Deputies, 1870–1914

		Party	Yeas	Nays	Cohesion	Average Cohesion	General Cohesion
1870	Brame Interpellation	Bonapartist	13	155	84.5		
		Center Left	12	31	44.2	58.1	70.1
		Moderate Republican	3	18	71.4		
1872	Tax on Raw Materials	Extreme Right	8	20	42.9		
		Bonapartist	2	14	75		
		Right	61	67	4.7		
		Center Right	67	59	6.3		
		Center Left	55	45	10	24.5	65.8
		Moderate Republican	75	27	47.1		
		Union Republican	24	21	6.7		
1878	Treaty with Italy	Bonapartist	20	54	45.9		
		Right	45	3	87.9		
		Center Left	23	28	9.8		
		Moderate Republican	94	87	1.6		

Year	Tariff	Party					
1892	Meline Tariff	Union Republican	20	26	13		
		Radical	16	19	8.6	29.7	64
		Extreme Right	16	18	5.9		
		Right	117	5	91.8		
		Moderate Republican	183	27	74.3		
		Radical	52	48	5.5	47.1	66.2
1910	Tariff	Independent	24	1	92		
		Liberal Alliance	50	4	85		
		National Republican	5	5	0		
		Progress Republican	17	7	41.7		
		Republican Union	26	4	73.3		
		Democratic Republican	30	7	62.2		
		Democratic Left	26	3	79.3		
		Radical	83	7	84.4		
		Socialist-Radical	117	11	82.8		
		Parliamentary Socialist	19	4	65.2		
		Revolutionary Socialist	11	35	52.2	62.5	83.9

Sources: Verdier (1894), *Annales de la chambre des députés* (1871–1910), and Jolly (1977).

Smith 1980, 151–81). The compromise hinged not only on the government keeping protectionists among industry and agriculture happy with the balance between them but in not alienating the still sizable number of industrial and commercial interests that depended on trade and exports.[11]

The compromise removed the trade issue from the political spotlight and helped the Republicans dominate the French parliament until World War I. The success of the compromise also encouraged rent seeking by individual industry groups. Lobbies succeeded in generating a proliferation of laws after 1892 that modified duties on one product or a few similar items at a time. Approximately thirty such modifications were made between 1892 and 1910 (Golob 1944, 234–35).

6.3 THE INTERWAR YEARS

In the years after 1919, parliament extended war-time legislation that authorized the government to adjust tariffs in line with exchange-rate changes, and industry groups were able to wield enormous influence over the advisory committees in charge of setting tariff rates (Verdier 1994, 164.)[12] The governing Republicans and Radicals sought to maintain the balance between competing interests that had been cemented in the Méline Tariff. Representatives of labor, however, began expressing a more coherent form of class sentiment: the Socialists and Communists, along with the union peak association, the Confédération générale du travail (CGT), all favored greater openness (Verdier 1994, 162).

The first major challenge to the old compromise came in 1924 when industrial interests successfully pushed for export controls on a range of primary and semi-finished goods as a way to deal with the inflationary consequences of currency depreciations.[13] The aggrieved export industries rallied quickly in opposition, with supporters of farmers among both the Republican and Radical parties leading the way. The stabilization of the franc in 1926 and the subsequent lifting of export controls put an end to the standoff, and in 1928 the parliament passed new industrial duties and farm duties negotiated with Germany. The party voting patterns in the Chamber reveal only that most parties supported this patched up version of the old compromise and that levels of intraparty cohesion had risen from previous years (see Table 6.3).

It took a sharp decline in commodity prices in 1930 to break the Republican grip on power. The Steeg government collapsed in 1931, paralyzed by

---

[11] As Smith (1980, 21) points out, the 1892 tariff, "served to mitigate strife amongst capitalists in different lines or in different sectors by producing an explicit government commitment to a mixed, variegated, and balanced economy in which all major interests could enjoy a certain level of security."

[12] In fact, between 1919 and 1922 the calculation of duty multipliers was handled by a committee staffed largely by representatives of trade associations (Naudin 1928, 89–91).

[13] The controls covered such items as lumber, seeds, charcoal, leather, and woolen and cotton cloth and yarn. See Guillen 1978, 64.

TABLE 6.3
Voting on the Tariff of 1928 in the Chamber of Deputies

	Legislation	Party	Yeas	Nays	Cohesion	Average Cohesion	General Cohesion
1928	Tariff	URD	114	7	88.4		
		Left Republican	76	7	83.1		
		Radical	16	6	45.5		
		Socialist Radical	117	5	91.8		
		Republican Socialist	19	6	52		
		Socialist	26	6	62.5		
		Communist	0	21	100	72.5	81.5

Sources: *Annales de la chambre des députés* (1871–1910) and Jolly (1977).

its unwillingness to choose between urban and rural interests. The new Radical government imposed import quotas on a range of farm products (to avoid violating treaty commitments on tariff rates), and tightened them in 1933, but could not avert economic crisis. In 1936 the Radicals joined with Socialists (under Blum) and Communists in a novel "red-green" coalition, the *Front Populaire* (Wright 1964, 64; Dupeux 1959).

The new alignment, ostensibly pitting farmers and workers against business (and fascism), was plagued by conflicts. The government's economic policy revolved around a simple bargain: Workers were prepared to accept agricultural price supports in exchange for farmers accepting social welfare provisions and union rights. The Matignon Accords did establish union rights, limited the work week, and introduced retirement benefits and paid vacations. But tensions surfaced quickly. The Communists refused to approve a devaluation of the franc unless quotas on food imports were lifted and import duties cut (Verdier 1994, 162–63). Radicals delayed the Socialist plan for state control of wheat prices and the adjustment of the floor price of wheat in line with the devaluation (Wright 1964). Conflict grew over plans by the Socialists to promote reforms that would favor farm laborers and tenants in their dealings with landowners. By the end of 1936, farmers were protesting in Paris and agrarian groups were objecting to the Radicals' support for the Popular Front.

In early 1937, Blum requested wide-ranging emergency powers from parliament to set economic policy. In anticipation that agricultural protection would be reduced, Radicals in the Senate deserted the Popular Front and voted down the legislation. When Blum tried again in June, and met with the same opposition, he resigned. A new Radical government under Chautemps took over, restored old duties and quotas, and courted support from Republicans and business interests (Sauvy 1984, 151).[14]

---

[14] In the vote on granting the Chautemps government power to adjust tariffs in 1937, the average party cohesion index was 84.9. Socialists and Communists voting unanimously against the bill, while Republicans were split.

6.4 TRADE POLITICS IN THE FIFTH REPUBLIC

Under the continued dominance of the right and center-right, trade politics in the 1950s and 1960s developed little partisan flavor. A system of national economic planning, which placed a high priority on heavy industry and import substitution, grew from the initial program for postwar reconstruction designed by Jean Monnet. The creation of the European Economic Community in 1958 placed limits on discretionary changes in the tariff and shifted the focus to industrial policy. With the Gaullists firmly in control after the constitutional change in 1958, backed strongly by business interests, policy increasingly began to reflect pressures from industries for both protection and export promotion.

The planning process was powerfully shaped by industry groups, as bureaucratic agencies quickly began to act as internal lobbyists for their sectoral "clients" (Hall 1986). Indeed, in the 1960s and 1970s, many trade associations actually merged with the government agencies created to supervise them (see Mytelka 1982).[15] By the 1970s, trade associations in the footwear, watch, clock, and television industries were formulating the plans for those industries and even negotiated directly with foreign producers and governments to establish voluntary restraints on imports (Milner 1988, 198).

Among the parties, divisions soon began to emerge over the appropriate level of intervention and over European integration—although in the votes on the creation of the EEC in 1957 the parties actually held together quite well (see Table 6.4). But the core party constituencies were increasingly fractured. The business peak association, the Conseil national du patronat français (CNPF), backed the Gaullists solidly, but the business community was divided over trade and industrial policy issues. As in Britain, there was a clear split between the large, concentrated industries, which tended to do very well in lobbying for rents, and small business which did not (Hall 1986, 169–70). Responsibility for administering subsidies was held by the Ministry of Finance, which was already overwhelmed with applications for aid by the 1960s, and firms and groups with enough political clout simply avoided the process altogether and appealed for assistance directly to the cabinet or president (Verdier 1994, 248). It was the small businessmen who pushed through the liberal manifesto, adopted by the CNPF in 1965, which denounced planning. Larger industries were quick to reject this position, and the CNPF actually dissolved in 1968, reforming under the control of larger firms in 1970 to play a role in the negotiation of the Sixth Plan.

Among farmers, opinions about policy were also divided. The peak association, the Fédération nationale des syndicats des exploitants agricoles

---

[15] For instance, the agency created by the Ministry of Finance to monitor the textile industry, the Centre interprofessionnel de rénovation des structures industrielles et commerciales de l'industrie textile (CIRIT), was controlled by a board dominated by the industry trade association.

TABLE 6.4
Voting on the Treaty of Rome in the Chamber of Deputies, 1957

	Legislation	Party	Yeas	Nays	Cohesion	Average Cohesion	General Cohesion
1957	Treaty of Rome	Poujadist	35	1	94.4		
		Gaullist	16	0	100		
		Peasant	4	10	42.9		
		Independent	2	81	95.2		
		Overseas	0	6	100		
		MRP	0	74	100		
		RGR-Radical	2	23	84		
		Radical	19	25	13.6		
		UDSR-RDA	1	20	90.5		
		Socialist	0	100	100		
		Communist	149	0	100	81.2	84.8

Sources: Verdier (1894) and Jolly (1977).

(FNSEA), comprised around forty specialized farmer groups that took very different positions on trade (Safran 1985; 107–18). While many of these, including the grain and dairy producers, favored protection and lobbied to maintain price supports in the face of foreign pressures, export-oriented wine and oil seed growers were also vocal members; the FNSEA tended to back away from taking general positions on trade matters.

Reflecting these divisions within the business and agricultural communities, Gaullist and Republican party members were increasingly divided over trade and industrial policy in the 1970s and 1980s (Gourevitch 1986, 186). The Gaullist response to the economic crisis of the 1970s was to hand out more state monies to ailing industries even while nominally pursuing "deplanification" (Hall 1986, 189). The steel, shipbuilding, and textile industries were heavily subsidized against foreign competition, and makers of shoes, leather goods, clocks and watches, and machine-tools also received generous attention.[16] To provide aid to financially strapped firms in struggling industries, a Comité interminsteriel pour d'amènagement des structures industrielles (CIASI) was established in 1974, and in the late 1970s Giscard announced a new policy aimed at providing special assistance to high-technology growth industries.[17]

The prolonged recession increased support for the Socialists and led in 1981 to Mitterrand's presidential victory and the formation of a coalition government of Socialists and Communists under Mauroy. The Socialist plat-

---

[16] By 1972, in fact, over 30 percent of the French budget was allocated to industrial subsidies; twice the proportion spent on subsidies in 1953 (see Caron 1979, 346).

[17] Six industries were initially identified, including consumer electronics, robotics, biotechnology, synthetic textiles, office automation, and underwater exploration. See Green 1984. Separate development plans were devised for aeronautics and computers, and the textile industry was added to the list of those targeted for state aid.

form emphasized the importance of keeping traditional French industries alive and promised to protect employment in shipbuilding, mining, and metal works, which were by then in great distress (Verdier 1994, 246). The new government set about nationalizing the largest industrial groups and investment banks and extended industrial policy, mounting rescues for a range of industries including steel, chemicals, textiles, leather goods, automobiles, machine tools, electronics, and furniture.

A drastic deterioration in economic conditions in these first years of Socialist rule forced a radical change in macroeconomic policy in 1983, splitting the left over whether austerity measures were necessary and revealing deeper divisions over trade and industrial policy. Among Socialists there was strong support for European integration and liberalization from leading figures of the "second left" who had closer ties to the main non-Communist union confederation, the Confédération française démocratique du travail (CFDT). Left wingers associated more closely with blue-collar unions, and the Confédération Générale du Travail championed protection and intervention and argued that the economic problems could be solved instead by the imposition of much higher import barriers combined with French withdrawal from the European Monetary System and devaluation of the franc. Mitterrand eventually affirmed his support for European integration, even though several Socialist ministers opposed it and the Communists called for French withdrawal from the EC altogether.[18]

When the center-right won a majority in the National Assembly in 1986 and formed a government under Chirac, they focused chiefly on privatization and financial deregulation during an uneasy period of "cohabitation" with Mitterrand. The return of the Socialists to power in 1988, under Rocard and later Bérégovoy, brought little alteration to trade and industrial policy. The *nouvelle politique industrielle* focused again on aiding national champions and expanding them to "critical size" in the world market (Verdier 1994, 254). No new industry plans were formulated, but large amounts of government funds continued to be poured into protecting major sectors of the economy from international competition. The government also strained to accommodate the demands of several powerful agricultural groups when the EC agreement with the United States on reducing subsidized farm exports (the so-called Blair House accord of 1992) led to blockades of Paris by angry farmers.

In the 1993 election, the conservatives took a similar position on trade matters generally and on the Blair House accord in particular. In the midst of France's worst recession since World War II, selective use of import

---

[18] Mitterrand continued to target aid to high-technology sectors; his list of favored sectors, from robotics to computers, was virtually identical to Giscard's. For the electronics industry, which Mitterrand referred to as "our weapon of the future," government procurement was guided by the aim of reversing the trade imbalance and creating 80,000 new jobs (see Hall 1986, 207).

barriers was favored by both conservatives and Socialists, and each side promised to protect farmers who might be injured by any EC reforms or multilateral agreements.

6.5 CONCLUSIONS

This brief account of the evolution of French trade politics over the last two centuries reveals fewer big shifts in cleavage patterns than occurred either in Britain or the United States. This is what one would expect based on the generally low levels of interindustry factor mobility reported for the French economy for most of the period. The evidence indicates that class-based conflict over trade never really escalated in French politics to the heights it reached in the United States or in Britain in the later years of the nineteenth century. The success of Méline's compromise tariff in 1892, and the subsequent dominance of the political scene by the Republicans, effectively removed trade from partisan competition in France, and industry lobbies took a very active role in shaping a trade policy. In the postwar era, these groups formed close relationships with the bureaucracy and exercised a powerful influence over the economic planning process. The major parties, split by factions, gravitated toward very similar types of trade and industrial policies based on selective state aid for major industries.

Sweden

The evidence discussed in chapter 2 indicates that levels of interindustry factor mobility rose dramatically at the turn of the century in Sweden and remained quite high in later decades. According to the theory developed in chapter 1, we should thus anticipate a rapid reshaping of Swedish trade politics around class cleavages late in the nineteenth century. And, since factor mobility remained relatively high in the years after 1930, in contrast with the experience in the United States, Britain, and France, the formation of industry-based coalitions in these later periods was much less likely. While the latter development fits better with previous discussions of class-based politics in Sweden (Rogowski 1989) than with group-based approaches, the theory advanced here has the advantage of predicting change over time in the pattern of political cleavages.

Expectations and a summary of the basic findings are reported in Table 7.1. Again, the match between the effects anticipated by the theory and the changes observed is very good. There is quite a case here for a Swedish exceptionalism that runs counter to the French extreme examined in the preceding chapter: Swedish trade politics has been characterized throughout most of its recent history by bargaining between broad-based, factoral coalitions. Very high levels of interindustry factor mobility since the 1920s, due in part to policies aimed directly at encouraging flexibility in the economy, have gone hand in hand with the political dominance of cohesive class-based coalitions in Sweden. The distinctive feature of the Swedish case since the 1930s, of course, has been the compromise between these class coalitions that embedded trade openness as a central element of a broader plan to manage the Swedish economy.

7.1 EARLY NINETEENTH-CENTURY TRADE POLITICS

Since we have little data on wages and profits for Sweden in the first half of the nineteenth century, it is difficult to make clear predictions about politics in this early period. Testing the theory is also difficult given the absence of democratic institutions and political parties. The sketch drawn here must be a rough one. The Riksdag did allow for some representation of interests in this period, however, and it seems that the greatest support for the liberalizing reforms begun by Oscar I in the 1840s came from a mix of specific agricultural and business interests. In particular, timber and lumber interests,

TABLE 7.1
Anticipated and Observed Outcomes in Sweden

Period	Factor Endowments	Mobility	Prediction[a]	Outcomes	
				Class-based Parties and Associations	Industry Groups
1815–1869	Abundant labor; scarce land and capital	Intermediate?	Mixed?	n/a	Evidence of some group pressures on Riksdag; craft guilds opposed liberal reforms
1870–1914	Abundant labor; scarce land and capital	High	Class coalitions	Ruralists and Conservatives supported protection; Social Democrats championed free trade	Few groups actively lobbied on trade
1919–1939	Abundant capital; scarce labor and land[b]	High	Class coalitions	Parties adhered to old platforms, LO and SAF supported free trade; "cow trade" between Social Democrats and Agrarians	Accommodation between parties and peak associations left little room for lobbying
1945–1994	Abundant labor and capital; scarce land[c]	High	Class coalitions	Dominant Social Democrats, opposition parties, and peak associations all held to free-trade consensus	Little activity; more lobbying in 1980s

[a]Class coalitions are expected to imply that class-based organizations are internally unified on trade and adopt coherent platforms while groups are inactive. Industry coalitions imply that class-based organizations are internally divided on trade and adopt ambiguous positions (see Table 3.1).

[b]Here Rogowski's classification is problematic. He argues that the evidence on factor endowments indicating labor abundance belies an effective scarcity due to "familial self-exploitation" within the peasant population. The evidence alone (which is consistent with later data—see point c. below) would actually lead us to predict that workers (and the organizations representing them) would support free trade not protection, as the analysis here seems to bear out.

[c]Using 1966 data, Bowen, Leamer, and Sveikauskas (1987) find Sweden to be abundant in capital and all types of labor (except agricultural workers) and scarce in arable land.

producers of iron ore and pig iron, and the commercial centers were all strong supporters of reform and especially of elimination of the protectionist Produktplakat (Rustow 1955, 24; Heckscher 1954, 218, 224–25).[1] Grain, meat, and dairy producers, and burghers in the tightly regulated textile and iron industries, were vocal opponents (Montgomery 1939, 114; Heckscher 1954, 233). The craft guilds associated with the iron industry, mostly located in isolated communities, were also strong opponents of liberal reforms.

Oscar's most radical reforms were implemented by his finance minister, Johan Gripenstedt, a vigorous champion of liberal ideas. In the 1850s and 1860s he did away with all prohibitions against imports and exports, abolished export duties, greatly reduced tariffs on manufactures, and established free trade in agricultural products (Heckscher 1954, 237). To avoid consulting with the Riksdag Gripenstedt resorted to the same tactics employed by Louis Napoleon in France, entering Sweden into a treaty system that cemented the trade reforms in international commitments. The reforms met with hostility from the Riksdag, and helped weaken support for the old regime. In 1866 the Riksdag was transformed into a bicameral parliament with elected representatives and the first real parties began to form.

7.2 From Oscar I to World War I

In the 1870s, lingering economic depression generated new protectionist demands among a large section of the agricultural population, especially in the grain-growing regions of Svealand and northern Götaland. The Liberal Themptander government, backed strongly by urban voters and business interests, negotiated a new liberal treaty with France in 1882, and the political conflict over trade quickly escalated. A protectionist league and a rival Association Against a Tariff on Foodstuffs formed, and in 1887 two elections to the lower chamber of the Riksdag were fought on the tariff issue. In the first election, free traders won a majority. In the second they were denied victory by an electioneering blunder.[2]

Oscar II initially put up a fight, appointing a new mixed ministry of free traders and protectionists. But parliamentary opposition ultimately forced the removal of the free traders, and Gustav Boström was appointed head of the new Ruralist government. Boström imposed high tariffs on agricultural products, and when the French treaty expired in 1892, raised tariffs again

---

[1] The *Produktplakat* prohibited any foreign vessel from importing to Sweden any goods other than those produced in its home country, and raised duties by 40 to 50 percent for imports and exports carried on foreign ships. The laws were officially repealed in 1857, but by then had long since been rendered redundant by treaties with major trading partners.

[2] In Stockholm, a stronghold of free-trade sentiment, protectionists discovered an irregularity in the tax records of one of the candidates and succeeded in having all the free-trade representatives invalidated (Rustow 1955, 36).

(Verney 1957, 108–9). Opposition came not only from the Liberals but from the Social Democratic clubs and trade unions representing the still-disenfranchised working class. In 1889, these elements founded the Social Democratic Party, which took a firm stand against protection and turned the deepening class cleavage into a clear partisan battle (Rustow 1955, 42). In 1898 the Landsorganisationen (LO), the national labor organization, was established after less than two decades of union activity. In 1902 Swedish business organized into the Svenska Arbetsgivarföreningen (SAF), a national employers' federation.[3] Both organizations solidly opposed the Ruralist tariffs.

By the turn of the century, the Ruralists and newly formed Conservatives, both relying on an agrarian base of support, were allied together in favor of protection, but were under immense pressure to reform policy and extend the franchise. The Conservative-Ruralist alliance eventually adopted a compromise plan for electoral reform in 1907 based on proportional representation, considerably slowing the political ascent of the Social Democratic and Liberal parties. When a coalition of the Social Democrats and Liberals finally won control of government in 1917, they immediately liberalized Swedish trade policy.

7.3 THE DEPRESSION AND THE PACT OF SALTSJÖBADEN

The alliance between Social Democrats and Liberals broke apart in 1920 over the issue of tax reform and was followed by a string of short-lived, minority governments in which the Liberals held the balance of power between the Conservatives and Agrarians on one side and the Social Democrats on the other. The Liberals crippled Social Democratic governments in 1920, 1923, and 1926 by splitting from them on tax and unemployment benefits issues to align with the right; they defeated the Conservative government in 1924 by siding with the left on defense spending (Rustow 1955, 96–97). The Liberals themselves were hardly a cohesive group and counted among their supporters both urban and rural constituencies.

In 1929 and 1930, with a farm crisis growing, the coalition government of Conservatives and Agrarians (under Arvid Lindman) attempted to pass new protectionist legislation but was defeated by strong opposition from Social Democrats and urban Liberals.[4] By the autumn of 1931, the broadening economic distress had forced the government to follow Britain off the gold

---

[3] In 1910, business also formed a Federation of Swedish Industries (SI), consisting of twenty-six trade associations that had virtually the same membership as the SAF, but focused its political activity on issues of policy rather than management/worker relations.

[4] Though records are unavailable, legislative voting behavior in the Riksdag in this period apparently exhibited very high levels of cohesion among the parties, and particularly in the ranks of the Conservatives and Social Democrats. See Sternquist and Bjurulf 1970.

standard in order to abandon deflationary policies. The election of 1932 yielded large gains for the parties representing the groups most affected by the economic crisis: workers and farmers. The Social Democrats and the Agrarians became the two largest parties in parliament. The leader of the Social Democrats, Per Albin Hansson, formed a minority government and presented a program to combat unemployment (with public works spending) and to relieve agricultural distress (with price supports). For the first time, large numbers of Agrarians were willing to accept expansionist fiscal measures and, led by Axel Pehrsson i Bramstorp, they developed an informal alliance with Hansson. The government passed tariff cutting legislation in 1932, with the support of both Liberals and many Agrarians.

Strong Agrarian support for the antidepression spending program in 1934 cemented the new "red-green" coalition of workers and farmers. Some strains developed in 1936, however, over industrial relations policy and pensions; the Agrarian support flagged and the Hansson ministry resigned. The election later that year gave his Social Democrats a majority in the lower chamber of the Riksdag for the first time. They still needed Agrarian support in the Senate, however, and Hansson was now more assiduous in tending to the "cow trade," broadening his proposals for agricultural price supports as a compromise for strengthening workers rights in industrial disputes and increasing pension benefits and unemployment insurance (Sainsbury 1980, 33). The Social Democrats were also prepared to allow for a range of specific tariffs and subsidies to aid agriculture in the 1930s. The costs of the agricultural protection for workers were acknowledged explicitly in order to accent the bargain that had been struck between the two classes: The 1936 party manifesto assured the Agrarians that "the Swedish working class will pay the price necessary to guarantee workers in agriculture and small farmers a tolerable living standard" (Mabbett 1995, 87).[5]

In 1938, in an effort to be included in the accommodation that was taking place, business associations met with labor and farming organizations and concluded the famous Pact of Saltsjöbaden. Business associations endorsed the government's labor and social welfare policies, and a fiscal policy aimed at full employment, in exchange for labor commitments to peaceful industrial relations and continued private control of property. The broad accommodation between class interests included a commitment to liberal trade policy and left little room at all for industry groups in the trade policymaking process.

---

[5] Rogowski has attempted to explain the alliance by reference only to trade politics, suggesting that labor in Sweden might be considered a scarce factor at this time (due to "familial self-exploitation" among the peasantry) like land, and so was aligned with farmers in favor of protection (1989, 84–86). The problem with this interpretation is that Swedish labor and the Social Democrats continued to support open trade in these years and only made specific concessions to farmers in order to preserve the alliance. The deeper origins of the alliance may well lie as Katzenstein (1985, 167) suggested, in the extensive intermingling of farming and working populations due to the dispersion of industrial production among small towns.

7.4 SWEDISH TRADE POLITICS UNDER THE SOCIAL DEMOCRATS

In the years after 1945, the dominant Social Democrats and the Conservative parties all backed a liberal approach to trade policy that emphasized the need for smooth adjustment to the demands of the international market, aided by vigorous retraining and adjustment assistance policies (Jones 1976, 22–25; Katzenstein 1985, 65). The parties and peak associations, including the LO and the SAF, remained unified internally on the trade issue (supporting the pro-trade approach), and on economic issues in general, and group lobbying was severely limited (Sjoblom 1985, 24–25, 51).

To a large degree, the Social Democrats' policy of wage equalization took the trade issue out of politics, since it meant that the differential effects of trade on wages in particular sectors were minimized. This level of solidarity was made feasible by extensive mobility-enhancing policies—the hallmark of Swedish policy in the postwar period (Jones 1976, 39–42). Retraining programs administered by the National Labor Market Board provided workers with generous allowances for living expenses while undertaking training courses, for living away from home to study, for exploring new employment opportunities in other towns, for relocating permanently, and for suffering separations from family. All pension rights were, by law, completely transferable to new employment so that relocating workers were not disadvantaged.

When these policies were devised in 1951 by economists Gösta Rehn and Rudolf Meidner, the LO leadership embarked on a campaign to persuade the major unions to support them (Heclo and Madsen 1987, 49–50). After some hesitation, even the protectionist-leaning textile workers agreed to retraining and relocation benefits as an alternative to attempts to preserve jobs in their declining industry (Milner 1989, 109). This, as Rehn described it, was exactly the plan's objective: "to avoid protective and protectionist palliatives when changes in the world trade situation or other trade conditions create difficulties for various groups" (Rehn 1985, 1).

Another key component in postwar Swedish policy was the investment reserve, developed in concert with the SAF in the 1950s.[6] The reserve was designed to ease adjustment and smooth out fluctuations in the business cycle. In periods of growth, firms could avoid taxation by placing some of their profits in a reserve fund. On request, monies were released from these funds for specific investment projects approved by the supervising Labour Market Board. In addition, generous assistance was made available in the form of grants to firms seeking to adapt to foreign competition by modernizing or shifting production to more profitable areas (Jones 1976, 22–25; Katzenstein 1985, 65). In their report to the sixteenth federation's congress in 1961, the LO economists argued that "the factors of production must be

---

[6] For detailed discussions see Lindbeck 1974, 773, 97–104; and Jones 1976, 16–17, 151–62.

made more adaptable," and called for further expansion of all the programs designed to increase firm and worker mobility (Johnston 1963, 42).

The policymaking system that subsequently emerged in Sweden is regarded widely as a "corporatist" exemplar (Wilensky 1976, 53). The central feature of the system was the bargaining between peak associations that was institutionalized in the policymaking process and represented a broad "social partnership" to limit conflict between capital and labor (Korpi 1978). Rather than the "sectoral interpenetration" of state bureaucracies by interest groups evident in nations such as France, trade politics in Sweden was marked by a process that Katzenstein refers to as "trans-sectoral co-ordination" (1985, 92). Independent participation by groups was severely limited and structured. Most of the formulation of trade and economic policy was delegated to temporary commissions of inquiry (*utredning*) with representatives appointed from the civil service, the Riksdag, and the peak associations (Premfors 1983). The same makeup was given to the directors of the permanent National Board of Trade (*Kommerskollegium*), which existed within the Ministry of Commerce and was responsible for researching trade policy issues and making policy recommendations.

Presiding over the bargaining between peak associations, and under the firm leadership of Tage Erlander and then Olof Palme, the Social Democrats enjoyed a dominant position in Swedish politics until the recession of the 1970s. The government reacted to that crisis by imposing temporary import restrictions to help ease the pressure on the textile and footwear industries and provided some selective aid to industries in crisis, notably the steel and shipbuilding industries in which bankruptcies would have created enormous local impacts (Lawrence and Bosworth 1987, 73–74). But these interventions were abandoned quickly. They were aimed at buying time for adjustment rather than altering the government's overall approach to trade (Pontusson 1991, 176). More politically significant was the Meidner Plan of 1975, an attempt to deal with economic recession and the dissatisfaction among labor, while avoiding nationalization that would tear apart the political accommodation with business. The plan proposed that a proportion of the profits of major companies be diverted to purchase shares for union-managed funds, with ownership passing to workers over the long term (Gourevitch 1986, 202). The opposition this raised among business groups and white-collar unions contributed in 1976 to the first postwar electoral defeat suffered by the Social Democrats.

A coalition of parties of the center and right formed a government under Torbjörn Fälladin in 1976, promising to reform economic policy by reducing taxes and expenditures on social services. The Conservatives and Liberals were joined by the Agrarian Party.[7] The coalition succeeded in changing economic policy very little between 1976 and 1982. The stability in policy

---

[7] Responding to the decline in the farming population, the Agrarian Party had restyled itself the "Centre" Party under Gunnar Hedlund in the late 1950s. The Conservative Party changed its name to the "Moderate" Party. I have used their old names here for simplicity.

after the change in government indicates just how constrained governments were by the bargain struck between the peak associations (Gourevitch 1986, 199). The new center-right government remained firmly committed to open markets and continued to support adjustment assistance and retraining programs despite the troubled economic circumstances faced by Swedish producers.

The Social Democrats returned to power in 1982 under Palme. The new government avoided the controversial proposals made in the Meidner Plan and focused instead on re-emphasizing the need for smooth adjustment to market forces among labor and business. Unlike the leftist governments in Britain and France in the 1970s and 1980s, the Social Democrats undertook no large-scale nationalization of industry and shied away from an interventionist industrial policy. And in marked contrast to governments in most other advanced economies, those in Sweden did not resort to extensive use of nontariff barriers to imports. Only in the late 1980s were there signs of a change when the LO and SAF began to face growing challenges from member groups (Weaver 1987, 305).[8]

7.5 CONCLUSIONS

Swedish trade politics evolved over the last two centuries in a distinctive fashion that fits well with predictions based on the theory advanced in chapter 1 and the evidence on changing levels of interindustry factor mobility reported in chapter 2. During the late nineteenth century and the first decades of the twentieth century, trade was an important part of the class conflict that developed at the heart of Swedish politics. The Social Democratic and Liberal parties that represented the urban classes took strong and unified positions in favor of free trade. Protection, along with the preservation of royal authority and religious orthodoxy, was advocated by the Conservative and Agrarian parties. In the interwar period, the famous Pact of Saltsjöbaden negotiated a broad accommodation between business, labor, and agrarian class interests and endorsed liberal trade policy. Both the Social Democrats and the Conservative parties stood behind this approach to policy in the postwar era, emphasizing the need for smooth adjustment to the demands of the international market aided by vigorous retraining and adjustment assistance policies. Drawing from the theory developed in the first chapter, it seems clear that this approach, unique to the Swedish case, has only been possible as long as levels of interindustry factor mobility have remained high enough that the competition for industry "rents" has not splintered broad factoral coalitions along sectoral lines.

---

[8] Labor unions in the export-oriented engineering industries began to grow increasingly discontent with centralized wage bargaining. Similarly, SAF members began to push harder for more freedom to bargain with their workers independently (see Pontusson and Swenson 1993).

CHAPTER EIGHT

Canada

Canadian trade politics is perhaps less familiar to most readers than the well-worn trail of the U.S., British, and French histories. Existing accounts tend to emphasize the role of industry groups in pressuring the Canadian government to alter tariff policy in different historical eras (McDiarmid 1946; Forster 1986). The theory advanced in this book suggests that a group-based approach is generally appropriate for the Canadian case, although there are some significant changes over time that affect the formation of political cleavages. As indicated by the evidence in chapter 2, levels of interindustry factor mobility have remained quite low in the Canadian economy, in relative terms, throughout most of the last two centuries. According to the theory, we should anticipate strong industry cleavages in Canadian trade politics, with a deviation perhaps in the interwar years when the data indicate that mobility levels rose to marginally higher levels.

Table 8.1 summarizes the expectations for the Canadian cases and reports observed outcomes for each case, again stated in terms of levels of cohesion among the parties and peak associations, and the degree of industry-group lobbying. The match between the effects anticipated by the theory and the observed outcomes is again quite reasonable. The Canadian story is, in key ways, very similar to the French experience. Relatively low levels of factor mobility have tended to foster narrow, industry-based coalitions, often concentrated in particular regions, and have made it difficult for political parties and peak associations to overcome internal divisions over the trade issue.

8.1 Trade Politics in Canada from Union to Confederation

After the Act of Union in 1840, which united Upper and Lower Canada, the beginnings of a Canadian party system emerged, and rough distinctions were made between Conservatives and Liberals in the British tradition. With Mac-Donald's Tories dominating politics in the early nineteenth century, trade policy was shaped significantly by patronage and group pressures (Coleman 1988, 19; Forster 1986, 17–18; Ethier 1988, 224). The chief supporters of free trade were grain growers and timber producers in the western provinces, while farmers in the eastern provinces, and the iron and textile industries, lobbied vigorously for protection.[1] Industry and regional divisions appear to have cut across broad factor classes (Palmer 1983, 20).

---

[1] On the lobbying patterns, see Easterbrook and Aitken 1956, 224.

TABLE 8.1
Anticipated and Observed Outcomes in Canada

Period	Factor Endowments	Mobility	Prediction[a]	Outcomes	
				Class-based Parties and Associations	Industry Groups
1815–1869	Abundant land; scarce capital and labor	Low	Industry coalitions	Tories favored high tariff and Liberals opposed, but both split along regional lines	Highly active; many groups petitioned the Assembly
1870–1914	Abundant land; scarce capital and labor	Low	Industry coalitions	Liberals divided; Tories more united on protectionist National Policy	Groups petitioned House and lobbied Dominion Board of Trade
1919–1939	Abundant land and capital; scarce labor	Intermediate; rising	Mixed	Liberals and Tories supported National Policy, but split by western agrarian movement	Little evidence of group lobbying
1945–1994	Abundant land and capital; scarce labor[b]	Low	Industry coalitions	Both major parties supported GATT process, but divided over CUSFTA and NAFTA	Groups active in pushing for special deals

[a] Class coalitions are expected to imply that class-based organizations are internally unified on trade and adopt coherent platforms while groups are inactive. Industry coalitions imply that class-based organizations are internally divided on trade and adopt ambiguous positions (see Table 3.1).
[b] Using 1966 data, Bowen, Leamer, and Sveikauskas (1987) find Canada to be abundant in capital and all types of land, and scarce in all types of labor except agricultural workers.

In 1842 the grain farmers in the West, anxious to boost their exports to the British market and aware that a food crisis persisted there, petitioned the British government to allow the free admission of Canadian wheat. Britain rejected the idea and instead introduced sliding-scale duties on grain imports to provide some relief at home from soaring food prices. At the suggestion of the British Colonial Secretary that Canadian exporters might be granted trade preferences if Canada first imposed duties on U.S. wheat, the Tories engineered the first protectionist agricultural tariff in late 1842 (McDiarmid 1946, 54–55). In the aftermath, a barrage of petitions from industry groups poured into the Assembly in the 1840s pleading for increased duties on manufactures. Many of these were granted in the 1845 tariff.[2]

Starting with the repeal of the Corn Laws in 1846, trade liberalization in Britain effectively removed all trade preferences granted to Canadian producers of grain and timber that had enabled them to compete with Baltic suppliers to the British market. Increasingly, these producers looked south to the U.S. market for export sales. Even farmers in the East, driven out of wheat production by wheat rust and midge, began exporting growing quantities of oats, barley, poultry, and dairy products to the United States (Easterbrook and Aitken 1956, 291). Under increasing pressure from these groups, and especially from the influential timber interests, the Tories ended preferences for British imports and pushed instead for a new trade relationship with Canada's southern neighbor, negotiating a Reciprocity Treaty with the United States in 1854 that provided for free trade in selected agricultural and mineral products including grain, fish, lumber, and coal.

The recession in 1857 sharply reduced government revenues and led the Tories to raise duties again through the Cayley-Galt Tariff of 1858.[3] Led by manufacturers from the Toronto and Hamilton areas, protectionist industries formed the Association for the Promotion of Canadian Industry to help orchestrate their lobbying effort. Others, principally those producers dependent on imports of raw materials, formed the Tariff Reform Association to lobby against further protection and any threats to reciprocity (Easterbrook and Aitken 1956, 372; Forster 1986, 35, 47). Neither organization survived after 1858, however, and the political scene was still mostly dominated by regional and local industry organizations, often separated on religious and ethnic grounds and lobbying independently to influence policy.

In 1867, the British North America Act united the provinces of Canada, New Brunswick, and Nova Scotia into a single confederation and instituted a single national tariff. The year before, the United States announced that it was abrogating the reciprocity treaty (a post–Civil War snub to Britain as much as to Canada). Both the Liberal and Conservative parties stated their

---

[2] As in the United States in these years, such petitions were often jointly delivered to representatives from farmers and artisans from the same cities and towns, advocating increased (or reduced) tariffs on specific items; see Forster 1986, 17–18.

[3] Tariffs still provided two thirds of revenues at this time. See Ethier 1988, 224.

support for reciprocity nevertheless, and their shared position after 1867 was to maintain a standing offer to negotiate a new treaty with the United States. The first tariff of the confederation, the Dominion Tariff of 1868, represented a basic compromise between protectionist and free-trade interests—lopsided, as it was, in favor of protectionists (Pinchin 1978, 3).

8.2 NATIONAL POLICY AND THE DOMINION TARIFF

The tariff became more of a partisan issue in Canada after confederation when the Liberals, drawing strong support from agrarians (especially in the western provinces), advocated large tariff reductions. They were no match, however, for the eastern-urban electoral strength of the Tories. Under Mac-Donald's leadership, the Tories actually courted support from the nascent worker movement, pushing through passage of the Trades Union Bill in 1872 and backing the first worker elected to federal parliament.[4] MacDonald made protection a central issue in the 1872 election campaign and won handily.

The Tories had only one lapse in their political management of the three decades after 1867, when the revelation of kickbacks to party members from railway contractors (the "Pacific Scandal") handed control to the Liberals in 1874. Led by Mackenzie, the Liberals initially steered clear of the tariff issue. With the deepening of the economic recession after 1873, however, industry groups began to lobby hard for new protection, and the House faced a slew of petitions from industries seeking assistance (McLean 1895, 19; Forster 1986, 114; Coleman 1988, 20). Groups also sent delegations to lobby the Dominion Board of Trade at its meeting in Ottawa and contributed heavily to the parties in hopes of influencing their position on the tariff as the election approached in 1878.[5]

Mackenzie advocated a tariff for revenue purposes only and issued a stern attack on protectionism. But the issue divided Liberals sharply, and many party members stood down altogether or actually maintained their old protectionist stance when running for election (Forster 1986, 175). The Tories won easily again and moved quickly to establish their "National Policy" aimed explicitly at building up manufacturing, attracting scarce capital and immigrants, and enlarging the domestic market by westward expansion. High tariffs were an integral part of the plan, and the new duties were passed in 1879. The votes on the bill in the House are shown in Table 8.2.[6]

---

[4] The worker, H. B. Witten, became known as the "Tory mechanic" (Forster 1986, 93).

[5] Although Forster (1986) listed many of these groups, he ultimately concluded that their "number and persistence were beyond all calculation" (189).

[6] Data on votes and parliamentary affiliations are from *Hansard Parliamentary Debates* and the *Canadian Parliamentary Companion* and *Annual Register* and the *Canadian Parliamentary Guide (1879–1993)*. General cohesion indexes are calculated from 10 percent random samples drawn by the author from all votes in the given year.

TABLE 8.2
Divisions on Trade Bills in the House of Commons, 1870–1914

		Party	Yeas	Nays	Cohesion	Average Cohesion	General Cohesion
	Legislation						
1879	National	Conservatives	81	22	57		
	Policy	Liberals	19	35	30	45.2	52.5
1897	Dominion	Conservatives	10	46	64		
	Tariff	Liberals	73	58	12	35.3	58.6

Sources: Hansard Parliamentary Debates and *Canadian Parliamentary Companion and Annual Register.*

Both parties, but particularly the Liberals, were divided in the voting. The most strenuous opposition to the tariffs came from representatives from the Maritime provinces. The greatest push in favor of the policy came from representatives from Toronto, Montreal, and Quebec City, centers for highly protected industries such as iron and steel, textiles, machinery, furniture, footwear, and glass (Easterbrook and Aitken 1956, 393–94).

In 1893, after spending more than a decade in opposition, the Liberals adopted a platform calling for "tariff for revenue only" but took a public position on trade vague enough that it allowed them to attract farmer support without actually committing to major tariff reform (McDiarmid 1946, 204).[7] They won office at last under Wilfred Laurier in 1896, promising to make no major tariff changes. Laurier restyled the party, turning his back on the old republican position, courting manufacturers in Ontario and Quebec for support, and effectively accepting the National Policy developed by the Tories. In office, Laurier made only minor changes in trade policy, cutting iron and steel duties slightly while providing new subsidies to those industries as compensation. To address the complaints from export-oriented agrarians in the West, Laurier raised the possibility of a new reciprocity treaty with the United States. In 1896 he made the proposal for a new treaty to the U.S. government, but was turned down flat. Declaring that "there will be no more pilgrimages to Washington," Laurier introduced the "Dominion Tariff" in 1897. The new bill increased many duties, imposed separate rates for the United States (to allow Canada to retaliate against the Dingley tariff passed that same year), and gave unreciprocated preferences to British imports (Thorburn 1985, 4–5).

By 1910, however, grain farmers in western Canada were again demanding that the government seek a reciprocity treaty with the United States. In

---

[7] It should be noted that divisions among manufacturers, workers, and farmers across different regions and industries were significant enough to hamper the development of class-based peak associations in these years. On the difficulties faced by nascent labor organizations in these years, see Palmer 1983. On the Canadian Manufacturers' Association, see Coleman 1988, 22.

1911 a new reciprocity agreement was negotiated, providing for free trade in most primary products and a small number of manufactures, as well as reciprocal reductions on many items. The lengthy debate over the bill in parliament forced the Liberals to call an election in September. In the ensuing campaign the Conservatives, emphasizing the importance of preserving imperial links with Britain, won power easily and scuttled the treaty.

8.3 INTERWAR YEARS

The Liberal Party regrouped quickly after the war, and at its convention in 1919, the leadership reins were passed to Mackenzie King. The party broadened its base of support among both French Canadians in the eastern provinces and farmers and workers in the West, and began a long period of political dominance. The major challenge the Liberals faced when taking control after the 1921 election was the growing discontent in the prairies that Laurier had tried to assuage with the promise of reciprocity in 1911. The problem was exacerbated by the sharp decline in world prices for wheat and other grains in the early 1920s and the severe hardship this imposed upon indebted farmers. By 1921 western farmers had formed their own Progressive Party, which quickly dominated provincial governments in the prairies and formed a government in Ontario. The Progressives attacked the National Policy and its continuing protectionist tradition supported by Liberals and Tories alike.

King responded by engineering a series of modest reductions in duties on farm machinery in the early 1920s and eliminating sales tax on all farm inputs (McDiarmid 1946, 264). In 1925, King campaigned on a platform stating that tariffs should be used to raise revenue rather than for protection, and criticized Conservative proposals for higher duties (Neatby 1963, 69). But the Conservatives made large gains in the election, and King was forced to form a minority government with the aid of the Progressives. The Tories attempted to bring down the government by quickly forcing a vote on the tariff, but the Progressives voted with King. The Progressives cooperated with Liberals in the elections of 1925, 1926, and 1930, and were steadily absorbed into the Liberal Party itself.

In 1929 and 1930 the Conservatives, led by Richard Bennett, put growing pressure on King, demanding that he use the tariff to divert trade toward Britain and away from the United States, where the Republicans in Congress were seeking to pass a new protectionist trade bill (the Smoot-Hawley Act). When it became clear in 1930 that new hikes in U.S. tariffs were on the way, King actually preempted them by raising Canadian duties on U.S. goods (see McDonald, O'Brien, and Callahan, 1997, 807–9). But the Conservatives charged him with not going far enough and won control of government later in the year. Their attempts to deal with the growing economic crisis ultimately proved ineffective, however, as Bennett offered his "Iron

TABLE 8.3
The Division on the Ottawa Agreement in the House of Commons, 1932

	Legislation	Party	Yeas	Nays	Cohesion	Average Cohesion	General Cohesion
1932	Ottawa Agreement	Conservatives	114	20	70.2		
		Liberals	75	10	76.5		
		Progressive-CCF	4	8	33.3	69.4	82.5

Sources: *Hansard Parliamentary Debates*, and *Canadian Parliamentary Guide*.

Heel" to workers. At the Ottawa Conference in 1932, the Liberals, back in government, readily agreed to Imperial Preferences aimed at increasing trade between members of the Commonwealth. The legislation was passed with bipartisan support (see Table 8.3). In 1935 the Liberal government ultimately reached an agreement with the United States to extend it most-favored-nation status.

Meanwhile, a new radical movement had formed in the West among labor groups, farmer organizations, and socialists: the Cooperative Commonwealth Federation (CCF). The CCF was founded in 1932 with the stated aim of eradicating capitalism in Canada via nationalization.[8] The movement thrived in Saskatchewan, where drought and the extreme specialization in wheat growing had produced devastating conditions in the 1930s.[9] King responded to the new challenge with the same kind of approach that had worked for him in the past: a program providing hefty subsidies and relief payments to the farmers.

Differences in the positions of the major parties on trade had all but disappeared by the 1930s (McDiarmid 1946, 8). Industry-group lobbying still appears to have played a dominant role in shaping trade policy throughout this period, though policy innovation was driven mainly by the first appearance of urban-rural conflict as the Progressives and the CCF challenged the policy status quo. Careful management and compromises by the King government helped to keep the old system in place.

8.4 POSTWAR TRADE POLITICS AND NORTH AMERICAN FREE TRADE

The Liberal dominance of Canadian politics continued into the 1950s, based on their two traditional strongholds of support in the eastern provinces, among the French-speaking population of Quebec in particular, and among the farmers in the West. The continuing electoral problem for the Conservatives, who drew support predominantly from urban business interests, was

[8] Although the CCF attacked the National Policy, it focused most of its attention on breaking the private monopolies that controlled the transportation and marketing of grain.
[9] It failed to gather much support in the industrial heartland of Ontario; see Palmer 1983, 228.

that they were not able to compete effectively among the French Catholic community, which constituted four fifths of the Quebecois population. Both the major parties occupied the middle ground on a broad range of economic policies, including the tariff. Both parties had accepted the high levels of protection before the war, and afterward both had accepted the international mandate for gradual liberalization, though Liberals typically emphasized the benefits of trade slightly more than their rivals (Winn 1976, 234).

Labor's voice in policy was quite weak until the New Democratic Party (NDP) was founded in 1961. Although it shied away from the doctrinaire socialism of the CCF in favor of a more moderate approach, the new party failed to secure a broad base of support (Palmer 1983, 289). In 1969 it was forced to expel its militant leftist faction, known as the "Waffle," which had written a manifesto for a socialist Canada that included economic independence from the United States (via rigid trade and capital controls) and nationalization. The NDP was dealt another severe blow in 1974 when Trudeau's Liberals campaigned hard against the wage and price controls that the Tories were advocating as a solution to inflation. The issue split the NDP in half: Western and rural members favored the controls while eastern and industrial members were vehemently opposed (Palmer 1983, 291).

The two major parties were heterogeneous mixes of regional, ethnic, and economic groups, and their caucuses were dominated by bargaining between these diverse memberships (see Thorburn 1985, 17). In this environment, group lobbying pressure and contributions to campaigns played an important and growing role (see Underhill 1961). The trade policymaking process, in particular, had much less to do with any class or ideological differences between the parties than with "ins versus outs" (Thorburn 1985, 338). Policy was formed on a case-by-case basis, shifting in response to demands from groups that were directed predominantly toward members of the bureaucracy rather than toward members of parliament.[10]

The importance of groups in the policy process was accentuated by regional concentrations and the interaction between industry and sectional divisions. Agricultural producers remained split over the trade issue with export-oriented grain and beef producers in the prairie provinces at loggerheads with dairy, fruit, and vegetable farmers hurt by import competition in Quebec and Ontario (Protheroe 1980, 36). Manufacturers were also divided over trade: Producers of telecommunications equipment, autos, pulp and paper, and agricultural machinery were much more amenable to liberalization than the older, import-competing textile and footwear producers in Ontario. In fact, although the Canadian Manufacturers Association represented some 75 percent of domestic firms, it backed away from taking any general position on trade. Most notably, it opposed the use of general tariff-cutting formulas in international negotiations in favor of an industry-by-industry approach. The Canadian Labor Congress made a cautious statement

---

[10] This is the conclusion reached by Presthus (1973), who documented an intricate process of elite accommodation in postwar Canadian economic policy making.

in favor of liberalization, but many unions were openly critical of this stance (Protheroe 1980, 39–41).

As early as 1978 there had been discussion in Canada of a possible free-trade agreement with the United States. In that year, a report issued by the Senate Standing Committee on Foreign Affairs (the Van Roggen Report) recommended serious consideration of a bilateral free-trade deal. In 1984, with the Conservatives back in power under Mulroney, a series of disputes with the United States led to repeated threats of U.S. retaliation for alleged Canadian transgressions and provoked alarm among many large producers who were dependent on sales to the U.S. market. Taking advantage of the 1984 congressional authorization for the president to negotiate a free-trade deal with Israel, U.S. officials and Canadian officials began negotiations in 1986 aimed at securing better access to the U.S. market (Cameron and Tomlin 2000, 6). Significant opposition to the Tory initiative came from manufacturing and farming groups in the eastern provinces, particularly in Quebec.

The trade pact became an important issue in the 1988 elections. The Conservatives supported the final version of the pact and ultimately won the election by a wide margin. The Liberal opposition, led by Turner, referred to the agreement as the "Sale of Canada Act" and warned of severe job losses in the textiles, footwear, and clothing industries. Despite Turner's heated rhetoric, however, the votes on the legislation in the House indicate that the parties were still divided internally over the trade issue (see Table 8.4).

Mulroney and the Conservatives ultimately joined the negotiations over the NAFTA in 1991, but as the most reluctant partner at the table (Cameron and Tomlin 2000, 63–66). In May of 1993, with an election on the horizon, Mulroney steered the NAFTA bill through the House of Commons over significant opposition from members of his own party as well as from the Liberals. A lingering recession had left its political mark, and Mulroney made way for Kim Campbell to take over as prime minister before the election in October, downplaying the trade issue. At the polls, Jean Chrétien's Liberals picked up a massive ninety-nine seats in the House of Com-

TABLE 8.4
Divisions on North American Free Trade in the House of Commons, 1988, 1993

	Legislation	*Party*	*Yeas*	*Nays*	*Cohesion*	*Average Cohesion*	*General Cohesion*
1988	Canada-U.S.	Conservatives	152	30	67		
	Free Trade	Liberals	22	18	10		
	Agreement	NDP	12	16	14.2	40.4	88.9
1993	North American	Conservatives	143	41	55.4		
	Free Trade	Liberals	8	15	30.4		
		NDP	11	14	12	42.6	88.3

Sources: *Hansard Parliamentary Debates* and *Canadian Parliamentary Guide.*

mons, leaving only two elected Conservatives. During the campaign, Chrétien had promised to renegotiate the NAFTA treaty after the election. He did
soon request that the United States and Mexico reopen discussions on several of the treaty's provisions, but was predictably rebuffed. In the end, he
supported the treaty and even went so far as to propose a grand NAFTA-EU
free-trade deal and the expansion of NAFTA southward to include nations
such as Chile.

8.5 CONCLUSIONS

The evolution of Canadian trade politics over the last two centuries has a
distinctly French flavor, although the importance of regional divisions in the
economy and in politics is perhaps more unique to Canada. With relatively
low levels of interindustry mobility in a regionally separated economy, trade
debates in Canada have rarely been delineated by any kind of clear class
cleavage and instead have been dominated by industry-group pressures. Industry and regional divisions over the trade issue cut across broad factor
classes, and Canadian parties and peak associations have been internally
divided over the tariff issue. Although class coalitions were more visible in
the 1920s and 1930s, when radical agrarian movements in the western provinces challenged the protectionist policy endorsed by the major parties, a
series of concessions by King's Liberal government checked the conflict. In
the years after 1945, with the parties (and peak associations) relying on
heterogeneous combinations of regional, ethnic, and economic groups for
support, the policymaking process was shaped more by group demands and
"ins versus outs" than simple class cleavages.

CHAPTER NINE

Australia

The Australian story is a particularly interesting case in terms of the theory advanced in this book. As indicated by the evidence reported in chapter 2, levels of interindustry factor mobility rose precipitously at the turn of the century in the Australian economy and remained quite high in relative terms in later decades. The pattern is similar to that followed by the Swedish economy. According to the theory, we should thus expect that Australian trade politics since the late nineteenth century would be marked by a fairly robust class cleavage, pitting owners of abundant land against urban interests.

Expectations and a summary of the basic findings are reported in Table 9.1. In general, the Australian evidence tends to confirm the expectations and fits well with previous class-based interpretations (Rogowski 1989; Tsokhas 1984), although such accounts do not themselves explain the apparent patterns of change over time that fit well with the theory advanced here. Clear, class-based cleavages only emerged in Australian trade politics at the close of the nineteenth century when interindustry factor mobility rose to high levels. After the formation of the federal government in 1901, the parties began to assume coherent class positions: Rural interests backed the Free Trade Party, business and the urban middle classes supported the Protectionists, and the Labor Party gradually adopted a unified stance in favor of tariffs. Rural interests ultimately elected to compromise, however, joining forces with the Protectionists in order to check Labor at the polls, and this effectively took the trade issue out of electoral politics in Australia for most of the twentieth century.

9.1 Trade Politics in the Colonies

The colonies became self-governing in the 1850s and 1860s, and early debates over trade policy were characterized by fierce lobbying by local industry groups in each state's legislature, with different sets of manufacturers and workers taking opposing positions on the tariff issue (Serle 1971, 31–32; Atkins 1958). Although individuals were often identified as "liberals" and "conservatives" in the British manner, there were no mass-based parties until much later, and shifting alliances and personal loyalties were key features of a political arena dominated by self-absorbed regional constituencies.

At the time that self-government was granted, existing tariffs were levied for revenue purposes only, and import duties were by far the most important

TABLE 9.1
Anticipated and Observed Outcomes in Australia

Period	Factor Endowments	Mobility	Prediction[a]	Outcomes	
				Class-based Parties and Associations	Industry Groups
1815–1869	Abundant land; scarce capital and labor	Low	Industry coalitions	n/a	Highly active; many groups testified before committees on trade policy and petitioned state assemblies
1870–1914	Abundant land; scarce capital and labor	High	Class coalitions	Protectionists and Free Traders fought over trade issue until merger in 1909; Labor protectionist	Fewer groups actively lobbied trade commissions
1919–1939	Abundant land and capital; scarce labor[b]	High	Class coalitions	Liberal-Country coalition and Labor both protectionist	Little evidence of lobbying on trade
1945–1994	Abundant land and capital; scarce labor[b,c]	High	Class coalitions	Coalition and Labor, along with AFB and ACTU, committed to protection; some Country Party dissent in 1980s	Major groups lobbied Tariff Board for alterations to rates

[a]Class coalitions are expected to imply that class-based organizations are internally unified on trade and adopt coherent platforms while groups are inactive. Industry coalitions imply that class-based organizations are internally divided on trade and adopt ambiguous positions (see Table 3.1).

[b]Here Rogowski's classification is problematic. The evidence on endowments employed by Rogowski compares factor proportions in each nation with world averages. Given the overwhelming bias in Australia's dependence on trade with Britain (for political and historical reasons), and after 1945, on trade with the United States, a strong case can be made for considering the economy to be scarce in capital relative to its main trading partners. Data from later years is consistent with this view; see point c. below. This would lead us to predict that business (and the organizations representing them) would support protection, as the analysis here seems to confirm.

[c]Using 1966 data, Bowen, Leamer, and Sveikauskas (1987) find Australia to be very scarce in capital, in contrast to Rogowski's findings, and in all types of labor (except agricultural workers) and abundant in arable land.

item of taxation in each colony. Economic pressures in the 1850s and 1860s rapidly altered the way tariff policy was set. In the two largest colonies of Victoria and New South Wales, a large inflow of immigrants attracted by the gold rushes began to swell the ranks of the unemployed when the boom subsided. In Victoria, the strains were particularly severe. The need for the infrastructure to keep pace with population growth created an urgent demand for new revenue, and the opportunity was seized upon by protectionist interests. When a Select Committee was appointed to consider changes in the tariff in 1860, it was deluged with appeals for new tariffs from a multitude of industries.

Groups representing a vast array of nascent manufacturing interests in industries like coach building, boot making, saddle and harness making, flour milling, and furniture, lobbied vigorously for new protection (Patterson 1968, 12–14). Farming groups and commercial interests, including tobacco dealers, raised the only opposition. Pamphleteers became active in calling for new tariffs and a loose Tariff League was formed by protectionist groups to publicize their cause (Whitfeld 1950, 52–59). Tariffs were increased by the short-lived Heales government in 1862, but when the economic situation failed to improve another Select Committee on Manufactures was appointed in 1865, and a new round of special pleading began.[1]

The problems were less severe in New South Wales, but rising rates of metropolitan unemployment were evident in the late 1850s, and the Parkes government established a Select Committee in 1860 to investigate the state of the working class. Like its Victorian counterpart, the committee was subject to numerous appeals from industry groups from Sydney and a variety of townships and recommended an upward revision of the tariff to foster growth in manufacturing (Patterson 1968, 24). The proposal received a hostile reception in the state legislature, however, where agricultural interests held more weight. To the squatters, the most important issue was the cost-of-living effects of trade barriers for themselves and their employees, and they strongly opposed new protection.

Demands for tariff hikes became louder, however, in the 1860s. The Parkes government received a wide range of petitions from localized industry groups (Patterson 1968, 25). In 1862, it established a new Committee on the State of Manufactures and Agriculture which heard testimony from a large number of groups.[2] In 1863, the Cowper government proposed a new protectionist tariff, but could not pass it in the House. Strong opposition came from farming groups and the city's commercial interests, who feared that the new duties (without provision for drawback) would ruin the Sydney *entrepôt* trade with New Zealand and Queensland. In the wake of this de-

---

[1] See Victorian Legislative Assembly 1865. Over forty separate groups appear to have given testimony to the committee.

[2] See New South Wales Legislative Assembly 1862.

feat, the House was again bombarded with petitions for and against new tariffs. Temporary legislation in 1863 and 1864 raised tariffs on revenue items (alcohol and tobacco) to stave off a financial crisis as a variety of governing coalitions were formed and dissolved. Moderate protective measures were finally passed into law in 1866 (Loveday, Martin, and Parker 1977, 38–40).

9.2 TRADE POLITICS AND FEDERATION

Trade became the central political issue in the colonies when economic recession hit hard in the late 1880s. The different colonies dealt with the economic problems in very different fashions. In New South Wales, the Free Trade Party led by Parkes formed a coalition to keep markets open, using revenues from auction sales of Crown land and property taxes to redistribute income from landowners to workers (Anderson and Garnaut 1987, 42). Similarly, in Western Australia and Queensland, where farmers and graziers dominated politics, governments adhered to free-trade policies. In Victoria, on the other hand, where the flood of immigration had been greatest, a large pool of unemployed workers formulated radical demands for protection to increase employment in manufacturing (Loveday, Martin, and Parker 1977, 28).[3] Victorian governments, like those in South Australia and Tasmania, became strongly protectionist in response to these urban demands and provided high tariffs to fledgling manufacturing industries.

By the 1880s, a coherent form of class politics had taken shape in Victoria, where large numbers of workers belonged to Protection leagues and combined with manufacturers to oppose the Free Trade League. Melbourne's powerful Trades Hall Council was dominated by craft unions from manufacturing trades, which strongly supported protection, and the labor movement formed a comfortable alliance with protectionist Liberal governments that dominated politics in the 1880s and 1890s.

The decline in special pleading among industries, apparent from the 1880s and coincident with the rise of class coalitions, was reflected in the lobbying before official commissions in this period. Commissions on the tariff in Victoria, which had attracted large numbers of groups in the 1860s, were faced with far less pressure from narrow interests by the 1890s. Far fewer groups appeared before the Royal Commission on the Tariff, set up in 1883, and the 1895 Board of Enquiry appointed to examine the fiscal system of Victoria in light of objections (especially from rural interests) to high tariffs.[4]

---

[3] Victoria also lacked the large tracts of arable crown land that generated so much revenue for the government in New South Wales. For a detailed discussion of Victorian politics at the time, see La Nauze 1948.

[4] See Victorian Legislative Assembly 1883 and 1894. Fewer than forty groups appeared

In New South Wales the negative effects of trade on wages were offset by Parkes' redistribution policies, and workers were far less inclined toward protection. Stepping up land sales in the 1870s, Parkes even repealed many revenue duties that had been imposed in the 1860s and was presented with a gold medal from the Cobden Club! Advocates of free trade vied with protectionists for support in the Sydney Trades and Labour Council, and the Council's position on the issue remained ambiguous (Nairn 1957, 435). The Council divided twelve to ten in a vigorous debate over whether to support the new Protection and Political Reform League (PPRL) in May 1885. A similar vote split the Council in 1887, this time favoring the free traders, and many individual Labor candidates continued to maintain close ties with the Protectionists or the Free Trade Association through the 1880s (Nairn 1957, 436).

The trade issue began to galvanize opposing interests in the New South Wales elections in the late 1880s when the recession grew worse. The PPRL, under the leadership of the "mad teetotaller" Richard Charles Luscombe, achieved its greatest success in 1886 by setting aside its usual work on pamphlets and debates to organize a large demonstration in Sydney.[5] A crowd of about six thousand turned out to watch Protectionist parliamentary members, manufacturers, and trade unions march through Sydney and hear speeches with titles like "The Curse of Cobden."[6] The president of the Trades and Labour Council described it as a "grand wedding, the wedding of capital and labour" (Loveday and Martin 1966, 135). A fiscal crisis in 1886 gave the Protectionists enough leeway to form a cabinet, led by Jennings, and pass new tariffs. But, when the Jennings government collapsed the following year, Parkes took the reins again and repealed the measures. In 1889 a new Protectionist ministry took office and raised tariffs when it won a majority in 1891. Again, the new duties were swiftly repealed in 1895 when the Free Traders took control under Reid.

The continuing economic distress of the 1890s transformed Australian

---

before the Royal Commission in 1883, an even smaller number (around twenty) gave testimony to the Board of Inquiry in 1894.

[5] Luscombe's nickname was bestowed by the free-trade *Sydney Morning Herald*, February 2, 1889. The PPRL had also played a major role in the short-lived Land and Industrial Alliance, which had organized a conference in Sydney the year before, attracting about forty delegates from regional branches, trade unions, and several Free Selectors' Associations and Farmers' Unions (see Loveday and Martin 1966, 123–24). The Alliance resolved to cooperate to "confront the dominant influence of the pastoral and importing interests," but it was soon clear that the participating farm groups were opposed to wholesale protection (Loveday and Martin 1966, 125).

[6] Their advertisement appealed to:

tradesmen and mechanics of all kinds, to seaman and to labourers, to attend and show by their presence whether the people of Sydney and suburbs are satisfied with the policy which has made our interior a sheep walk and Sydney a receptacle for the shoddy goods of Europe, while thousands of skilled and unskilled labourers are out of employment. (quoted in Atkins 1958, 242)

politics. Falling international wool prices led graziers to cut wages of shearers, and when the well-organized shearers' union resisted, a series of strikes in other industries followed in 1890 and 1891 and threw industrial relations into turmoil. New industrial unions organized large numbers of less skilled workers, were more militant and class conscious, and advocated a central labor leadership and political representation for workers (Gollan 1955, 18). When the maritime strikes ended, the unions had failed to secure most of their goals and turned instead to electoral politics. Labor Electoral Leagues were created to sponsor candidates, and with success at the polls these quickly developed into parliamentary Labor parties in each state.[7] In 1899 the Federal Labor Party was formed.

Yet, workers remained divided over trade policy along regional lines. At the first conference of the Labor Party in 1900, a simple platform was drawn up that sidestepped the trade issue and focused instead on immigration restriction and old-age pensions. In the first federal election in 1901, the party leadership decided that trade policy should be an open question for its candidates (Loveday, Martin, and Parker 1977, 388). Led by Watson, the party actually had no set policy on protection throughout the first and second Parliaments and allowed its members to vote freely on such matters in the House.[8] Over time, however, a growing proportion of Labor members moved into line behind support for import barriers. The healing rift among Labor is apparent in the voting patterns among their members, both in the New South Wales Legislative Assembly in the 1890s (where Labor members split their allegiance between the more cohesive Free Traders and Protectionists) and in the new Federal parliament after 1901 (see Table 9.2).[9]

The tariff issue had been hotly debated at the Constitution Conventions of

---

[7] Interestingly, the birth of a Labor Party in Victoria was more protracted than in N.S.W. and elsewhere since the Liberals had already won the regular support of the working class in the early political battles over land, taxes, and protection. Although tensions between employers and workers were rising, the tendency to think that labor might just be seen as a wing of the Liberal Party was reinforced by the consolidation of the electoral alliance with Deakin's Liberals in 1894 in order to avoid any chance of dividing the anti-Free Trade vote (Gollan 1955, 23).

[8] Although protection for sugar and tobacco was linked to the more unifying immigration issue. Growers of sugar cane and tobacco in Queensland had come to rely heavily on Melanesian labor in the late nineteenth century, and at Federation, the Protectionist and Labor parties were concerned about alienating their Queensland delegates with the "White Australia" restrictions on immigration demanded by their urban supporters—so they simply coupled these with high import barriers and subsidies to sugar and tobacco producers.

[9] Data on votes are from the New South Wales Legislative Assembly, *Votes and Proceedings of the Legislative Assembly* (1892, 1895), and from the Parliament of the Commonwealth of Australia, *Votes and Proceedings of the House of Representatives* (1906–1971). Data on party affiliations are from the *Members of the Legislative Assembly of New South Wales 1856–1901* (Martin 1959) and the *Biographical Register of the Commonwealth Parliament 1901–1972* (Rydon 1975). General cohesion indexes are calculated from 10 percent random samples drawn by the author from all votes in the given year.

TABLE 9.2
Divisions on Trade Bills in the New South Wales Assembly and the House of
Representatives, 1870–1914

	Legislation	Party	Yeas	Nays	Cohesion	Average Cohesion	General Cohesion
1892	Customs Duty Bill	Free Trade	2	37	89.7		
	(NSW)	Protectionist	56	6	96.5		
		Labor	8	5	23.2	84.1	82.5
1895	Customs Bill	Free Trade	44	5	79.6		
	(NSW)	Protectionist	0	28	100		
		Labor	7	3	40	88.2	83.4
1906	Excise Tariff	Free Trade	0	29	100		
	Act	Protectionist	28	0	100		
		Labor	12	6	33.3	96.5	86
1908	Lyme Tariff	Free Trade	1	24	92		
		Protectionist	32	1	93.9		
		Labor	19	2	81	91	88.3

Sources: New South Wales Legislative Assembly (1892, 1895), Parliament of the Commonwealth of Australia (1906, 1908), Martin (1959), and Rydon (1975).

1900, which prepared the way for federation, with pro-trade interests expressing grave concerns about the likely consequences of federation for trade policy. Western Australia, highly dependent on export-oriented primary industries, maintained until the last moment that the loss of tariff discretion was grounds for it to reject federation (Warhurst 1981, 191). Indeed, the farming and mining vote behind the Free Trade Party was no match for the urban electoral strength of the Protectionists, led by Edmund Barton, in the first federal election in 1901, and a highly protective national tariff schedule was quickly enacted. After the election of 1903, in which Labor won an increased number of seats, a new minority Protectionist government under Alfred Deakin was formed and sought support from Labor for a policy that was christened the "New Protection." Implemented in the Excise Tariff Act of 1906, this policy imposed a substantially higher tariff on imports, and an excise tax on domestic manufactures in the same amount, with the excise refunded for those firms that paid "a fair and reasonable wage," as judged by the Court of Conciliation and Arbitration (Alexander 1980, 26–27). The policy forged a coalition between capitalists and workers, obviating the struggle, in the words of the Court's Justice Higgins, between "the pressure for bread on the one side and the pressure for profits on the other."[10] Import duties were raised again in the Lyme Tariff of 1908.

The urban coalition of business and labor was an uneasy one. After losing

---

[10] Quoted in Gollan 1955, 168. The Court's famous "Harvester Judgement" of 1907 defined a fair wage as one sufficient to support a worker with a nonworking wife and three children. The legislation was eventually ruled unconstitutional in 1908.

their majority in 1903, Deakin and the Protectionist leadership hesitated about whether they should join forces with Labor or with the Free Traders. They were strongly influenced by business organizations, including the powerful employers associations and the national Chambers of Manufactures, which passed resolutions rejecting nationalization and promising to oppose any party supporting socialist legislation (Loveday, Martin, and Parker 1977, 402–26). By 1904, the Free Traders were prepared to accept existing tariff levels to secure a united stand with business against socialism, and their leader, George Reid, was by then directing all his energies to "stalking the socialist tiger." The electoral success of the Labor Party in 1906, and its increasing appeal to a militant class consciousness, eventually brought the Free Trade and Protectionist parties together. In 1909 they formed a single anti-Labor Party under Deakin, the Liberal Party, based on a coalition of landowning and business interests.[11]

The new coalition was not strong enough, however, to prevent Labor winning office for the first time in 1910. Under the leadership of Andrew Fisher, the Labor Party finally took a clear position in favor of protection. With no party advocating free trade, protection thus became firmly established in Australian politics as an uncontested area of economic policy. Industry associations and labor unions, preoccupied with industrial disputes, played little part in the "new protection" or the subsequent tariff hikes prior to World War I. Even the formidable Amalgamated Shearers' Union, the oldest and strongest labor group bound to the exporting wool industry, accepted protection as necessary for the general good of the working class. Political activity by business interests was channeled into the Chambers of Commerce and Chambers of Manufacturers, which stood uniformly behind protection (Loveday, Martin, and Parker 1977, 17–18).

9.3 THE INTERWAR YEARS IN AUSTRALIA

The Liberals acted promptly at war's end to protect manufacturers against revived import competition by passing the Green Tariff in 1921, which provided for a large increase in duties on industrial goods. Votes on the bill and subsequent legislation in the interwar period are shown in Table 9.3. The Labor Party strongly backed protection—the divisions that had marked the party in 1901 having disappeared—and there was little dissent from Liberals or members of the new Country Party.

The Country Party, founded in 1920, had accepted the need for industrial protection in the name of bolstering the anti-Labor coalition. It did not hurt

---

[11] The anti-Labor "fusion" was fraught with tensions. The Free Traders sought assurances about future trade policy. When pro-fusion members of the N.S.W. and Victorian Chambers of Manufactures did assure them that there would only be limited adjustments to existing policy, protectionist members roundly denounced them. See Glezer 1982, 6.

TABLE 9.3
Divisions on Trade Bills in the House of Representatives, 1919–1939

	Legislation	Party	Yeas	Nays	Cohesion	Average Cohesion	General Cohesion
1921	Greene	Liberal	32	0	100		
	Tariff	Labor	23	1	92		
		Country	4	2	33.3	88.2	87
1930	Special	Liberal	25	2	85.2		
	Duties	Labor	31	0	100		
	Bill	Country	2	1	33.3	90.7	89.4

Sources: Parliament of the Commonwealth of Australia (1921, 1930) and Rydon (1975).

that farmers in many areas, particularly in the more labor-intensive fruit, sugar, and dairy industries of northern New South Wales and Queensland, were threatened by cheap imports from Latin America, the Philippines, and New Zealand. But there was a growing concern in the 1920s, especially with the worldwide decline in grain and meat prices, about the rising costs to farmers of imported machinery and chemicals. The Liberal governments responded by granting direct subsidies to agricultural producers for the purchase of farm machinery and chemical fertilizers.

The Liberal prime minister, Stanley Bruce, also sought to deflect agricultural complaints by appointing a committee of economists to report on the tariff in 1927. The Brigden Commission produced a comprehensive argument for protectionism while arguing that the existing levels were probably high enough. Generous protection for manufactures was justified, according to Brigden, on the grounds that such a policy maintained a higher real wage than would be possible under free trade.[12] The report provided the origins of the "Australian case for protection" that helped inspire Stolper and Samuelson in their later work on the distributional effects of trade.

Bruce lost the general election in 1929, and a new Labor government took office under James Scullin. It was soon confronted with unprecedented levels of unemployment and a balance of payments crisis and, ignoring the Brigden report, imposed a wholesale tariff increase in 1930. The government could not survive the economic crisis, however, and fell in December 1931. By that time, agitation against higher tariffs had begun among rural interests and importers, and Tariff Reform Leagues had formed in most of the states. In the election campaign the Liberals, propelled by the widespread fear of socialism and nationalization, were savvy enough to promise to have the Tariff Board review the new protection that had been granted in

---

[12] See Copland 1931 and Anderson 1938. Both articles were cited by Stolper and Samuelson in their original paper in 1941.

1930 (though none of the increases were subsequently reversed).[13] In Western Australia, where export-oriented grain producers and mining industries had expressed the most outrage at the tariff hikes, talk now turned toward secession. Harking back to complaints in 1900, they characterized high external tariffs and internal free trade as "Western Australia's greatest burden under Federation" (Warhurst 1981, 191).

Rural concerns were eased somewhat in 1932 when the government committed Australia to the system of imperial preferences negotiated with Britain at the Ottawa Conference. The British market still accounted for half of Australia's exports, so British preferences for imperial products offered at least some advantage for aggrieved farmers, although not against Canadian competition. It did not help that Australian tariffs had been bumped up prior to the granting of preferences to British imports (the Ottawa commitment was to reduce tariffs to about 15 percent below those levied on nonimperial imports).

9.4 AUSTRALIAN TRADE POLITICS IN THE POSTWAR ERA

The coalition between the Liberal and Country parties dominated politics in the two decades following World War II, holding power from 1949 to 1972. The Liberals' core base of support lay among owners of capital in urban areas who remained the driving force behind the party's protectionist position (Millar 1978, 39). In opposition in 1948, when the Labor government signed on to the GATT, the Liberals condemned the terms of Australia's participation strongly (Glezer 1982, 22). Once in power, they introduced an elaborate system of highly restrictive import quotas to effectively opt out of GATT-mandated liberalization, arguing that as long as barriers to agricultural exports remained, Australia was justified in protecting its manufacturing (Arndt 1965; Rattigan 1986, 5). This was a position acceptable to both agricultural exporters and industrialists relying on import barriers.

Perhaps most surprising is that the coalition's protectionist policies were supported so strongly in these years by the Country Party, when land-abundant Australia was a large exporter of low-cost agricultural products. The party was united with Liberals in its opposition to socialism, and the need for anti-Labor solidarity explains a large part of the puzzle. With agricultural producers accounting for a declining share of population, employment, and national income in the postwar period, the coalition was crucial if the party was to have any great influence over policy outcomes (Rattigan 1986, 5). There were other forces, however, that pushed the Country Party away from free trade.[14] The most competitive farmers were those producing

---

[13] Subsequent reviews by the Board during the rest of the 1930s were very sympathetic to the protectionist cause, and the Liberal prime minister Robert Menzies praised the "sturdy Australianism" with which the Board conducted its inquiries. See Glezer 1982, 19.

[14] This account draws heavily from Anderson and Garnaut 1987, 47–48.

wool, grain, and beef for world markets. These types of farming were extremely land intensive and employed workers (most notably shearers) who typically pledged their allegiance to the Labor Party. Far more of the rural population worked in the less land-intensive sugar, dairy, fruit, and tobacco industries, which were heavily dependent on protective policies. The Australian climate was not suited to large-scale dairying and citrus-growing, especially in the years before irrigation projects extended the areas of pasture, and farmers in these fields relied on subsidies to compete with imports from New Zealand and Latin America. Protection for sugar and tobacco producers was linked historically with immigration policy: The Labor and Protectionist parties had granted heavy protection to these industries after Federation, in part to make up for prohibitions on the inflow of Melanesian workers in the north. These protected farm industries formed an important component of the Country Party's electoral support.

The leader of the Country Party in the 1960s, John McEwen, took the position of Minister for Trade and Industry (rather than the traditional deputy's position as treasurer), and actually attempted to use protection to broaden his party's electoral base (Jupp 1982, 80). He vigorously advocated what he called "all-round protection" for both industry and agriculture. His attention was directed in particular toward industries located partly in country towns where he hoped to extend his party's electoral base. Farmers were compensated in this system by subsidies for chemical fertilizers and generous depreciation allowances on farm machinery. After the conclusion of the Japanese Trade Agreement in 1957 and the removal of import licensing in the early 1960s (in line with GATT mandates), McEwen pushed through emergency protection on a broad range of products in the 1960s.[15]

The general approach applied by McEwen and the coalition in these years was to make a broad commitment to protection, while keeping the specifics vague and letting the independent Tariff Board be responsible for advising on particular tariff rates and adjustments to the structure of protection (Glezer 1982, 26–27). The Board sent out questionnaires to gather information on an industry and typically made its recommendations with little active participation from industry groups and little real political debate.[16] The broad con-

---

[15] He also pressed repeatedly for currency devaluation, a move that united both import-competing manufacturers and rural exporters, and he denounced the coalition cabinet's decision not to devalue with sterling in 1967. See Glezer 1982, 203. In 1962 the government set up the Special Advisory Authority (SAA), which was charged with the task of recommending emergency protection for industries on the premise that the Tariff Board would later conclude a full inquiry. Textile and chemical industries used this route to obtain a string of temporary duties in the 1960s (Glezer 1982, 63). The stated approach of the head of the SAA, Frank Meere, was "You make it and I'll protect it" (quoted in Glezer 1982, 71).

[16] The Board had the power to summon witnesses, but never resorted to this, even though it was increasingly the case in the 1960s that interested parties did not appear at all before it and refused to supply information on production costs. During the Board's 1960 review of coated steel strip, for instance, the chief domestic producer did not appear and the Board did not send a request (Glezer 1982, 55).

sensus on the need for high protection for industrial development, coupled with acceptance of a routine administrative channel by which fixing of tariff rates could be accomplished, meant that with only a few exceptions (mostly in rural and textile districts) parliamentary members were typically inactive on the trade issue and the Board's reports seldom even occasioned debate.

The one challenge to the coalition's cozy system came in the shape of Alf Rattigan, the civil servant appointed to head the Tariff Board from 1963, who soon adopted an activist conception of bureaucratic leadership and began a public campaign for reform in the late 1960s (Rattigan 1986; Glezer 1982, 78–109). Following up the recommendations of the Vernon Committee in 1965, he argued in favor of a comprehensive review of the structure of Australian protection, rather than the old ad hoc approach, which would begin with the most highly protected industries. Not one industry group or firm supported Rattigan's proposals and the Associated Chambers of Manufacturers (ACMA) vigorously opposed it (Glezer 1982, 100).[17] While rural groups, such as the woolgrowers and graziers, did offer their support, McEwen himself became a major opponent.

The Labor Party, meanwhile, remained firmly committed to protection. When Labor won office under Whitlam in 1972, after twenty-three years in opposition, the party's official platform had endorsed protection for more than six decades. Whitlam, however, was ready to experiment in the heady aftermath of his electoral success. In 1973, at the suggestion of several prominent economic advisers, he pushed a 25 percent tariff reduction through a surprised cabinet, framing it as an anti-inflation measure. Outrage among Labor Party members and the union movement was widespread and long-lasting. The tariff cut aroused especially intense opposition among large unions in the textile, clothing, and footwear industries. Union leaders (and the Liberal opposition) held it accountable for the sharp rise in unemployment in 1974. Whitlam backtracked quickly by imposing new import quotas on clothing, textiles, and footwear in 1974 and by devaluing the dollar 13.5 percent; he took a firm position in favor of protection in the elections of 1974 and 1975. The political damage had been done, however, and the tariff cut contributed to the growing perception that Labor had recklessly mismanaged the economy.[18]

---

[17] In the normal course of Tariff Board investigations, in fact, there was a strong code of non-opposition to protection among manufacturers. Users were generally confident that protection for raw materials and inputs would feed into higher protection for their own industries, and the ACMA had long taken the position that it would not extend its services to support any members seeking to lower tariffs (see Glezer 1982, 230).

[18] Rogowski (1989, 178) has suggested that the tariff cut may have been part of a calculated attempt by the Labor leadership to court white-collar voters by moving away from protectionism. But the tariff cut was not part of any grand plan. It was the outcome of careful maneuvering by a group of economists capitalizing on their unusual access to policy making in the early months of the Whitlam government, and it might have been derailed at several points along the way had more of the party leadership known about their plans. See Hiscox 1989. Whitlam,

Led by Fraser, the Liberals made protection a major issue in the election of 1975 and appealed directly to those industries most harmed by increased imports. The volume of competing imports in textiles, clothing, and footwear had increased by 75 percent in the twelve months to June 1974, and the number of employees fell 22 percent in the six months to December 1974 (Anderson and Garnaut 1987, 81). Fraser promised to introduce new protection to increase employment in these industries, blaming Labor's tariff reduction for their problems. After assuming office again in late 1975, the Liberal-Country coalition imposed more restrictive import quotas and higher duties for each of these industries and for producers of motor vehicles and auto parts in 1976. Using a mix of tariffs and tariff quotas, these new restrictions were broadened prior to the election of 1977, and just months before the 1980 election they were extended for seven years. Effective rates of protection for these industries, already high, tripled between 1975 and 1982 (see Krause 1984, 290; Gregory 1984).

Labor returned to power in 1983, led by Hawke, with the shadow of the 1973 tariff cut still hanging over its position on trade policy. After that political disaster, the Labor leadership took a staunch, unified stand on trade policy that stressed the need to avoid job losses. Union leaders, including Hawke, who had headed the Australian Council of Trade Unions in 1973, tolerated no dissension from Labor's traditional platform (Tsokhas 1984, 26). The parliamentary voting on legislation in this period reveals that high levels of party cohesion were maintained on both sides (see Table 9.4). Labor's cautious approach upon returning to power focused on maintaining employment in troubled industries and differed little from that taken by the previous government. Labor's only major initiatives in trade policy involved new subsidies for the ailing steel industry and extended protection for the automobile industry.

Among the opposition parties some cracks began to form in the consensus on protection during the mid-1980s. The National Farmers' Federation, created in 1977 by graziers and grain exporters, began to make the reduction of barriers to manufactured imports a key component of its lobbying and public education programs (Anderson and Garnaut 1987, 74). The Rural Committee of Liberal Party members also called for a review of the tariff and supported the Rattigan-inspired Tariff Board reforms. Support for reform also grew in the mining sector (Krause 1984, 289; Tsokhas 1984, 42–44). Until the 1980s, most mining companies also had large investments in protected manufacturing industries. During the resources boom of the early 1980s, however, many large companies began concentrating only on mining, and in particular on the export-oriented iron ore, bauxite, and lead industries, and they soon began voicing more support for trade liberalization.[19]

---

convinced that the upper echelon of the bureaucracy harbored anti-Labor convictions, gave these economic advisers great leeway early in his tenure. See Whitlam 1985, 49–50, 184, 191.

[19] See the *Australian Financial Review*, 19 January 1982.

TABLE 9.4
Divisions on Trade Bills in the House of Representatives, 1945–1994

	Legislation	Party	Yeas	Nays	Cohesion	Average Cohesion	General Cohesion
1948	International Trade	Liberal	22	5	63		
	Organization	Labor	11	2	69.2		
		Country	3	15	66.7	67	80.2
1957	Disapproval of	Liberal	2	34	88.9		
	Treaty with Japan	Labor	13	1	85.7		
		Country	0	33	100	89.4	88.4
1979	Tokyo Round	Liberal	62	0	100		
	Agreement	Labor	24	3	77.8		
		Country	38	2	90	90.1	87.2

Sources: Parliament of the Commonwealth of Australia (1948–1979) and Rydon (1975).

Lobbying by industry groups for protection did increase at the same time, but both parties were pushed toward supporting gradual trade reforms (Anderson and Garnaut 1987, 73).

9.5 CONCLUSIONS

The Australian experience, at least since the 1920s, yielded a resilient compromise between coherent class coalitions in favor of protectionism—what amounts, at least in the eyes of the trade economist, to the evil twin of the Swedish case. After the Australian colonies became self-governing in the 1850s and 1860s, debates over trade policy were characterized initially by fierce lobbying by local industry groups. But the lines of cleavage were redrawn around classes at the turn of the century, with owners of the abundant factor, land, providing coherent political support for free trade in opposition to the demands for protection emanating from urban workers and business interests. Urban "Protection" leagues battled with rural "Free-Trade" leagues in each colony during the 1890s and in the new federal parliament after 1901, where they became national Protection and Free-Trade parties. It was only in response to Labor's growing electoral success and its radical plans for tax reform and nationalization that Protectionists and Free-Traders ultimately formed a coalition that endorsed the prevailing high tariff and effectively shelved the trade issue in 1909. The protectionist compromise—as unique, in its own way, as Sweden's free-trade counterpart—remained solidly in place in the decades that followed, as both sides voiced unified support for existing policy.

CHAPTER TEN

Lessons from the Case Studies

The aim in this chapter is to very briefly sum up the evidence presented so far and to shift the focus away from historical trends within nations to emphasize some of the most compelling cross-national comparisons that can be made. The evidence presented in chapter 2 indicated that levels of interindustry factor mobility in these six Western economies have been powerfully affected by economic and technological changes associated with industrialization. While these changes were felt in each of the economies, the extent of their impact (and their timing) varied substantially across nations in accord with differences in rates of industrialization and factor-market regulations. France, for instance, with its legacy of heavy industrial regulation, never displayed the high levels of factor mobility that characterized the British and U.S. economies at the turn of the century. The Australian economy remained several steps behind the others in the industrialization process in the twentieth century, relying less on advanced human and physical capital and large-scale production, and it experienced a less marked decline in measured factor mobility in recent decades. The Swedish experience in the twentieth century stands out in even more pronounced fashion, as programs aimed directly at increasing factor mobility helped keep the costs of factor movement relatively low.

10.1 CROSS-NATIONAL DIFFERENCES IN EACH PERIOD

The different nations examined here have experienced quite different types of changes at various times during the last two centuries. In the early part of the nineteenth century, rising levels of factor mobility had a marked impact on political conflict over trade in Britain and the United States. Localized industry-based coalitions, which tended to take center stage in politics in the early years of the nineteenth century in both economies, had ceded that place to broader class-based coalitions by the 1840s in Britain and by about the 1850s in the United States.

By contrast, the French system appears to have remained relatively isolated from these changes. Deeply rooted barriers to the movement of factors of production within the French economy helped ensure that industry-based coalitions retained their strength and primacy. Trade politics in France in 1870 appears to have had more in common with politics in less-advanced economies of the time (like Sweden, Canada, and Australia) than with politics in its great economic rival across the channel.

Rapid industrialization in all the Western economies late in the nineteenth century was associated with a general shift toward greater class conflict over the trade issue. The fight was carried on, in most cases, by highly unified political parties and peak associations. The competition between the Tories and the Liberal-Labour coalition in Britain, and between Republicans and Democrats in the United States, are particularly clear examples. Lobbying activity by industry groups declined, and the parties and peak associations generally stood firm on unambiguous platforms favoring either free trade or protection.

In France and Canada, where the costs of movement within the economy remained relatively high even at the turn of the century, older industry-based patterns in coalition formation remained. In Sweden and Australia changes arrived later. By 1914, levels of factor mobility had risen to historical highs in these small economies, greater even than the highest levels reached earlier in Britain and the United States. The trade issue thus generated clear class-based cleavages in both these political systems, pitting Social Democrats against Agrarians and Conservatives in Sweden and the Free-Traders against Labor and the Protectionists in Australia.

The tumultuous interwar period witnessed something of a sea change in trade politics in the United States. As levels of interindustry factor mobility began to fall in the U.S. economy in the first decades of the new century, broad-based trade coalitions began to unravel, internal divisions appeared in both major parties over how to address the trade issue, and there was a marked rise in industry-group lobbying in the trade policymaking arena. Similar changes took place in Britain, where splits over the trade issue began to emerge among both Tory and Labour party members, and in business and labor peak associations, in the 1930s.

In Canada and France, where levels of mobility rose slightly, there was some indication of increased class tensions over trade—the short-lived Popular Front in France and, more compellingly, the radical agrarian movements in Canada's west. Such tensions seem pale, however, by comparison to the overwhelming class character of politics in Sweden and Australia. In these two economies, parties and peak associations were very highly unified on trade matters and group lobbying had a minimal role in policy making. By the end of the 1930s, class coalitions had produced a coherent free-trade approach to policy in Sweden and an equally coherent protectionist approach in Australia.

In the decades after 1945, rising barriers to the movement of productive factors between industries in the U.S. economy and in Britain coincided with an especially marked disintegration in class coalitions in trade politics. The class conflict and partisanship on trade issues that characterized past eras gave way, in both nations, to policymaking processes dominated by intense lobbying from industry-based unions and management associations.

The change was particularly stark in the United States, where deep divisions appeared among both Republicans and Democrats, and where both parties gravitated toward ambiguous policy positions aimed at balancing demands from industries on either side of the trade debate.

By contrast, old class coalitions proved quite durable in Sweden and Australia, where levels of interindustry factor mobility remained much higher. Swedish and Australian parties maintained high levels of internal unity on trade issues, and industry groups were generally subordinated in the policymaking process to parties and peak associations. Broad bargains between class coalitions ensured that trade policy remained coherently liberal in Sweden and protectionist in Australia.

10.2 CONCLUSIONS

The historical analysis of trade politics in the United States, Britain, France, Sweden, Canada, and Australia indicates substantial support for the argument advanced in chapter 1. The investigation reveals a strong association between general levels of interindustry factor mobility and coalition formation in these nations. In the next two chapters I examine statistical evidence on congressional voting on trade legislation in the United States to test the argument in more rigorous fashion.

PART III

Conflict in the U.S. Congress over Trade

The historical descriptions presented in the previous chapters were painted, by necessity, in rather broad brush strokes. They covered a great number of years, and a great number of events, in order to give a sense for how well the theory's predictions fare against the general evidence.

In the following two chapters, as a complement to this analysis, I present a more detailed treatment of the quantitative evidence on political conflict over the trade issue in the U.S. Congress. Congress is a splendid producer of political data, and the aim in these chapters is to use the most relevant data to full effect. Chapter 11 provides an analysis of the trends in congressional voting on trade legislation between 1824 and 1994 and group testimony before congressional committees. Chapter 12 presents a statistical analysis of congressional votes on the major trade bills that examines evidence on the relative importance of different factors and industries in the electoral districts of members of Congress. Combined, these chapters provide clear evidence that changes in coalition patterns (and the relative utility of class- and group-based models) are related in the expected fashion to changes in levels of interindustry factor mobility. The results indicate that congressional behavior more clearly reflects class cleavages when factor mobility is relatively high, and is more consistent with a group model when levels of mobility are low.

CHAPTER ELEVEN

Historical Changes in Coalitions

Chapter 4 described long-term changes in U.S. trade politics that fit well with predictions based on the theory. According to the theory, the formation of broad factor-owning class coalitions should have been most likely during periods when interindustry factor mobility was relatively high (around the turn of the century), while narrow industry-based coalitions should have been most likely in periods when mobility was relatively low (early in the nineteenth and late in the twentieth centuries). U.S. trade politics did indeed possess a predominantly local, group-based flavor at the beginning of the nineteenth century. The emerging political parties were split over the tariff issue along regional lines, and trade legislation reflected the competing pressures placed on Congress by a vast array of locally organized groups. In the years following the Civil War, however, trade became the great partisan issue in U.S. politics, as Republicans, drawing broad support from business and labor, supported protectionist tariffs over the vehement opposition of Democrats and their largely rural constituency. More recently, at least since the 1950s, growing rifts have been apparent in both parties and peak associations over the trade issue, and industry groups again appear to have been exercising a powerful role in shaping policy outcomes.

This story can be retold in sharper detail by focusing on the major trends in the quantitative data. In this chapter, I first provide an analysis of the trends in congressional voting on trade legislation between 1824 and 1994, concentrating on measures of partisanship and party cohesion. I consider various alternative explanations for the observed trends that have nothing to do with changes in factor mobility and cleavage patterns. In particular, I present data on general levels of party cohesion in Congress in order to discuss institutional stories about party development and "decline," and data on the industry composition of party constituencies to discuss the effects of partisan realignment. Later sections examine trends in group testimony before congressional committees on trade legislation in a similar vein. I pay particular attention to the impact of the Reciprocal Trade Agreements Act of 1934 on industry lobbying. Overall, the quantitative evidence fits well with the theory advanced in chapter 1 and cannot be accounted for by alternative arguments that focus on institutional and other changes in the U.S. system.

11.1 Partisanship and Party Cohesion

According to the analysis in chapter 4, the trade issue generated the deepest class cleavages, and hence more partisanship, in U.S. politics in the last two decades of the nineteenth century and the first two decades of the twentieth century, when levels of interindustry factor mobility reached historical peaks. This picture emerges more starkly when we examine trend data on congressional votes on trade legislation. Figures 11.1 and 11.2 show the percentages of party members voting for trade liberalization—or against new protection—on major trade legislation in Congress since 1824.[1]

In both the House and the Senate, Republican preferences became more cohesively protectionist during the nineteenth century and then became more liberal on trade beginning in the 1940s.[2] The preferences of Democrats have shifted in the opposite directions, becoming more strongly free trade throughout the nineteenth century and more protectionist after World War II. Significant divisions appeared within the parties on the trade issue during the antebellum period and in the years since 1945.

A simple gauge of the change in party unity over time is provided by examining the cohesion indices calculated from the votes on trade legislation. These indexes were reported separately in chapter 4, but charting them together makes it much easier to see the long-term trends. Figures 11.3 and 11.4 show party cohesion scores derived from House and Senate votes on the major trade bills between 1824 and 1994. Clearly, there have been significant changes. Party cohesion rose steadily throughout the nineteenth century to peak around the turn of the century and declined significantly afterward.

It is plausible, of course, that these scores are simply a reflection of general party discipline. Exogenous changes in parties and party discipline have undoubtedly influenced partisanship on trade votes. Low levels of party unity in the antebellum period must surely reflect, in part, the weak organizational character of the parties that, until the 1840s, did not hold national conventions or adopt explicit platforms. Recent low levels of party cohesion on the trade issue might plausibly reflect a general party decline since the beginning of the twentieth century. This latter trend has been the focus of a great deal of attention and debate among students of U.S. politics (see Burnham 1965, 1970; Crotty 1980; Wattenberg 1984).[3]

---

[1] See appendix C for extensive discussion of these bills.

[2] Note that, in the antebellum period, "Republican" stands in for Federalist, Adams, and Whig party members; "Democratic" refers to Democratic Republicans and Jackson Democrats.

[3] The change is often traced to the rise of a highly autonomous committee system at the expense of the Speaker and party power, the introduction of the Australian ballot, which allowed voters to split tickets more easily, direct primaries, which reduced party control of nominations, and the direct election of senators (see Polsby 1968). For early studies indicating

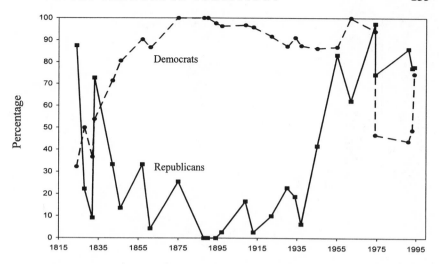

FIGURE 11.1 Percentage of party members voting for freer trade, Senate 1824–1994

Prior to the Civil War, party unity on trade does appear to track general party cohesion well. The dotted lines in Figures 11.3 and 11.4 show Rice scores for all votes in corresponding sessions of the House and Senate, and general party unity and cohesion on trade do move together closely in the first half of the nineteenth century. In later periods, however, the fit is quite poor. In particular, the recent decline in cohesion on trade does not appear to simply reflect any general party "decline" in the American system. The change that has taken place has been particular to the trade issue.

11.2 INDUSTRY COMPOSITION OF PARTY CONSTITUENCIES

The trends in party cohesion on the trade issue fit quite well with the argument about shifts in interindustry factor mobility. But perhaps they can also be explained by changes in the industry composition of party support bases. As noted in chapter 3, for any level of factor mobility, the extent to which the trade issue divides legislative parties will depend on the diversity in the industry composition of the electoral districts of different party members. Industry-based divisions among the electorate can create divisions among legislative parties only to the degree to which party members have constituencies composed of different types of industries. Since industries tend to be concentrated regionally, such differences should be profound—but they can vary significantly with geographic partisan realignments.

a "decline," see Clubb and Traugot (1977) and Brady, Cooper, and Hurley (1979). For recent dissenting views indicating that party decline was overstated, Rohde (1989), Cox and McCubbins (1993), and Aldrich (1995).

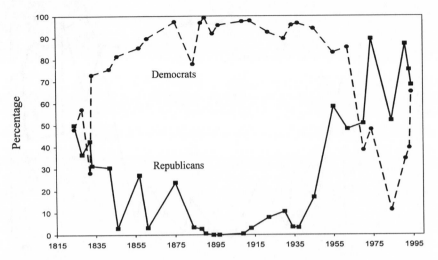

FIGURE 11.2 Percentage of party members voting for freer trade, House 1824–1994

Simply put, intraparty cohesion on trade should be related negatively to diversity in the industrial composition of electoral districts of party members. All else constant, the less diverse the industry makeup of party-held districts, the more unified the parties should be on pro-trade (when biased toward export industries) or protectionist (when biased toward import-competing industries) platforms.[4] Partisan realignments might have large ef-

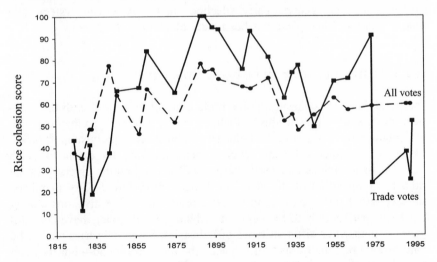

FIGURE 11.3 Party cohesion on trade votes in the U.S. Senate (weighted averages)

[4] These effects are conditional on some degree of factor specificity. If factors are perfectly mobile within the economy, Stolper-Samuelson effects should ensure that whole factor classes have highly unified views on trade regardless of the industry in which they are employed.

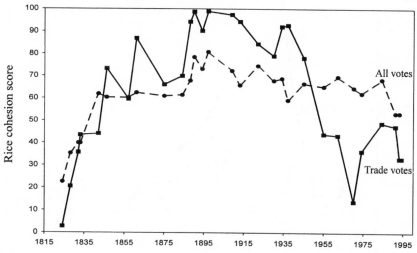

FIGURE 11.4 Party cohesion on trade votes in the U.S. House (weighted averages)

fects on party unity on the trade issue if they reshuffle party support bases in such a way as to increase or decrease their economic diversity. To what extent can this account for the observed trends in legislative voting?

Data on the geographical distribution of industrial and agricultural production in the United States paints a clear picture. Figures 11.5 and 11.6 report measures of the importance of the major export and import-competing industries in the states held by Republicans and Democrats in the Senate for each year in which a major trade vote was taken. I calculated the percentage of total state income accounted for by the leading export and import-competing industries in each state.[5] The median scores among members of each party in the Senate provide indicators of the distribution of industries in each party's support base.[6]

Clearly, the economic composition of each party's support base has been subject to change over time. Throughout much of the nineteenth century and the early part of the twentieth century, export industries were more important in Democratic districts than in Republican ones; differences are less clear for import-competing industries. According to these simple indicators, the economic character of the Republican support base did mandate a more protectionist position for the party, in contrast to that of the Democrats, at

---

[5] The ten leading export and import-competing commodities for each year in which a vote occurred were selected using official data on net exports and imports. See appendix C for a full discussion of the method and data sources.

[6] The median score is chosen here for its particular role in spatial voting analysis, as well as to discount outliers. In fact, the results are almost identical using mean scores for party members. The median scores for party members in the House exhibit the same trends, though there is much less volatility in each series.

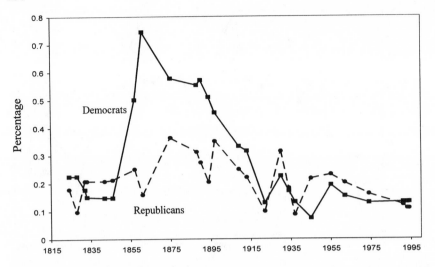

FIGURE 11.5 Value of export industries for median party member in Senate (output as percentage of state income)

least until the 1920s. Around that time the partisan differences in district composition began to diminish rapidly.

After the 1920s, the Republican Party began to draw electoral support increasingly from the South and West where export industries—including agricultural producers and newer manufacturing and service industries—

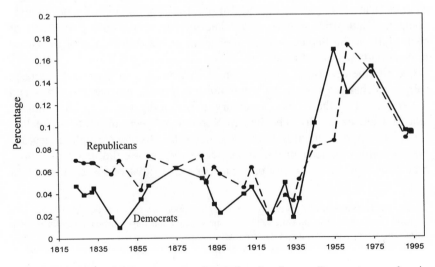

FIGURE 11.6 Value of import-competing industries for median party member in Senate (output as percentage of state income)

accounted for larger shares of the economy. The Democrats, once a minor force in the urban and commercial centers of the East, began to draw heavy support from the large northeastern cities and the cities of the Midwest.[7] Even as many Republicans continued to shift away from protectionism in the postwar era, many Democrats shifted in the other direction. Led by powerful unions in the textile and steel industries, which came under growing pressure from imports in the 1960s, the AFL-CIO stated its opposition to trade openness and persuaded many members of the Democratic Party to do likewise.

These changes are shown in Figures 11.5 and 11.6. By the 1930s, the distinction between the industry composition of the party constituencies had all but disappeared, and Republicans in the postwar period were elected from a set of districts in which export and import-competing industries were distributed in more or less identical fashion to their importance in districts represented by Democrats. The growing similarity in the industry composition of party constituencies is striking. It likely reflects not just changes in the regional strengths of the parties but a general, long-term decline in the regional concentration of the U.S. economy.[8]

While these changes may help explain the shift in party platforms on trade over time—Republicans became less protectionist over time, Democrats more so—they do not themselves explain the decline in party cohesion. What we need to look at is the diversity in the industry makeup of the districts of members of each party and whether this has changed over time. Figures 11.7 and 11.8 report the coefficients of variation in the proportion of income accounted for by export and import-competing industries in the districts of Republicans and Democrats in the Senate since 1870.

The data reveal that variation among members of each party in the industry composition of their districts has not changed in ways that explain the trends in party cohesion. There has been no clear long-term trend in the intraparty variation in the importance of export industries, although it did decline briefly around the turn of the century and then rise briefly during the 1930s and 1940s. The same can be said about the importance of import-competing industries, although the variation among Republicans actually rose around the turn of the century and variation among Democrats fell. The importance of both export and import-competing industries among party members actually appears to have grown more similar over recent decades for both Republicans and Democrats rather than less similar—suggesting that, all else constant, there has been less cause for internal division in the parties over the trade issue.

---

[7] See Sundquist 1983. The realignment of the 1930s, of course, had thrown labor support firmly over to the Democrats, and the party consolidated its strength in the largest urban centers in the East and North in the 1950s and 1960s.

[8] This decline is seemingly coincident with the waning significance of external economies of scale and the demise of "rust belt" industries. See Kim 1992.

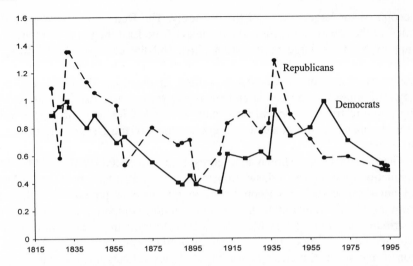

FIGURE 11.7 Intraparty variation in the value of export industries (coefficient of variation across members in Senate)

From the evidence it seems clear that while regional party strengths became less salient in defining partisan differences over trade over the course of the last century as a result of partisan realignment, changes in the geographical strengths of the parties cannot be blamed for helping to fragment the parties internally over the trade issue.

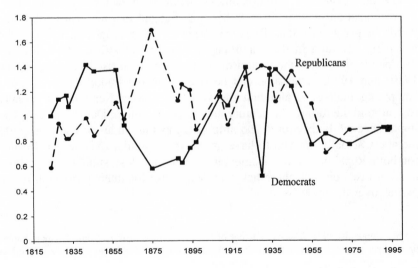

FIGURE 11.8 Intraparty variation in the value of import-competing industries (coefficient of variation across members in Senate)

11.3 GROUP LOBBYING

The findings in chapter 4 indicated that the trade issue generated the deepest industry cleavages, and hence more group lobbying, in U.S. politics during the early part of the 1800s and late 1900s, when levels of interindustry factor mobility reached historical lows. Figure 11.9 charts the data (presented separately in chapter 4) on groups testifying before House committees on the major pieces of trade legislation between 1824 and 1994. For 1824 to 1842, these are memorials and oral testimony provided to the Committee on Manufactures; from 1884 they refer to oral and written testimony to the Ways and Means Committee.[9] Although the pattern is interrupted in 1934, when the Reciprocal Trade Agreements Act (RTAA) was passed, lobbying fell off during the late nineteenth century and grew rapidly beginning in the 1920s and 1930s.

The RTAA had an important effect on lobbying on trade bills before the House committees. Until 1934, the congressional hearings were pivotal in shaping the trade legislation voted on in the House and Senate. The hearings format, which assigned particular days for receiving testimony on the treatment of different commodities, was especially convenient for industry-group lobbying. This system was changed completely in 1934. After the RTAA, hearings were typically limited to general discussions about whether to extend the president's negotiating authority and, after 1974, whether to implement previously negotiated agreements (under "fast-track" provisions that prohibited amendment). What is particularly interesting in the data, however, is the gusto with which industry groups returned to the hearings in the years since 1945. It seems that groups have been appearing not in order to demand a particular tariff rate or quota in a bill but to signal the seriousness of their position on a change in policy and (in concert with lobbying directed to the administration and parties more generally) in hopes of being granted exceptions and special deals.[10]

Figure 11.10 presents a breakdown of the industry groups according to factor ownership. As we might expect, owners of capital are the most proficient lobbyists. Since owners and managers of firms are fewer in number than all the workers (and farmers) engaged in each industry, they face lower costs in organizing for collective action (Olson 1965). Management associations are by far the most common type of group lobbying Congress in each historical period. Perhaps as a consequence of prohibitions on labor organization, labor groups were less active than other types in the antebellum period.

---

[9] See appendix C for further details.

[10] Measuring only lobbying aimed at Congress, it should be noted, means underestimating group activity in recent times relative to the past, when lobbying efforts directed toward the administration, bureaucracy, and national party committees were probably less important for groups.

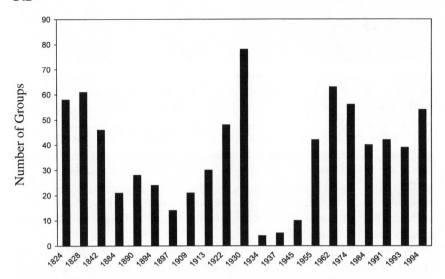

FIGURE 11.9 Industry groups testifying before House committees on trade legislation, 1824–1994

Figure 11.11 compares the number of groups lobbying for higher protection with those lobbying in favor of freer trade. Again, as might be expected, protectionist groups outnumber those lobbying for trade liberalization. In the political-economy literature, the standard explanation for inefficient protectionism is that the benefits of tariffs are concentrated

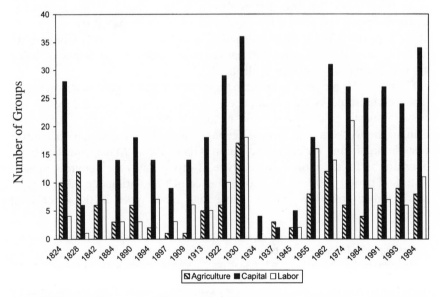

FIGURE 11.10 Types of groups testifying before House committees on trade legislation, 1824–1994

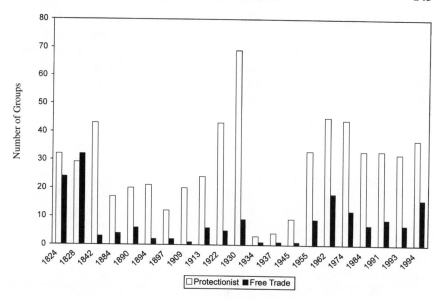

FIGURE 11.11 Policy preferences of groups testifying before House committees on trade legislation, 1824–1994

among producers in import-competing industries, while the costs are dispersed among producers in other industries and consumers; so the former find it easier to organize collectively to influence policy to their advantage.

The conventional wisdom on the RTAA relies on two versions of this same claim. The first version focuses on how delegating authority to the president eliminated protectionist logrolling and made more salient the costs of tariffs to consumers that would otherwise have been neglected because they were dispersed across electoral districts (Lohmann and O'Halloran 1994). The second version emphasizes how empowering the president to negotiate trade agreements that elicited reciprocal tariff reductions from other nations generated larger gains for, and thus more political support from, export interests (Bailey, Goldstein, and Weingast 1997). Ordinarily, the odds are against export interests having much of an impact on trade politics. To organize for political action would require overcoming severe collective action problems: As long as domestic tariff cuts are not directly linked to market access for their products, exporters *all* share a general preference for lower tariffs (to avoid closure in foreign markets and to lower costs of inputs), and so the benefits of any political action are greatly dispersed. By instituting that policy making proceed on the principle of reciprocity, the Democrats, in Destler's words, "shifted the balance of trade politics by engaging the interests of export producers, since tariff reductions could now be defended as direct means of winning new markets for American products overseas" (1992, 16).

There appears to be very little support for this claim, however, in the evidence on group lobbying before congressional committees. The ratio of groups lobbying for free trade versus those lobbying for greater protection did not rise noticeably after 1934. A growing number of groups did lobby for trade liberalization in the years after World War II, but a growing number also lobbied for protectionism. It is not clear at all that the RTAA fundamentally altered the political balance.[11]

11.4 CONCLUSION

In this chapter, I have briefly examined trends in the key quantitative indicators of shifts in trade cleavages in U.S. politics over the last two centuries. The data make clear that these shifts coincide with simple expectations based on long-term changes in levels of factor mobility in the U.S. economy. The most plausible alternative explanations for these changes in party and group behavior—associated with exogenous changes in party discipline, partisan realignments, and changes in the institutions of trade policy making in 1934—do not fare well against the evidence. In this next chapter, I examine congressional voting on trade legislation more rigorously to test for changes in the relative utility of the class and group approaches.

[11] For a critique of the conventional wisdom on the RTAA and its role in U.S. trade liberalization in the postwar era, see Hiscox 1999.

CHAPTER TWELVE

Quantitative Analysis of Voting on Major Trade Legislation—1824 to 1994

The study of legislative voting on trade bills provides a unique window on the political economy of international trade. It offers an opportunity to examine the types of coalitions that shape the choices made by legislators and define the political conflict over trade policy. This chapter analyzes voting on thirty major pieces of trade legislation between 1824 and 1994 in order to assess changes in coalition patterns (and the relative utility of class- and group-based models) in different historical periods. The presumption here is that legislators' voting decisions reflect their response to pressures from societal coalitions. If the theory is correct, voting decisions should more clearly reflect legislators' ties to broad factor classes when levels of interindustry factor mobility are high, and demands from protectionist and free-trade industries within their districts when mobility levels are low.

A number of studies of legislative votes on trade policy have appeared in the literature. Most of these have been limited to examining a specific piece of legislation, usually in the U.S. Congress, and usually in recent years. They include studies of the votes on the automobile domestic content legislation of 1982 (Coughlin 1985; McArthur and Marks 1988), the Trade Act of 1974 (Baldwin 1985), the textile quota legislation of 1985 (Tosini and Tower 1987), the Export Facilitation Act of 1987, and the omnibus trade legislation of 1987 (Marks 1993). The votes on the NAFTA have been given special attention in recent work (see Baldwin and Magee 2000; Kahane 1996; Steagall and Jennings 1996; Holian, Krebs, and Walsh 1997; Uslaner 1998). Only a few studies have looked at votes in earlier times or in other nations. These include analyses of the 1890 McKinley Tariff (Conybeare 1991), roll calls in the British Parliament in the 1840s on the Corn Laws (McLean 1995), and votes on trade bills in the German Reichstag between 1879 and 1902 (Schonhardt-Bailey 1991). One excellent analysis that covers twelve bills in Congress between 1890 and 1988 has been provided by Gilligan (1997).

The findings from these studies shed some light on the coalitions issue, but only indirectly. In all the recent votes, for instance, measures of the importance of import-competing industries in a district have significant, positive effects on the likelihood that the legislator will vote in favor of protection, especially when the bill includes particular provisions targeted at industries concentrated in the legislator's district. District ties to export industries, however, generally make legislators more likely to vote for free trade. These relationships (which fit with an industry-based approach) are much less clear in the studies of earlier votes, with some findings suggesting strong industry effects and others weak industry effects.[1] Evidence on the effects of factoral or class variables is even less clear. Some recent analyses have indicated that votes against NAFTA were positively associated with levels of contributions received from labor political action committees (Baldwin and Magee 2000; Steagall and Jennings 1996). But it is difficult to draw clear inferences from this without knowing the extent of the bias in the industry composition labor groups—import-competing industries are more unionized and thus are likely to be the primary source of contributions.

12.1 DATA

The approach taken here involves relating voting patterns among members of the Senate and House on major trade legislation to measures of the class and industry makeup of their constituencies. The dependent variable is the legislator's vote for protection (1 = for a protectionist bill or against a liberalizing bill, 0 = against a protectionist bill or for a liberalizing bill). The explanatory variables are class or industry characteristics of each state in each year in which a vote was taken. For factor classes, several measures are derived from the available *Census* data.[2] As a basic measure of the importance of farmers in each state, I used the total value of agricultural production as a fraction of state income. As a measure of the importance of labor, I calculated the proportion of total employment in manufacturing in each state's population. Measuring the importance of capital poses somewhat greater problems, since the Census data on capital invested in manufacturing industries ends in 1919. Using an aggregate measure such as total manufacturing production in each state is one possible approach, but does not permit distinctions between the amounts of capital and labor engaged in that production. I have used profits earned by capital in manufacturing (measured as value added minus wage payments) as a fraction of state income on the assumption that these profits vary from state to state largely as a function of the total magnitude of investments.[3] For industries, I have

[1] See Conybeare 1991 for the former and Gilligan 1997 for the latter.
[2] The state economic data are drawn from the *Censuses of Manufacturing, Agriculture*, and *Mining* in years closest to the years of the votes. (Appendix C provides a detailed discussion). For years prior to 1840, the state data are extrapolated from later observations (state income data are from the Department of Commerce, *State Personal Income* and Kuznets, Miller, and Easterlin (1960); population data are from the *Statistical Abstract of the United States*).
[3] The measure is strongly correlated (at 0.92) with total capital invested as a fraction of state income for the period (1840–1919) for which data on the latter are available. I have performed the analysis using a range of alternative measures of the class variables, including the total value of land in agriculture and total land area (for farmers), aggregate wages in manu-

constructed measures of the economic importance of export and import-competing industries in each state using data on trade from the Department of Commerce and *Census* data on production in various manufacturing, mining, and agricultural sectors. For each state I calculated the total production in the ten leading export and import-competing industries in each year as a proportion of state income.[4]

The analysis includes dummy variables for each bill, in order to account for individual characteristics of particular bills (or years) when examining votes in favor of protection.[5] On the other hand, I have not included controls for the party affiliations and regional locations of members of Congress, even though previous work indicates that both types of variables have been good predictors of voting patterns on trade at different times. I exclude them here in order to provide the clearest imaginable test between the class and industry-group models. Party affiliations and regional locations are both strongly correlated with the measures of the class and industry characteristics of states at different levels in different periods. This is unsurprising: The competing parties have appealed to very different class-based constituencies over the years and to supporters in different geographical regions, and those regions themselves have often displayed marked differences in their economic composition in terms of both factor classes and trade-affected industries (Kim 2000). In the antebellum years, for instance, the Jackson Democrats in Congress were elected mainly from southern states in which farming outweighed manufacturing interests and exporting industries were far larger than import-competing concerns. My main concern is not to muddy the water when comparing the performance of the class and group-based models by inadvertently including class effects in the group-based model, or vice versa.

I have divided the main analysis into five parts, pooling the votes taken in five different historical periods: 1824–1860, 1875–1913, 1922–1937, 1945–1962, and 1970–1994. The aim is simply to provide some clear comparisons over time.[6] The estimations of each model have also been performed on a bill-by-bill basis, and the conclusions are substantively identical.[7] The

---

facturing (for labor), and total manufacturing production and production per worker (for capital). The key results, discussed in the next section, are substantively identical regardless of which combination of measures is employed.

[4] For a full description of methods used in compiling the data, see appendix C.

[5] I have also examined specifications of each model that include variables such as dummies for bills with provisions delegating authority to the president to negotiate tariff reductions with other nations and for bills that ratified trade treaties already negotiated. The key substantive results are identical to the ones reported below so the simplest specifications have been presented.

[6] The division of the post-1945 period just recognizes that U.S. trade patterns were quite volatile in the immediate postwar period, as the European and Japanese economies were rebuilding, and (not coincidentally) the two political parties switched sides on the trade issue in the 1960s.

[7] Note that since some members of Congress vote on more than one bill in each of the pools

TABLE 12.1
Probit Estimations for Senate Votes on Trade Bills—Class Model

	Estimation Results (Dependent variable = Vote for Protection)[a]				
	1824–1860	*1875–1913*	*1922–1937*	*1945–1962*	*1970–1994*
Value of farm production	−0.84 (0.50)	−0.82* (0.38)	−1.57** (0.53)	2.84** (0.73)	−1.26 (0.77)
Employment in manufacturing	9.32** (2.21)	16.02** (2.64)	9.38** (3.27)	3.00 (3.40)	2.11 (4.12)
Profits in manufacturing	−6.04** (2.10)	−8.69** (2.03)	−2.89* (1.43)	−2.02 (2.01)	0.08 (1.59)
n	372	532	367	280	382
Log-likelihood	−225.25	−324.51	−219.96	−121.49	−241.43
Pseudo R^2	0.1246	0.1189	0.1288	0.1329	0.0270

[a]Estimations include constant and dummy variables for individual bills (not shown). Standard errors in parentheses.

[b]Effects estimated for change in each variable from minimum (0) to maximum (1) values for equations including only that variable and bill dummies using *Clarify: Software for Interpreting and Presenting Statistical Results* (King, Tomz, and Wittenberg 2000).

*Significant at 5 percent; **significant at 1 percent.

class and industry models are estimated separately, and their performance in different periods is then compared.[8]

12.2 RESULTS

Table 12.1 reports the first set of results from probit estimations for the Senate votes in each period.[9] The first specification includes the three indicators of the importance of different factor classes: the value of agricultural production, employment in manufacturing, and profits in manufacturing. According to the basic class model, we would expect that the value of farm production, is negatively related to votes for protection, since the U.S. economy has been relatively well endowed with land, compared to other nations, and owners of land should thus have favored freer trade (in accord with the

---

considered, all observations are not independent and so the estimated standard errors are biased in a downwards direction in that analysis. I am grateful to an anonymous reviewer for making this point. Results for the bill-by-bill analysis are available from the author.

[8] Since the various class and industry variables are collinear in ways and degrees that differ over time, including them all in one estimation would make it extremely difficult to interpret the size and significance of their competing effects on voting patterns.

[9] The dummies for individual bills are omitted since the interpretation of these effects is not important for our purposes here.

Effects of Individual Variables on Probability of Vote for Protection[b]

1824–1860	1875–1913	1922–1937	1945–1962	1970–1994
−0.46	−0.62	−0.64	0.82	−0.31
(0.09)	(0.07)	(0.06)	(0.10)	(0.10)
0.53	0.69	0.74	−0.32	0.42
(0.04)	(0.03)	(0.04)	(0.07)	(0.27)
0.12	0.68	0.64	−0.38	0.34
(0.38)	(0.04)	(0.11)	(0.08)	(0.30)

Stolper-Samuelson model).[10] Owners of labor, on the other hand, should have favored protection, since the economy has been relatively poorly endowed with labor compared with its trading partners. Thus, employment in manufacturing in the districts of legislators should be positively related to votes for protection. According to Rogowski (1989), the United States was transformed from a capital-scarce to a capital-abundant economy by 1913, although it was capital scarce for most of the period between 1840 and 1914, and he is not precise about exactly when the change occurred (Rogowski 1989, 29). At a minimum, we should expect a change in the policy preferences of owners of capital between the second and third periods examined here: specifically, a shift away from support for protection. In terms of the estimated coefficients, that means that the value of profits in districts of legislators should be positively associated with votes for protection in the first and second periods, and negatively thereafter.

Table 12.1 reports two sets of results. On the left are the estimated coefficients and Pseudo-R^2 statistics from the probit estimations of the class model in each period, which can be compared with results from the alternative industry-group model (see Table 12.5). On the right, to give some idea of the magnitude of the different effects, are the first differences in the probability of voting for protection when each of the class variables changes from its theoretical minimum to maximum value (from 0 to 1). Interpreting the estimated coefficients in the full model (on the left) is actually rather difficult here because employment and profits in manufacturing are so highly collinear across states (they are correlated at approximately 0.7 in each period). Both directly reflect the size of the manufacturing sector in each state, and the separate effects of the different class variables are thus

---

[10] See Rogowski (1989) for quantitative evidence on U.S. factor endowments with deductions about class preferences on trade derived from the Stolper-Samuelson theorem. Rogowski's designations are applied here.

TABLE 12.2
Probit Estimations for Senate Votes on Trade Bills—Industry Group Model

	Estimation Results (Dependent variable = Vote for Protection)[a]				
	1824–1860	*1875–1913*	*1922–1937*	*1945–1962*	*1970–1994*
Exporting industries	−2.30** (0.31)	−1.09** (0.25)	−3.55** (0.43)	−2.80** (1.06)	−4.79** (1.41)
Import-competing industries	1.27 (1.03)	1.27* (0.56)	1.70 (1.06)	1.24 (0.92)	3.45* (0.79)
n	372	532	367	280	382
Log-likelihood	−199.80	−347.00	−226.24	−129.36	−229.52
Pseudo R^2	0.2249	0.0578	0.1041	0.0768	0.0750

[a]Estimations include constant and dummy variables for individual bills (not shown). Standard errors in parentheses.

[b]Effects estimated for change in each variable from minimum (0) to maximum (1) values for equations including only that variable and bill dummies using *Clarify: Software for Interpreting and Presenting Statistical Results* (King, Tomz, and Wittenberg 2000).

*Significant at 5 percent; **significant at 1 percent.

difficult to discern.[11] An interesting part of the problem here is that when both employment and profits are included in the one model, the estimated coefficients also measure the effects of variation in labor and capital *intensities* in manufacturing production (using more labor with the same amount of capital, and vice versa). As a partial corrective here I have simply calculated the first differences for each variable (on the right) when other variables are excluded from the model. The separate effects are less important, in the end, than the overall performance of the class model in each period and how it compares with the industry-group model.

As anticipated, in all but the fourth period, the value of farm production is negatively associated with votes for protection. The votes taken in the immediate post-1945 years seem to be anomalous in this regard, perhaps due to the new rural reliance on farm support programs introduced in the 1930s. The estimated effects of farming on votes (shown on the right) are smallest in the first and last periods; the largest negative effects appear in the periods between 1875 and 1937. Manufacturing employment is positively associated with protectionist votes, as expected, although the results are again less clear between 1945 and 1962, the postwar boom period for all kinds of U.S. manufacturing exports. While the class model anticipates that owners of capital favored protection until at least 1914, the coefficients for the profits

[11] For a discussion, see Gujarati 1999, 327–35. The problem is not just inefficiency, although the standard errors for the estimates more than double when all three variables are included in the model. It is also a question of effective sample size: There are hardly any observations, for example, in which state employment in manufacturing is high while state profits in manufacturing are low (or vice versa).

Effects of Individual Variables on Probability of Vote for Protection[b]				
1824–1860	*1875–1913*	*1922–1937*	*1945–1962*	*1970–1994*
−0.73	−0.48	−0.50	−0.26	−0.54
(0.05)	(0.07)	(0.04)	(0.05)	(0.10)
0.65	0.52	0.47	0.46	0.73
(0.04)	(0.06)	(0.09)	(0.26)	(0.06)

variable in the first three periods are negative. Since employment and profits are highly collinear, however, this may simply indicate that highly capital-intensive producers were less supportive of protection than others. The effects of profits on votes, calculated with employment excluded from the estimation (on the right), are positive until 1937, and largest between 1875 and 1937, as are the effects of employment on votes.[12]

Table 12.2 presents the results of estimations for the same set of votes on trade legislation in the Senate, but now using indicators of the importance of exporting and import-competing industries in each state as the explanatory variables. In line with a simple industry-group model, we anticipate that the importance of exporting industries should be negatively related to votes for protection, since individuals employed or invested in those industries benefit from trade liberalization, while the importance of import-competing industries should be positively related to votes for protection.

As expected, in each period the estimated coefficients for the exporting industries variable are negative, and the coefficients for import-competing industries are positive. We must exercise care here in interpreting the size and significance of the separate effects, since these two variables appear quite collinear across states in early periods (the correlation is around −0.4 between 1824 and 1913). Again (on the right), I calculated the first difference effects on the probability of voting for protection for a change in each variable from its theoretical minimum to maximum (0 to 1) when excluding the other variable from the estimation. Here the pattern in the size of effects

---

[12] It should be noted that I have tried variants of the basic class model for the recent periods that include measures of the skill level of the workforce in each state assuming, in line with Midford (1993) and Scheve and Slaughter (1998, 2001), that skilled workers, viewed as a separate class, oppose protection. Yet models that include measures of the proportion of the state's adult population with high school diplomas or higher levels of education (available from the *Statistical Abstract*) perform no better than the basic specification in Table 1. In none of the estimations are the coefficients on these variables significant and often they take the wrong (positive) sign. Since such data are unavailable for previous periods, I have only reported the simplest model here in order to provide straightforward comparisons over time.

TABLE 12.3
Probit Estimations for House Votes on Trade Bills–Class Model

	Estimation Results (Dependent variable = Vote for Protection)[a]				
	1824–1860	1875–1913	1922–1937	1945–1962	1970–1994
Value of farm production	−1.36** (0.26)	−0.53** (0.11)	−0.03 (0.31)	2.69** (0.43)	−1.72** (0.43)
Employment in manufacturing	6.47** (1.07)	8.46** (1.17)	15.57** (2.06)	8.95** (1.53)	4.04** (1.73)
Profits in manufacturing	−2.25* (0.99)	−1.32 (1.00)	−2.46** (0.72)	−0.31 (0.87)	0.19 (0.68)
n	1584	2656	1565	1262	2480
Log-likelihood	−985.28	−1658.12	−909.46	−754.86	−1605.73
Pseudo R^2	0.1001	0.0992	0.1552	0.0504	0.0638

[a]Estimations include constant and dummy variables for individual bills (not shown). Standard errors in parentheses.
[b]Effects estimated for change in each variable from minimum (0) to maximum (1) values for equations including only that variable and bill dummies using *Clarify: Software for Interpreting and Presenting Statistical Results* (King, Tomz, and Wittenberg 2000).
*Significant at 5 percent; **significant at 1 percent.

over time is the reverse of that for the class variables: Both industry variables have larger effects on voting in the first and last period, and smaller effects on votes in between.

Overall, the results of the analysis of the Senate votes are reasonably consistent with expectations based on changes in factor mobility over time. Voting decisions more closely reflect senators' consideration of the interests of broad factor classes when levels of mobility were higher (in the years between 1875 and 1937) than when mobility levels were lower (in the periods between 1824 and 1860 and from 1945 to the 1990s). The pattern works just the other way when we examine the responsiveness of Senate voting to demands from free-trade and protectionist industries within each state.

Tables 12.3 and 12.4 report the results of the analysis of House votes for each model. These must be treated with more caution since the measures of the importance of classes and industries are only available at the state level, rather than the district level, and so we are relying on an assumption that the class and industry composition of districts within states are similar. The results are very similar to those obtained from the analysis of Senate votes. The estimated coefficients are comparable for each class and industry variable in each period. The only clear difference is that the estimated effects of employment and profits on voting in the immediate postwar years, between

Effects of Individual Variables on Probability of Vote for Protection[b]				
1824–1860	1875–1913	1922–1937	1945–1962	1970–1994
−0.40	−0.68	−0.52	0.28	−0.49
(0.03)	(0.03)	(0.04)	(0.12)	(0.04)
0.64	0.73	0.81	0.81	0.69
(0.02)	(0.02)	(0.02)	(0.04)	(0.03)
0.45	0.80	0.71	0.68	0.45
(0.10)	(0.02)	(0.05)	(0.12)	(0.11)

1945 and 1962, are positive rather than negative (Table 12.3), suggesting that members of the House from states heavily dependent on manufacturing did not switch positions on trade as quickly after the war as senators. The estimated effects for the maximum possible change in each of the class variables are largest in the second and third periods, between 1875 and 1937. The estimated effects of changes in each of the industry variables again indicate a complementary result: They are largest in the earliest and latest periods and smaller in the periods in between.

A simple way to gain a better sense of the relative utility of the class and industry models involves a comparison of the Pseudo-R^2 values in each period (see Table 12.5). For votes in both the Senate and the House the pattern is the same; the class model performs much better than the industry model in periods two through four and does far worse than the industry model in periods one and five.

Table 12.5 also reports the results of formal tests to discriminate between the two competing models. Davidson and MacKinnon's (1981) "J test" is used to assess H_0 (the class model is appropriate) against H_1 (the industry model is appropriate) by an indirect linear combination of the two models. The test is conducted by estimating a combination of the class model and the predicted values from the industry model, where α_i is the weight on the industry model. If H_0 is true, then the true value of α_i is zero. We can then test for $\alpha_i = 0$ to judge whether H_0 can be rejected. The procedure is simply reversed to test for whether H_1 can be rejected. The results of these tests are shown in Table 12.5 (using the class and industry models from Tables 12.1–12.4). In periods one and five, the industry model dominates the class model in both the Senate and House; the class model dominates the industry model in period two in both chambers; while a clear winner (or loser) does not emerge in periods three and four. The votes in period four (between

TABLE 12.4
Probit Estimations for House Votes on Trade Bills—Industry Group Model

	Estimation Results (Dependent variable = Vote for Protection)[a]				
	1824–1860	1875–1913	1922–1937	1945–1962	1970–1994
Exporting industries	−1.86** (0.11)	−0.82** (0.10)	−3.21** (0.40)	−0.73* (0.30)	−2.16** (0.53)
Import-competing industries	1.62* (0.73)	1.27** (0.36)	0.63 (0.63)	1.34** (0.48)	2.56** (0.29)
n	1583	2656	1565	1262	2480
Log-likelihood	−880.49	−1727.72	−941.91	−782.01	−1576.60
Pseudo R^2	0.1954	0.0614	0.1250	0.0163	0.0808

[a]Estimations include constant and dummy variables for individual bills (not shown). Standard errors in parentheses.
[b]Effects estimated for change in each variable from minimum (0) to maximum (1) values for equations including only that variable and bill dummies using Clarify: Software for Interpreting and Presenting Statistical Results (King, Tomz, and Wittenberg 2000).
*Significant at 5 percent; **significant at 1 percent.

1945 and 1962) seem especially difficult for the models. While the class model appears to explain more of the variation in both the Senate and the House votes, the effects of two of the three class variables (farming production and profits in manufacturing) actually are counter to the direction anticipated in standard class-based accounts.[13]

It should be clear that these cross-time comparisons provide only an indirect test of the factor mobility hypothesis. We are, unfortunately, tightly constrained by the availability of data. If data were available on levels of factor mobility by electoral district for a substantial period of history, so that we could allow for spatial differences in mobility levels as well as temporal ones, we could do much more with the analysis of roll call votes and test the theory more directly. But the data on general levels of mobility examined in chapter 2 represents the first systematic measurement of interindustry factor mobility over any span of time in the literature—an astounding fact given the centrality of this variable in theories of political economy. It is enough to provide us with a set of basic predictions about how the relative utility of the class and group-based models should fluctuate over time. That these predictions are confirmed by the analysis of congressional voting patterns strongly suggests that further analysis of factor mobility (or its converse, specificity) holds real promise of helping to bridge the large gulf that exists between competing theoretical models currently used in political economy.

[13] Part of the reason may lie in the turbulence in patterns of world trade in the immediate post-war period and the diminished political salience of the trade issue.

Effects of Individual Variables on Probability of Vote for Protection[b]

1824–1860	1875–1913	1922–1937	1945–1962	1970–1994
−0.65	−0.37	−0.47	−0.22	−0.58
(0.03)	(0.03)	(0.04)	(0.11)	(0.05)
0.63	0.46	0.41	0.41	0.64
(0.02)	(0.02)	(0.14)	(0.15)	(0.03)

12.3 CONCLUSIONS

These cross-time comparisons provide only an indirect test of the factor mobility hypothesis. We are, unfortunately, tightly constrained by the availability of data. If we had data on levels of factor mobility by electoral district for a substantial period of history, so that we could allow for spatial differences in mobility levels as well as temporal ones, we could do much more with the analysis of roll-call votes and test the theory more directly. But the data on general levels of mobility reported in chapter 2 represent the first systematic measurement of factor mobility over any span of time in the literature—an astounding fact given the centrality of this variable in theories of political economy. It is enough to provide us with a set of basic predictions about how the relative utility of the class- and group-based models should fluctuate over time. That these predictions are confirmed by the analysis of congressional voting patterns strongly suggests that further analysis of factor mobility holds real promise of helping to bridge the large gulf that exists between competing theoretical models currently used in political economy.

Historical changes in levels of factor mobility within the U.S. economy appear to have coincided with significant shifts in the tenor of U.S. trade politics. Early in the nineteenth century, the tariff was fundamentally a local issue that generated vigorous lobbying among producer groups and divided politics along regional lines according to concentrations of exporting and import-competing interests. By the close of the century, however, trade policy lay at the center of a fierce partisan contest between pro-tariff industrialists and workers and free-trade farmers. In recent decades, another change in the nature of political cleavages has become apparent. Broad class coalitions have become more divided over the trade issue and industry lobbies have dominated recent debates over the NAFTA and GATT agreements.

TABLE 12.5
Comparison of Performance of Class and Industry Models[a]

	1824–1860	1875–1913	1922–1937	1945–1962	1970–1994
A. Senate Votes					
Ratio of Pseudo R^2 in class vs. industry group model	0.55	2.06	1.23	1.73	0.36
Results of J-tests[b]					
α_i	3.93**	−0.53	1.90**	3.79**	3.17***
	(0.52)	(0.71)	(0.67)	(1.44)	(0.63)
α_c	0.53	3.21**	2.41**	3.06**	0.49
	(0.71)	(0.49)	(0.53)	(0.68)	(1.45)
Models rejected	class	industry	neither	neither	class
B. House Votes					
Ratio of Pseudo R^2 in class vs. industry group model	0.51	1.62	1.24	3.09	0.85
Results of J-tests[b]					
α_i	3.95**	−0.30	1.54**	1.34	2.92**
	(0.29)	(0.39)	(0.43)	(0.92)	(0.34)
α_c	−0.16	3.18**	2.76**	2.80**	1.26
	(0.39)	(0.26)	(0.30)	(0.37)	(0.87)
Models rejected	class	industry	neither	industry	class

[a]Specifications as shown in Tables 12.1–12.4.
[b]α_i and α_c are estimated coefficients for predicted values from industry and class models, respectively, in linear combination with the alternative model. Model test applies 95% confidence interval. Standard errors in parentheses.
*Significant at 5 percent; **significant at 1 percent.

The analysis of congressional votes on major trade legislation between 1824 and 1994 confirms this stylized account and provides clearer evidence that changes in coalition patterns (and the relative utility of class- and group-based models) are related in the expected fashion to changes in levels of factor mobility. The results indicate that voting decisions reflect more clearly class effects when factor mobility is higher, and they are more consistent with a group model when levels of mobility are low.

PART IV

Conclusion

CHAPTER THIRTEEN

Conclusions, Qualifications, and Implications

This book has addressed one of the oldest debates in political economy—that between class- and group-based approaches to the analysis of politics—and has provided a simple theoretical synthesis that outlines the conditions under which one approach is more appropriate than the other. I have argued that the types of political coalitions that form in trade politics depend to a large degree upon one basic characteristic of the economy: the extent to which factors of production are mobile between industries. Class coalitions are more likely where interindustry factor mobility is high, whereas narrow industry-based coalitions are more likely where mobility is low.

The evidence reported here indicates that levels of interindustry factor mobility have varied considerably historically and cross-nationally among a number of Western economies, in line with different stages of industrialization and differences in regulation. The investigation of trade politics in each case reveals a strong correlation between general levels of interindustry factor mobility and coalition formation. Overall, class coalitions appear stronger—and class-based parties and peak associations are more unified on trade—when levels of mobility are higher. Industry coalitions appear stronger—and lobby groups take a more active role in policy making—when levels of factor mobility are lower.

These findings offer a solution to the persisting division in the scholarly literature on trade politics between those analysts who point to the political role of industry groups in the policymaking process (for example, Gourevitch 1986) and those who focus on class conflict (Rogowski 1989). Both types of approaches—that is, both types of assumptions about the distribution of policy preferences among individual economic agents—can be justified under different conditions. Concentrating on industry groups will yield more inferential power to a study of trade politics when levels of interindustry factor mobility are relatively low: in France during the nineteenth century, for instance, or in the United States and Britain since the 1960s. Focusing on broader class coalitions will generally lead to greater insight when levels of mobility are relatively high: in Britain in the nineteenth century, for example, and in Sweden and Australia from World War I until the 1980s.

For the study of political economy, the findings carry profound implications. Depending on the assumptions one makes about levels of interindustry mobility, general equilibrium models produce very different predictions about the distributional implications of any policy that affects relative commodity prices (and thus the demand for different factors of production) and any policy that affects the supply of those different factors. The distributional effects of a vast range of policies thus hinge on levels of factor mobility: exchange-rate policy, controls on foreign investment (both outward and inward), all forms of industrial policy and industry regulation (subsidies, tax incentives, labor and environmental laws), a range of welfare policies (especially training and education policy), and immigration policy. Attention to levels of interindustry factor mobility is thus crucial for understanding the political-economic origins of a vast range of policies. The conflicts of interest that take shape over these various policy issues, the preferences of individual economic agents invested or employed in different locations in the economy, will vary greatly depending on how easy it is for them to move their assets between industries. Factoral coalitions will be far stronger in all areas when levels of mobility are high, while the incentives for industry "rent-seeking" will be stronger when mobility is low.

The findings reported in this study also carry important implications for predictions about the evolution of trade policies. When the trade issue becomes a more internally divisive force in major parties and peak associations, party leaders will have an incentive to gravitate toward incoherent positions aimed at balancing competing demands from the strongest groups on either side of the debate. Ambiguity in policy facilitates the compromise that becomes essential for party leaders faced with competing demands. This insight helps describe what has been happening in the United States and other Western economies in recent years. Faced with increased lobbying pressure from industry groups on both sides of the trade issue, leaders have used an array of nontariff instruments to undercut multilateral liberalization without actually abandoning the process.

It is difficult not to look at the different experiences of these nations and question whether one of them has, due to wisdom or good fortune, steered a better course through the shifting currents of the international economy over the last two hundred years. Some have been torn apart more violently by class conflict. The fierce battle over the direction of policy in Britain in the 1840s stands out in this regard, but the Populist revolt in the United States in the 1890s and the prairie radicalism in Canada in the 1930s were tumultuous in their own right. Still, it is difficult to look at the French case, where class cleavages were routinely eclipsed by the strength and political tenacity of a multitude of industry-based lobby groups, and imagine that this was the better end of the stick. At its worst, intense group lobbying in trade politics in France, and in the United States and Britain in recent years, brings to mind an Olsonian nightmare of resources squandered on the political contest of distribution (Olson 1982).

Sweden's experience from the 1950s to the 1980s provides more inspiration. The Social Democrats were able to put together a stable compromise between class coalitions built around a liberal trade policy aimed at maximizing welfare gains for the economy as a whole. The economists at the Landsorganisationen were prescient: They anticipated technological pressures for increased factor specificity and how that would undermine their economic strategy by increasing incentives for rent-seeking by narrow groups. They championed a set of mobility-enhancing policies that were designed to resist these trends by providing generous forms of adjustment assistance to workers and firms, and the strategy performed admirably. From this perspective, the Australian case really does resemble an evil twin: a protectionist compromise between class coalitions that succeeded in weighing down the small economy with immense efficiency costs.

There are reasons to be cautious about the findings and what we can make of them. I have not fully controlled for other variables that might plausibly explain some differences in coalition patterns and in the behavior of parties and groups. Variation in electoral and policymaking institutions are likely to have significant effects. Political organizations geared to representing broad types of coalitions are more likely when the franchise is extended more widely among society, for instance, and parties may be expected to act more cohesively, in general, in parliamentary systems and under proportional representation than they do in presidential systems and under plurality rule.[1] Verdier (1994) and Alt and Gilligan (1994) have argued that policymaking rules that allow more access for lobby groups are less likely to encourage formation of broad class coalitions. Certainly these arguments warrant more empirical investigation. Given the evidence, however, as I argued in chapter 1, it is highly unlikely that such claims can satisfactorily explain much of the historical and cross-national changes seen in cleavages over trade policy. The findings in this book suggest that cleavages are powerfully shaped by levels of factor mobility. Future research may be able to specify just how underlying cleavages and political institutions interact to produce patterns in trade politics.

There are other reasons for proceeding with caution. The theory developed here is based on a model of the economy that assumes competitive markets and no international movement of factors. Relaxing these assumptions creates some complications. We may expect, for instance, that as economies of scale become more important in production, not only do broad class coalitions become less likely in trade politics, but divisions may also emerge between individual firms within the same sector.[2] Allowing that factors of production can be more or less mobile internationally would also require a reformulation of the theory.[3] Also, no allowance has been made for

---

[1] See Duverger 1954; LaPalombara and Weiner 1966; Cox 1987; Turner and Schneier 1970. I have gone some way toward controlling for these effects by measuring levels of party cohesion in votes on trade legislation in each case relative to general party cohesion in all votes during the same legislative session.

[2] Individual firms may lobby on their own account or form ad hoc coalitions with firms from other industries with similar preferences. This pattern seems more common in recent years in the United States. The 1994 debates over the Uruguay Round of the GATT, for instance, witnessed the formation of the Coalition of Service Industries, the Intellectual Property Committee, and the Alliance for GATT Now, all with diverse memberships of large firms.

[3] For a formal treatment of this issue, see Hiscox 1998. Whether international factor mobility reinforces class or industry cleavages over trade turns out to depend on the degree of

164   *CHAPTER THIRTEEN*

variation in ownership structures in capital markets. In particular, deeper equity markets make it easier to trade ownership of capital assets in different industries and for owners of capital to diversify their portfolio of investments across industries. To the extent that capitalists own diversified portfolios, they should be less concerned about individual industry returns and how they are affected by trade, and so less inclined to form industry-based coalitions in trade politics.[4]

Finally, since factor mobility clearly can be affected by regulations, we must question the degree to which it is endogenous to politics. Very little systematic research has been done on the political origins of restrictions on factor movements and adjustment assistance and other mobility-enhancing policies.[5] Perhaps existing coalitions shape policies in ways that help determine future levels of mobility, suggesting a sequence of cause and effect between cleavages and mobility that would introduce a more complicated and dynamic component to the analysis. Bargaining between broad class coalitions in Sweden, for instance, does appear to have shaped the broad retraining and adjustment programs that kept interindustry mobility levels high in the postwar Swedish economy. Or, perhaps some third force shapes both coalitions and factor mobility at the same time. This is Verdier's (1995) argument about the importance of electoral competition in determining the extent to which politicians try to appeal to broader rather than narrower coalitions (and hence the degree to which they favor mobility-enhancing policies).[6]

The data speak quite clearly to this endogeneity question. The evidence indicates that levels of factor mobility in Western economies have been affected powerfully by exogenous economic and technological changes associated with different stages of industrialization. That these changes in measured levels of mobility appear to be associated, in anticipated fashion, with changes in coalition patterns in trade politics suggests that this is a line of inquiry worth pursuing with new energy.

---

factor mobility between industries and whether factors located in different industries are differentially mobile between nations.

[4] This raises some fundamental questions about the distinction between owners and managers and its political implications. Managers act only as agents for the capital invested in each firm. Since they, and the industry associations they form, make decisions about how much to spend on lobbying—and since they also comprise the direct memberships of business peak associations—it is not clear that we need to greatly modify the anticipated effects of variation in mobility outlined in Table 3.1. The implications for party behavior are perhaps less clear. To the extent that parties respond to group lobbying, the anticipated effects are unchanged; to the extent that they respond to preferences of capital-owning voters (who may own diversified portfolios), we should anticipate more unity on the trade issue.

[5] For a review, and a preliminary analysis of labor demands for adjustment assistance policies, see Burgoon and Hiscox 2000.

[6] Unfortunately, the vigorous mobility-enhancing policies in Sweden, employed by a Social Democratic government that dominated postwar politics, run counter to Verdier's competition thesis.

Appendixes

APPENDIX A

Mathematical Appendix to Chapter 1

The model developed here builds on Jones's (1971) three-factor model. It is a modified version of the traditional, 2×2 general-equilibrium model used in the trade literature.[1] Consider an economy in which two commodities, X_1 and X_2, are produced, and sector i uses only factors specific to it, L_i and K_i. Since only relative prices matter in this two-commodity model, X_1 is chosen as the numeraire for the analysis. Equilibrium is described by full employment of each factor (equations 1 to 4), and competitive profits (5 and 6):

$$a_{L11}X_1 = L_1 \tag{1}$$

$$a_{K11}X_1 = K_1 \tag{2}$$

$$a_{L22}X_2 = L_2 \tag{3}$$

$$a_{K22}X_2 = K_2 \tag{4}$$

$$a_{L11}w_1 + a_{K11}r_1 = 1 \tag{5}$$

$$a_{L22}w_2 + a_{K22}r_2 = p \tag{6}$$

where

a_{Lij} and a_{Kij} = the quantities of L_i and K_i required per unit output of X_j
w_j and r_j = returns to labor and capital in industry j in terms of the first commodity
p = the relative price of the second commodity in terms of the first.

Full employment requires that techniques of production are variable and, since competition ensures that unit costs are minimized, each a_{ij} depends on the ratio of factor prices in industry j: $a_{ij} = a_{ij}(w_j/r_j)$.

---

[1] Dealing with models with higher dimensions is rather tricky. Much work has been dedicated to proving the basic Stopler-Samuelson theorem in more complicated models. Ethier (1974) and Jones and Scheinkman (1977) proved a version of the theorem, known as the "friends and enemies" result, in a model with any number of goods and factors: specifically, an increase in the price of each good, ceteris paribus, will raise the real return to some factor and lower the real return to some other factor. Ethier (1982) proved that for any vector of changes in the prices of goods, the accompanying vector of changes in factor returns is positively correlated with the factor intensity-weighted averages of the price changes. Together, these two results confirm the basic Stopler-Samuelson insight in higher dimensions. For an excellent discussion of work in this area see Deardorff (1994).

Solving equations 1 and 2 for X_1, and equations 3 and 4 for X_2 yields:

$$\frac{a_{L11}}{a_{K11}} K_1 = L_1 \tag{7}$$

$$\frac{a_{L22}}{a_{K22}} K_2 = L_2 \tag{8}$$

Equations 5 to 8 provide a set of four relationships in the four unknown factor prices. Commodity prices are exogenous (in accord with the small-economy assumption) and, for the moment, endowments of specific factors are treated as parameters. The structure of the model is best examined by describing the manner in which the equilibrium is disturbed by changes in commodity prices. After differentiating totally, we can solve for the percentage change in each of the factor returns (results are stated in percentage terms in order to indicate, not only directions, but relative magnitudes of changes).

$$\frac{dw_1}{w_1} = -\frac{\theta_{K11}}{\sigma_1} \left(\frac{dL_1}{L_1} - \frac{dK_1}{K_1} \right) \tag{9}$$

$$\frac{dr_1}{r_1} = \frac{\theta_{L11}}{\sigma_1} \left(\frac{dL_1}{L_1} - \frac{dK_1}{K_1} \right) \tag{10}$$

$$\frac{dw_2}{w_2} = \frac{dp}{p} - \frac{\theta_{K22}}{\sigma_2} \left(\frac{dL_2}{L_2} - \frac{dK_2}{K_2} \right) \tag{11}$$

$$\frac{dr_2}{r_2} = \frac{dp}{p} + \frac{\theta_{L22}}{\sigma_2} \left(\frac{dL_2}{L_2} - \frac{dK_2}{K_2} \right) \tag{12}$$

where

σ_j = the elasticity of substitution between labor and capital in industry j

Θ_{Lij} and Θ_{Kij} = the distributive shares of factor i in the value of output of industry j

We have utilized the relation

$$\theta_{Lij} \left(\frac{da_{Lij}}{a_{Lij}} \right) + \theta_{Kij} \left(\frac{da_{Kij}}{a_{Kij}} \right) = 0$$

which is implied by the cost-minimizing choice of a_{ij} (Jones 1971, 6).

Now, to analyze the effects of factor mobility, we can consider each of the specific factors to be themselves outputs of productive processes whereby L_1 can be converted into L_2 and K_1 into K_2 at increasing opportunity costs. Total factor endowments, L and K, are fixed exogenously (where $L = L_1 + L_2$ and $K = K_1 + K_2$), but the ratios L_2/L_1 and K_2/K_1 respond positively to relative returns, w_2/w_1 and r_2/r_1, respectively. Mobility is then defined in terms of the elasticities of substitution, ϕ_L and ϕ_K, along the transformation loci connecting L_2 and L_1, and K_2 and K_1, respectively.

$$\varphi_L = \frac{\dfrac{d(L_2/L_1)}{L_2/L_1}}{\dfrac{d(w_2/w_1)}{w_2/w_1}}$$

also

$$\varphi_K = \frac{\dfrac{d(K_2/K_1)}{K_2/K_1}}{\dfrac{d(r_2/r_1)}{r_2/r_1}}$$

where

$$\varphi_L, \varphi_K \geq 0$$

These relationships can be used with equations 9 to 12 to derive full solutions for the percentage change in factor returns as a function of the percentage change in commodity prices ("hats" indicate percentage changes):

$$\hat{w}_1 = \left[\frac{-\theta_{K11}\sigma_2(\varphi_K\tau_{K2} - \varphi_L\tau_{L2}) - \theta_{K11}\varphi_L\varphi_K\Omega}{\Delta} \right] \hat{p} \tag{13}$$

$$\hat{r}_1 = \left[\frac{\theta_{L11}\sigma_2(\varphi_K\tau_{K2} - \varphi_L\tau_{L2}) + \theta_{L11}\varphi_L\varphi_K\Omega}{\Delta} \right] \hat{p} \tag{14}$$

$$\hat{w}_2 = \left[\frac{-\theta_{K11}\sigma_2(\varphi_K\tau_{K2} - \varphi_L\tau_{L2}) + \varphi_K(\sigma_1\tau_{K1} + \sigma_2\tau_{K2}) + \sigma_1\sigma_2 - \theta_{K11}\varphi_L\varphi_K\Omega}{\Delta} \right] \hat{p} \tag{15}$$

$$\hat{r}_2 = \left[\frac{\theta_{L11}\sigma_2(\varphi_K\tau_{K2} - \varphi_L\tau_{L2}) + \varphi_L(\sigma_1\tau_{L1} + \sigma_2\tau_{L2}) + \sigma_1\sigma_2 + \theta_{L11}\varphi_L\varphi_K\Omega}{\Delta} \right] \hat{p} \tag{16}$$

where

$$\Delta = \varphi_L(\theta_{K22}\sigma_1\tau_{L1} + \theta_{K11}\sigma_2\tau_{L2}) + \varphi_K(\theta_{L22}\sigma_1\tau_{K1} + \theta_{L11}\sigma_2\tau_{K2}) + \sigma_1\sigma_2$$
$$+ (\theta_{L11} - \theta_{L22})\varphi_L\varphi_K\Omega > 0$$

$$\Omega = \tau_{L1}\tau_{K2} - \tau_{L2}\tau_{K1}$$

and where τ_{Lj} and τ_{Kj} are the fractions of total labor and capital employed in industry j. Ω describes factor intensities: it is positive (negative) when production of X_1 is relatively labor (capital) intensive.

Equations 13–16 show that the relationships between p and factor returns depend on levels of labor and capital mobility. The Ricardo-Viner and Stolper-Samuelson results appear here as special cases. If we assume capital is completely specific, as in the standard Ricardo-Viner derivation, $\phi_K = 0$ and the solutions yield the standard results. Specifically, if p rises ($\hat{p} > 0$), both wage rates also rise but at a slower rate: $\hat{p} > \hat{w}_2 > \hat{w}_1 > 0$. (Note that $\hat{w}_2$ approximates $\hat{w}_1$ as ϕ_L rises). Further, the return on capital in the second industry increases at a faster rate than p, while in the first industry it falls: $\hat{r}_2 > \hat{p} > 0 > \hat{r}_1$. If we assume that labor and capital are infinitely mobile, as in the Stolper-Samuelson approach, $\phi_L = \phi_K = \infty$ and the model yields the familiar outcome: an increase in the relative price of the labor (capital)-intensive commodity produces a larger rise in wage rates (profits), and a decline in profits (wages). Specifically, if p rises, $\hat{w}_2$ and $\hat{w}_1$ are greater than $\hat{p}$ (< 0), and $\hat{r}_2$ and $\hat{r}_1$ are negative ($> \hat{p}$), if and only if $\Omega <(>) 0$.

The key relationship that concerns us here describes how the mobility of a factor influences class solidarity, as indicated by the difference between the effects of a price change on returns to the factor in each industry. For any change in p, the absolute difference between $\hat{w}_1$ and $\hat{w}_2$ is inversely related to ϕ_L; that is, $\partial(|\hat{w}_1 - \hat{w}_2|)/\partial\phi_L < 0$. Likewise, the absolute difference between $\hat{r}_1$ and $\hat{r}_2$ is inversely related to ϕ_K; that is, $\partial(|\hat{r}_1 - \hat{r}_2|)/\partial\phi_K < 0$. The implication is that, for any change in relative prices induced by a shift in trade policy or trade flows, the income effects for workers (capitalists) in different industries will be more similar when labor (capital) mobility is higher, all else equal.

Data and Sources for Chapter 2

The principal sources for data on wages and profits across industries in each nation (used in the derivation of Figure 2.1 in chapter 2) are described below. To offset some of the problems with each of the particular types of data available for different time periods, I have compared evidence on industry wages and profits from a wide range of different sources. Not all of the evidence I have gathered for each nation could be presented in Figure 2.1 without the charts becoming very difficult to read. In such cases, I selected series of data that spanned the longest time periods for the charts. All the different series of data on wages and profits for each nation (described below) are available from the author and on the web page for this book (http://www.pup.org). Also available are the detailed lists of industries covered by each data series for each nation.

B.1 THE UNITED STATES

The two most commonly used sources of data on wages in the nineteenth century are the Weeks (1886) and Aldrich (1893) reports, which provide data on daily wage rates for workers collected from the payroll records of firms in various manufacturing industries for a range of years (from 1801 to 1880, and 1860 to 1890, respectively). But these reports are quite limited in terms of their coverage of workers in the manufacturing sector (see Long 1960, 7–12). The primary data I have examined from the reports are the industry averages compiled painstakingly by Long. He drew a continuous time series of data on wages from sixty-seven establishments in eighteen manufacturing industries from the Weeks report, and from forty-nine establishments in thirteen manufacturing industries from the Aldrich report.[1] I have also calculated the average daily wage rates of "common laborers" in eighteen industries using the original data in the Weeks report.

An alternative source of early data on wages is the decennial *Census*.

---

[1] He first calculated weighted average wage rates across occupations in each establishment from the Aldrich data, and simple averages using the Weeks data (for which employment totals were lacking). Industry averages for each state were then calculated as simple means from the Weeks data and using employment weights for each establishment from the Aldrich data. Finally, industry averages were calculated from each sample by weighting those state industry wages by state employment in each industry (using figures taken from decennial *Censuses* and interpolating).

Several studies of wages in the nineteenth century use *Census* data on total wage payments and the average number of wage earners employed in each year to calculate average annual earnings for workers in different industries or locations (Long 1960; Rosenbloom 1994). This data has the advantage that it provides a broad coverage of the manufacturing labor force with comparable annual data on each major industry (categorized in approximates to the two-digit classifications later introduced by the Department of Commerce) and can be used to construct a long, continuous time series. To compile data on a consistent set of industries from the *Census* prior to 1914, I began with the list of seventeen categories for which Long (72–73) extracted data for the period 1860 to 1890. I amended this original list to extend the series for fifteen industries from 1820 to 1910 and added five more industries for which data were available over that entire period.[2]

After the turn of the century, evidence on industry wage rates is more readily available. The 5-yearly *Census of Manufactures*, and the *Annual Survey of Manufactures*, report data on total wage payments to production workers, and the average number of production workers, across major industry categories from 1900.[3] These series can be used to calculate average annual earnings for workers in each industry, like the data in the earlier *Censuses*, although at more frequent intervals. Hourly earnings for workers in the manufacturing industries, classified at the two-digit SIC level, are calculated from 1947 by the Department of Labor, based on annual earnings and total man-hours worked in each industry.[4] In addition, separate data on hourly wage rates for unskilled workers between 1920 and 1937 were compiled by the National Industrial Conference Board (see Glasser 1940, 36).

Data on rates of return to capital in different industries are harder to come by for early periods. Bateman and Weiss (1981) have used actual *Census* manuscripts to calculate profits (value-added minus wage costs) as a percent of capital invested for a sample of individual manufacturing firms in the southern states in 1850 and 1860. I have relied upon similar calculations using the industry-level data on value-added, wage costs, and capital invested to measure average profit levels for firms in each of the major manufacturing industries in each *Census* year.[5] After 1919, while the *Census of*

[2] Specifically, "Liquors, malt" and "Chewing tobacco" were cut from the list used by Long; boots and shoes, machinery, hardware, clothing, and printing were added to make up the longer list. The data for 1820 were entered for Massachusetts, New York, New Jersey, Connecticut, Rhode Island, Maryland, Virginia, and Pennsylvania only (since data in the 1820 *Census* are reported by establishment and industry totals must be calculated manually).

[3] These data are collected in Department of Commerce, *Historical Statistics of the United States* and *Statistical Abstract of the United States*, various years. Production workers can be treated as unskilled or low-skilled labor, since the non-production category includes all professionals and technicians. See Berman, Bound, and Griliches 1994.

[4] Department of Labor, *Employment and Earnings*, 1950–1990.

[5] One problem here is that the early *Censuses* are not very clear about the method of evaluating capital investments. It seems that the figures reported are undepreciated book values, although whether such values were revalued during periods of substantial inflation or

Manufactures and the *Annual Survey of Manufactures* continue reporting data on value added and wage costs by industry, they cease reporting data on capital invested. From 1947, however, data on total man-hours consumed per year are available for each industry, and these can be used as a crude proxy for total investments (in both fixed and working capital): that is, profit per man-hour can be regarded as an approximation to profit per dollar invested.[6] Beginning in 1933, direct data are also available on corporation profits (as percentages of net worth and equity) by two-digit SIC industries from the Securities and Exchange Commission.[7]

B.2 BRITAIN

Data on wages of six categories of skilled workers associated with different manufacturing industries in the nineteenth century are drawn from Mulhall (1899).[8] Williamson (1982) has compiled data on the annual earnings of skilled labor in six industries between 1810 and 1911.[9] Data on the weekly earnings of skilled workers in a range of industries between 1914 and 1935 is reported in the ILO's *Yearbook of Labour Statistics*.[10] The ILO also reports hourly earnings of employees in two-digit industries beginning in 1938. Data on total wages and salaries and the average number of employees in the two-digit industries are also available from the UN's *Industrial Statistics Yearbook* beginning in 1953. From 1924 data on weekly earnings for manual workers in two-digit industries are available from The Central Statistical Office's, *British Labour Statistics: Historical Abstract*. For calculations of industry profits, data on value-added, total wages and employment by two-digit industries are available from the UN's *Industrial Statistics Yearbook* beginning in 1953.

B.3 FRANCE

Data on wages of six categories of skilled workers in the nineteenth century are drawn from Mulhall (1899). He has compiled data reported by De

---

deflation is uncertain. The capital figures clearly refer to structures and equipment but exclude evaluations of working capital (inventories, cash, and accounts receivable), which appear to have represented significant investments in several industries. For a fuller discussion, and attempts to make allowances for these problems, see Hiscox (2002).

[6] The latter follows Alt et al. 1999.

[7] Securities and Exchange Commission, *Corporation Profits*, various years; and Department of Commerce, *Statistical Abstract of the United States*, various years.

[8] Specifically, cotton spinners, carpenters, masons, blacksmiths, and plumbers.

[9] The industries are textiles, printing, shipbuilding, engineering, and building. The data are reproduced in Mitchell (1988).

[10] Data are reported for sixteen categories of skilled workers in the engineering, shipbuilding, building, furniture, printing, and footwear industries.

Foville (for Paris only) and in the "French Economist's Table."[11] Data on the wages of skilled male workers across manufacturing industries between 1913 and 1935 are from the ILO's, *Yearbook of Labour Statistics*. From 1948 the ILO also provides data on hourly earnings of workers across two-digit industries. Beginning in 1953, average annual earnings for all employees in the two-digit industries are calculated from data on total wages and salaries and the number of employees in each two-digit industry reported in the UN's *Industrial Statistics Yearbook*. The data on annual salaries of workers in major industries, beginning in 1900, is from the Institute National de la Statistique et des Etudes Economiques, *Annuaire statistique de la France*. The UN's *Industrial Statistics Yearbook*, provides data on value-added, total wages and salaries, and average employment by two-digit industries from 1958, which is used to calculate the estimates of industry profits.

B.4 SWEDEN

Data on the hourly and annual earnings of male workers in ten industries between 1860 and 1930 are from Bagge (1936). The industry categories are close approximations of the standard two-digit classifications employed later. From 1927, data are available on the hourly earnings of male workers in two-digit industries from the ILO's *Yearbook of Labour Statistics*. Average annual earnings for all employees in the two-digit industries are calculated using data on wages and employees reported in the UN's *Industrial Statistics Yearbook* beginning in 1953. Estimates of industry profits are calculated using data on value-added, total wages and salaries, and employment in two-digit industries reported from 1953 in the UN's *Industrial Statistics Yearbook*.

B.5 CANADA

Average annual earnings of employees in two-digit industries from 1870 are calculated from Census data on total wages and employment reported in Urquhart (1965). From 1939, weekly earnings of workers are also reported for two-digit industries. Data on the hourly earnings of workers in seven industries from 1938 are reported in the ILO's, *Yearbook of Labour Statistics*. From 1961, the ILO also provides data on hourly earnings of workers across nineteen industries. Average annual earnings for all employees in the two-digit industries are calculated from data on total wages and the number of employees in each industry reported in the UN's *Industrial Statistics Yearbook* from 1938.

---

[11] The categories are carpenters, painters, blacksmiths, masons, builders, and plumbers.

Urquhart (1965) reports Census data on value-added, total wages, and employment by two-digit industries from 1870, and this data can be used to calculate estimates of profits in each industry. In addition, separate data on value-added, total wages, and employment across industries is provided, from 1938, by the UN's *Industrial Statistics Yearbook*. Data on corporation profits and assets are also available from Statistics Canada, *Corporation Financial Statistics*.

B.6 AUSTRALIA

Data on hourly earnings by industry in New South Wales from 1860 are drawn from the *Statistical Register*. Data on hourly earnings of male workers are reported for twelve industries beginning in 1914 by the ILO's *Yearbook of Statistics*. Average annual earnings for all employees in the two-digit industries beginning in 1938 are calculated from data on total wage payments and the number of employees in each industry reported in the UN's *Industrial Statistics Yearbook*. Data on value-added, total wages, and employment by two-digit industries are available from the UN's *Industrial Statistics Yearbook* beginning in 1938. These are the data used to calculate the estimates of industry profits.

Data and Sources for Chapters 11 and 12

The principal sources for data on U.S. congressional votes, committee hearings, and electoral districts (used in chapters 11 and 12) are described in detail below. Key data on each of the votes on major pieces of trade legislation, full lists of all groups testifying before committees considering bills, and data on the importance of import-competing and export industries in each state in each year are available from the author and on the web page for this book (http://www.pup.org).

C.1 CONGRESSIONAL VOTES

The full list of trade bills included for the House and Senate and how they have been coded (as either protectionist or liberalizing) is shown in Table C.1. I selected major pieces of legislation that directly raised or lowered barriers to imports. Approximately two bills for each decade were selected, for a total of thirty. I excluded product-specific legislation (the 1867 Wool and Woollens Act, for instance, and the 1988 Textile and Apparel Act) on the grounds that voting decisions on such bills are generally less representative of preferences with regard to the trade issue in general and are also more prone to logrolling. I have also excluded bills that were unclear or controversial in nature and difficult to interpret as either protectionist or liberalizing. The 1870 and 1872 Tariff Acts, and the 1883 "Mongrel Tariff," in which Republicans cut some (primarily revenue) duties in response to surplus revenues but with the aim of defending protection generally, are prime examples of bills that are difficult to characterize (Taussig 1931, 178–89, 232–50). The omnibus trade legislation voted on between 1986 and 1988, to which was attached a wide array of non-trade-related provisions, is another. I included the protectionist Trade Remedies Reform Act of 1984 rather than the omnibus Trade and Tariff Act of the same year, into which it was ultimately incorporated, since the latter contained a mixture of liberal and protectionist measures. Finally, two large "hurrah" votes in recent times, the 1979 Trade Agreements Act, which implemented the Tokyo Round agreement of the GATT, and the 1988 Canada–United States Free Trade Agreement have also been excluded on the grounds that there is almost no variation in the dependent variable.

Several other general pieces of trade legislation might have been included given more time and resources, and the decisions to exclude them (rather

TABLE C.1
Selected Trade Bills

Legislation	Coded
Tariff Act 1824	Protectionist
Tariff Act 1828	Protectionist
Adams Compromise Tariff 1832	Protectionist
Clay Compromise Tariff 1833	Liberal
Tariff Act 1842	Protectionist
Walker Tariff Act 1846	Liberal
Tariff Act 1857	Protectionist (H)/Liberal (S)
Morrill Tariff Act 1861	Protectionist
Tariff Act 1875	Protectionist
Morrison Bill 1884	Protectionist (H only)
Mills Bill 1888	Liberal (H)/Protectionist (S)
McKinley Tariff 1890	Protectionist
Gorman Tariff 1894	Liberal
Dingley Tariff 1897	Protectionist
Payne-Aldrich Tariff 1909	Protectionist
Underwood Tariff 1913	Liberal
Fordney-McCumber Tariff 1922	Protectionist
Smoot-Hawley Tariff 1930	Protectionist
RTAA 1934	Liberal
RTA Extension 1937	Liberal
RTA Extension 1945	Liberal
RTA Extension 1955	Liberal
Trade Expansion Act 1962	Liberal
Mills Bill 1970	Protectionist (H only)
Trade Reform Act 1974	Liberal
McIntyre Amendment 1974	Protectionist (S only)
Trade Remedies Reform 1984	Protectionist (H only)
Disapprove Fast-Track 1991	Protectionist
NAFTA 1993	Liberal
GATT Uruguay Round 1994	Liberal

than any of the listed bills) were made in light of the basic criteria described above (the generality and clarity of their provisions) and data availability. The Tariff Act of 1816, for instance, is often regarded as the first general protective tariff, but it was passed in the Senate without a division. The protectionist tariff bill of 1820, which was not passed, was excluded in favor of the more famous 1824 Tariff Act. Ratification of reciprocity treaties with Canada in 1854 and 1910, and the 1864 resolution to abrogate the former of these, were excluded since their impact was limited to a narrow range of imported raw materials. The 1877 Mills Resolution that the tariff should be for revenue purposes only is a possible candidate for study, but it was a symbolic gesture in the House and 146 representatives did not cast a vote.

The 1878 Wood bill to reduce duties on manufactures was more important, but it was defeated (by a motion to strike out the enacting clause) in the House, and I have included the 1875 Tariff Act in preference. The Morrison bills of 1886, which did not survive motions to proceed to their consideration in the House, were excluded in favor of the more successful, and almost identical, 1884 bill.

To avoid excessive duplication, I included only two of the numerous post-1945 votes on extension of the Reciprocal Trade Agreements negotiating authority, excluding the votes of 1948, 1949, 1951, 1953, 1954, and 1958. The 1948, 1949, and 1951 votes are also somewhat more ambiguous in their liberal character, since they introduced the peril-point and Escape Clause provisions designed to ensure that trade treaties would do no harm to domestic industries, and thus were supported by many protectionists (Pastor 1980, 96). The 1987 Gephardt Amendment to the omnibus trade bill of that year, requiring action against nations running large trade deficits with the United States, might have been included, although in political substance it approximates the 1984 Trade Remedies Reform bill which made the list. The 1993 vote to extend the president's authority to complete the Uruguay Round of GATT negotiations was excluded to make way for the 1994 vote to implement the actual agreement.

Most of the coding decisions on these bills were straightforward. The "Adams Compromise" act of 1832 is coded protectionist in accord with Taussig's (1931) interpretation since, while it did cut revenue duties and remove the "minimums" system, it retained all of the protective duties of 1828 and was thus regarded by opponents as a rejection of demands for a real compromise and by supporters as an endorsement of the "American system" as permanent policy (109–10).[1] The "Clay Compromise" of 1833, on the other hand, provided for drastic (albeit gradual) reductions in protective duties and is coded liberal. For the Tariff Act of 1857, I treated the House and Senate versions separately. In the House, the Campbell bill (known as the "manufacturers' bill") attempted to deal with the problem of surplus revenues by removing duties only on raw materials and thus actually raised levels of effective protection. In the Senate, the Democratic majority just substituted Hunter's bill mandating cuts in protective duties (the final act was an ambiguous compromise). Similarly, I split the House and Senate bills of 1888. The Mills bill in the House proposed large tariff reductions, but the Senate revised it completely, formulating a protectionist bill that was the blueprint for the McKinley Tariff of 1890.

For each trade bill, the votes used are those on final passage or, where applicable, those on the adoption of conference reports. The presumption is that earlier votes on amendments and procedural questions relating to bills are more likely to be affected by strategic concerns and vote trading. Votes

---

[1] See also Stanwood 1903, 383–86.

on the passage of legislation should generally be more accurate as a gauge of public position-taking on trade.

The votes were retrieved from the *Annals of Congress, Gales and Seaton's Register of Debates in Congress*, the *Congressional Globe*, and the *Congressional Record*. Calculations for general party cohesion on all votes in each session are based on the Rosenthal and Poole updated ICPSR data set.

C.2 COMMITTEES AND GROUPS

For each of the bills chosen for study, I examined the available records of testimony provided to congressional committees. I limited the study to House committees, since there is likely to be much duplication in Senate deliberations (and the Constitution provides that revenue bills must originate in the House). I have focused only on the lobbying efforts of organized groups, not individuals or individual firms, since the argument developed in chapter 1 is explicitly concerned with coalitions. In most cases, especially in the twentieth century, the distinction is clear-cut, since the groups are typically established labor unions and management associations represented by elected officers.

Identifying coalitions in other cases, especially in older records, can be a little more difficult. Schattschneider (1935) devoted a great deal of attention to investigating just how representative of particular coalitions were the lobbyists pressuring Congress in the 1930 hearings. Obviously, witnesses have an incentive to claim they are representing a large number of people or interests, whether or not they are actually doing so in any real formal sense. Schattschneider found that: "Very commonly a portion of the industry assumed the right to speak for the whole, often without pretense of having consulted the rest. It was not unusual for a single producer to speak in the name of an entire industry solely by virtue of the fact that he was engaged in the business concerned" (267).

Even worse, Schattschneider found that claims to speak for an industry were sometimes implied but not explicitly avowed, seemingly as part of a calculated effort to deceive. For instance, the 1930 brief of the "American Soap Manufacturers' Association" (which Schattschneider notes was not listed in the Commerce Department's list of associations) has appended to it a list of soapmakers implying, but carefully avoiding to state, that these were being represented (1935, 267). Some lobbyists listed names of associations of which they were merely members, implying that they were speaking on behalf of these associations, even though when pressed they were not. The only way to weed out these cases is by a very careful study of the hearings. The rule applied was not to count lobbyists who did not claim to be *formally appointed representatives* of other factory owners in their industries (from at least three firms), where their appointment was indicated by the office they held in an existing organization or by reference to resolutions voted on at meetings convened by workers and owners to organize a special lobbying effort.

I counted both oral and written testimony given to House committees as evidence of lobbying efforts. It is arguable that letters sent to committees cost so little when compared with organizing personal representation before the committee that they should be discounted. But this is not always clear. The authorization and approval for a letter from a group may require almost as many deliberations and resolutions as the process that sends a representative of the group to Capitol Hill. The distinction is even less important for groups with representatives permanently housed in Washington. It is also meaningless when committees, unable to accommodate all the witnesses prepared to give oral testimony, encourage groups to submit written materials instead to save time. I excluded instances when witnesses were summoned by committees. I also excluded cases where groups revealed that they were asked to appear or write to the committee by a member of the House or Senate (including individual committee members).

The policy position adopted by each group when lobbying was coded as either Free Trade, Protectionist, or Ambiguous. The coding is based on whether the group voiced support or opposition for the bill in question (and whether that bill was protectionist or liberal) or, if no general position was taken on the whole bill, whether the group demanded an increase or decrease in protection as part of any specific component of the legislation being considered. Groups that requested duty-free raw materials or inputs for their own industry, but demanded that duties on their own products be maintained or increased, were coded as Protectionist since any combination of their demands would increase the effective protection for their industry. Groups that pleaded for a switch from ad valorem to specific duties were typically hoping to increase levels of protection (as a consequence of falling prices) and were coded Protectionist.

Full lists of the groups testifying before each committee and the positions they took are available on request from the author and on the web page for this book (http://www.pup.org). Specific sources and coding decisions are described in the following sections.

C.3 THE COMMITTEE ON MANUFACTURES

The Committee on Manufactures was responsible for deliberating on tariff legislation in the antebellum House. Records of the testimony (oral or written) considered by the Committee were seldom compiled in these early years. But memorials submitted to the House on the tariff question were automatically referred to Committee for consideration and report in light of proposed legislation. These memorials provide a reasonable approximation to the written testimony submitted in later hearings.

Forty of the memorials submitted to the House for consideration before the passage of the 1824 Tariff Act (18th Congress, 1st Session) were printed by the House. The first twenty are reproduced in *American State Papers* (Finance, volume V) and the *Annals of Congress* (18th Congress, 1st Session). The second twenty were located in the National Archives and listed by Pincus (1977). The remaining were drawn directly from the *Annals*, which recorded their presentation and referral in the House. Pincus does not identify positions or industry attachments, but I have supplied them wherever possible from the *Annals* record. Industry-of-origin was either self-evident from the title or, in a few cases, was derived from the memorial itself, which identified the authors more narrowly than did the title.

The hearings held by the Committee in 1828 are better documented, with a record of the testimony of twenty-nine witnesses provided in the actual report (also reproduced in *American State Papers*, Finance volume V). But these hearings were unusual in that the Committee was granted permission to select the witnesses it would examine, and for this reason was later accused of being part of Martin Van Buren's plan to divide the Adams supporters by crafting a repugnant bill (see chapter 4). Of the witnesses, seven were current members of the House (all Jacksonians) who, since they were or had engaged in particular business pursuits (including the production of iron, wool, hemp, and spirits), were treated as experts. Among the others were some fifteen individuals engaged principally in woolen manufactures, three involved in making cotton goods, and three others from the glass, paper, iron, and spirits industries. With the exception of the iron producer, the witnesses were exceptionally placid and denied any need for additional protection unless it was to offset duty increases on raw materials. Aside from this suspect testimony, the Committee was formally charged with the task of reporting on all the memorials the House had referred to it (20th Congress, 1st Session). I have listed all the memorials that were printed in *American State Papers*. They may not comprise a complete list of all those considered by the committee, however, since the record of House proceedings at the time (*Register of Debates in Congress*) does not make a record of memorials or petitions presented and referred.

The reports made by the Committee in 1832 and 1833—the famous Adams and Clay Compromise reports—contain no listings of witnesses examined or any records of the memorials under consideration and were both written in response to a message from the president urging a change in policy. In addition, *Register of Debates in Congress* provides no record of memorials presented to or referred by the House to the Committee in its account of proceedings in Congress in these years.

The 1842 legislation is a little more amenable to study. The Committee's report states that, besides being referred the president's message on the tariff, it also received "a great number of petitions, memorials, and resolutions" regarding the same. The Committee actually preferred to select and summon whichever witnesses it saw fit, in the manner of the notorious 1828 committee, and put this to the House in the form of a resolution that was rejected. Thus, having been delayed, they "determined to receive written statements, and hear such persons as might appear before them." The groups providing testimony are listed in the final report (Report No. 461 March 31, 1842) and I have included these along with memorials presented to the House (27th Congress, 2nd Session in the *Congressional Globe*) referred to the Committee prior to its reporting the bill.

For the 1846 legislation, unfortunately, there is no record of a printed report and no listing of memorials on the tariff presented to the House in the index of the *Congressional Globe*, which appears to have stopped recording these in its account of congressional proceedings in these years. Data are likewise unavailable on efforts made by groups to influence the Committee in 1857 and 1861. The last hurrah for the Committee, at least as a forum for trade debates, came in 1870 with its "Examination of Statements in the Report of the Special Commissioner of Revenue," a heated response by protectionists to the 1869 report authored by David Wells, which had attacked the existing tariff rates in the wake of the Civil War. Grover Cleveland wrote the Committee's minority report backing Wells.

C.4 THE COMMITTEE ON WAYS AND MEANS

The Committee on Ways and Means took over the deliberation of tariff legislation in the postbellum House, aided no doubt by the particular circumstances of the time: The high war tariffs produced excessive revenues and the issue was framed by Republicans as a problem not of excessive protection but of finding the right balance between internal taxes and import duties. From 1884 onwards, there exists an accurate record of all the testimony provided to the committee (in oral and written form) in its hearings on trade legislation (see Committee on Ways and Means, *Hearings*, various years).

Note that in 1884, several regional associations signed a statement presented by the Iron and Steel Association but, except for the Eastern and Western Iron Ore Association and the Tinned Plate Association (which sent their own witnesses), I have treated these as members of the same industry group. Similarly, the Pennsylvania and Ohio Woolgrowers associations, since they testified in concert with the National Association, have not been counted separately. In 1890, notable among the exclusions from the list are Joseph Wharton's testimony on behalf of the Bessemer Steel Association (he did not address the tariff issue, only patents), and "representatives of American Pocket Cutlery Manufacturers" (only two companies signed the letter). Again, regional associations of wool growers, millers, tobacco growers, and canned goods packers joined forces when lobbying and are counted as single industry groups. Several groups appeared only to lobby on internal tax rates and one, the Women's National Industrial League (an "organization of wage-women") mounted a prescient early campaign against cigarettes.

C.5 TRADE AND STATE PRODUCTION DATA

The key economic data for the statistical analysis of congressional voting presented in chapter 12 includes trade data identifying the top ten export and import-competing industries along with data on levels of production for each of these industries in each state. The trade data are from the Department of Commerce (*Commerce and Navigation of the United States*, various years). In each case, net exports and net imports were used to identify the leading trade-affected industries in each year in which major trade legislation was voted upon.

State production levels for each of these industries were compiled from the *Census of the United States* (1820, 1840, 1850, 1860), the *Census of Manufactures* (1880, 1890, 1900, 1909, 1914, 1921, 1929, 1933, 1937, 1947, 1954, 1963, 1972, 1977, 1982, 1987, 1992), the *Census of Agriculture* (1890, 1899, 1910, 1925, 1929, 1935, 1939, 1945, 1950, 1964, 1969, 1974, 1978, 1982, 1987, 1992), the *Census of Mineral Industries* (1930, 1939, 1972, 1982, 1987), and the *Statistical Abstract of the United States* (1914, 1924). For data for the period 1890–1937, I followed Gilligan's (1997) methodology in most respects. Specifically, values for agricultural production in 1937 were interpolated from the 1934 and 1939 figures. In 1890, the *Census of Agriculture* only provided quantity data for animals and sugar, so values were calculated using prices from the Department of Commerce (*Historical Statistics of the United States* 1976). The same was done for values of wool and wheat production for 1914 using quantity data from the *Statistical Abstract*. Following Gilligan, values for sugar production in 1914 were extrapolated from 1899 and 1909 data.

A long-standing difficulty with this type of analysis is that the industry classifications used by the Department of Commerce in compiling trade data are not the same as the classifications it uses in compiling production data in the *Censuses*. The latter classifications gradually evolved into the Standard Industrial Classification. I matched the industries as closely as possible according to the different definitions. Full lists of the leading export and import-competing industries in each year, along with matching industry classifications for production data, are available on request.

Finally, to calculate measures of the economic importance of these industries in each state requires a measure of the size of each state economy. Aggregate production figures for the states are not available for a large portion of the period under examination here. I have thus followed Gilligan's (1997) lead in using available data on state personal income. This is provided for recent years from the Department of Commerce (*State Personal Income 1929–83* 1989). Kuznets, Miller, and Easterlin (1960), supply values for 1880, 1900, and 1920. I have interpolated values for 1890, 1909, and 1913, and extrapolated values for 1840 and 1820.

Acs, Z., and S. Isberg. 1991. Innovation, Firm Size, and Corporate Finance. *Economics Letters* 35:323–26.

Aitken, H. 1960. *Taylorism at Watertown Arsenal: Scientific Management in Action, 1908–1915.* Cambridge, Mass.: Harvard University Press.

Aldrich, John. 1995. *Why Parties? The Origins and Transformation of Political Parties in America.* Chicago: University of Chicago Press.

Aldrich, Nelson W. 1893. *Wholesale Prices, Wages, and Transportation.* Report by the Secretary of the Treasury. 52nd Cong., 2nd sess., S.R. 1394. Washington, D.C.: U.S. Government Printing Office.

Alesina, Alberto. 1989. Politics and Business Cycles in Industrial Economies. *Economic Policy* 8:55–87.

Alesina, Alberto, and Howard Rosenthal. 1995. *Partisan Politics, Divided Government, and the Economy.* Cambridge: Cambridge University Press.

Alexander, F. 1980. *Australia Since Federation.* 3rd ed. Melbourne: Thomas Nelson.

Alt, James, and Michael Gilligan. 1994. The Political Economy of Trading States. *Journal of Political Philosophy* 2:165–92.

Alt, James, Fredrik Carlsen, Per Heum, and Kare Johansen. 1999. Asset Specificity and the Political Behavior of Firms: Lobbying for Subsidies in Norway. *International Organization* 53 (1):99–116.

American State Papers: Finance. Vol. 5.

Anderson, K. L. 1938. Protection and the Historical Situation: Australia. *Quarterly Journal of Economics* 53 (4):86–104.

Anderson, R. Kym. 1980. The Political Market for Government Assistance to Australian Manufacturing Industries. *Economic Record* 56 (June):132–44.

Anderson, R. Kym, and Ross Garnaut. 1987. *Australian Protectionism.* Sydney: Allen and Unwin.

Arndt, H. W. 1965. Australia: Developed, Developing, or Midway? *Economic Record* 41 (95): 318–40.

Atkins, Barbara. 1958. Antecedents of the NSW Protectionist Party. *Proceedings of the Royal Australian Historical Society* 44:239–58.

Annals of the Congress of the United States, 1823–1824. Washington, D.C.: Gales and Seaton.

Australia. Parliament. House of Representatives. *Votes and Proceedings of the House of Representatives.* Canberra: Commonwealth Government Printing Office.

Bagge, Gösta. 1936. *Wages, Cost of Living, and National Income in Sweden, 1860–1930.* London: P. S. King.

Bailey, Michael, Judith Goldstein, and Barry Weingast. 1997. The Institutional Roots of American Trade Policy. *World Politics* 49 (3):309–38.

Bain, J. 1956. *Barriers to New Competition.* Cambridge, Mass.: Harvard University Press.

Baldwin, Robert. 1985. *The Political Economy of U.S. Import Policy.* Cambridge, Mass.: MIT Press.

Baldwin, Robert and Christopher Magee. 2000. *Congressional Trade Votes: From*

NAFTA Approval to Fast-Track Defeat. Washington, D.C.: Institute for International Economics.

Bartel, Ann P., and Frank Lichtenberg. 1987. The Comparative Advantage of Educated Workers in Implementing New Technology. *Review of Economics and Statistics* 69 (1):1–11.

Bateman, F., and T. Weiss. 1981. *Deplorable Scarcity: The Failure of Industrialization in the Slave Economy*. Chapel Hill: University of North Carolina Press.

Bauer, Raymond, Ithiel de Sola Pool, and Lewis Dexter. 1963. *American Business and Public Policy*. New York: Atherton.

Beer, Samuel. 1965. *Modern British Politics*. London: Alfred A. Knopf.

Berman, E., J. Bound, and Z. Griliches. 1994. *Changes in the Demand for Skilled Labor with US Manufacturing Industries*. NBER Working Paper 4255. Cambridge, Mass.: National Bureau of Economic Research.

Bhagwati, Jagdish. 1982. Directly Unproductive Profit-Seeking (DUP) Activities. *Journal of Political Economy* 90:988–1002.

Blank, Stephen. 1978. *Industry and Government in Britain: The Federation of British Industries in Politics*. Lexington, Mass.: Lexington Books.

Blewett, N. 1968. Free Fooders, Balfourites, Whole Hoggers, Factionalism within the Unionist Party. *Historical Journal* 11 (1):95–124.

Blewett, N. 1972. *The Peers, the Parties, and the People: The British General Election of 1910*. Toronto: University of Toronto Press.

Bloch, F. 1979. Labor Turnover in U.S. Manufacturing Industries. *Journal of Human Resources* 14 (2):236–46.

Block, R. 1978. The Impact of Seniority Provisions on the Manufacturing Quit Rate. *Industrial and Labor Relations Review* 31:474–88.

Bowen, Harry, Edward Leamer, and Leo Sveikauskas. 1987. Multicountry, Multifactor Tests of the Factor Abundance Theory. *American Economic Review* 77 (5): 791–809.

Boyce, Robert. 1987. *British Capitalism at the Crossroads, 1919–1932*. Cambridge: Cambridge University Press.

Bradford, Sarah. 1984. *Disraeli*. New York: Stein and Day.

Brady, David, Joseph Cooper, and Patricia A. Hurley. 1979. The Decline of Party in the U.S. House of Representatives, 1887–1968. *Legislative Studies Quarterly* 4:381–407.

Brawley, Mark. 1997. Factoral or Sectoral Conflict? Partially Mobil Factors and the Politics of Trade in Imperial Germany. *International Studies Quarterly* 41 (4): 633–54.

Brogan, Denis W. 1967. *The Development of Modern France*. New York: Harper Brothers.

Brown, Benjamin. 1943. *The Tariff Reform Movement in Great Britain 1881–1885*. New York: Columbia University Press.

Burgoon, Brian, and Michael J. Hiscox. 2000. Trade Openness and Political Compensation: Labor Demands for Adjustment Assistance. Paper presented at the 96th Annual Meetings of the American Political Science Association, September, Washington, D.C.

Burnham, Walter Dean. 1965. The Changing Shape of the American Political Universe. *American Political Science Review* 59:7–28.

———. 1970. *Critical Elections and the Mainsprings of American Politics*. New York: Norton.

Cain, Louis, and Donald Patterson. 1986. Biased Technical Change, Scale, and Factor Substitution. *Journal of Economic History* 46 (1):153–64.

Cameron, Maxwell, and Brian Tomlin. 2000. *The Making of NAFTA: How the Deal was Done*. Ithaca, N.Y.: Cornell University Press.

Canada. Parliament. Various years. *The Canadian Parliamentary Companion and Annual Register*. Ottawa: Citizen Printing and Publishing.

———. *The Canadian Parliamentary Guide*. Ottawa: Gale Canada.

Carey, John, and Matthew Shugart. 1992. *Presidents and Assemblies: Constitutional Design and Electoral Dynamics*. New York: Cambridge University Press.

Caron, Francois. 1979. *An Economic History of Modern France*. New York: Columbia University Press.

Carr, J., and W. Taplin. 1962. *History of the British Steel Industry*. Cambridge, Mass.: Harvard University Press.

Carter, S., and E. Savocca. 1990. Labor Mobility and Lengthy Jobs in Nineteenth-Century America. *Journal of Economic History* 50:1–16.

Caves, Richard, and Michael Porter. 1979. Barriers to Exit. In *Essays on Industrial Organization in Honor of Joe S. Bain*, edited by R. Masson and P. Qualls, pp. 39–69. Cambridge, Mass.: Ballinger.

Caves, Richard, Jeffrey Frankel, and Ronald Jones. 1990. *World Trade and Payments*. 5th ed. Glenview, Ill.: Scott Foresman.

Clapham, John. 1927. *Economic History of Modern Britain*. Cambridge: Cambridge University Press.

Clough, Shepard. 1939. *France: A History of National Economics*. New York: Octagon Books.

Clubb, Jerome M., and Sandra Traugot. 1977. Partisan Cleavage and Cohesion in the House of Representatives, 1861–1974. *Journal of Interdisciplinary History* 7 (3):375–402.

Coelho, R., and J. Shepherd. 1976. Regional Differences in Real Wages: The United States, 1851–1880. *Explorations in Economic History* 13:551–91.

Cole, Wayne. 1983. *Roosevelt and the Isolationists, 1932–45*. Lincoln: University of Nebraska Press.

Coleman, William D. 1988. *Business and Politics: A Study of Collective Action*. Montreal: McGill-Queen's University Press.

Commons, John R. 1909. Horace Greeley and the Working Class Origins of the Republican Party. *Political Science Quarterly* 24 (3):468–88.

Congressional Globe. 1841–1861. Washington, D.C.

Congressional Record. 1875–1994. Washington, D.C.

Conybeare, John. 1991. Voting for Protection: An Electoral Model of Tariff Policy. *International Organization* 45 (1):57–81.

Copland, D. B. 1931. Neglected Phase of Tariff. *Quarterly Journal of Economics* 46 (4):289–308.

Coughlin, Cletus. 1985. Domestic Content Legislation: House Voting and the Economic Theory of Regulation. *Economic Inquiry* 23 (3):437–48.

Cox, Gary. 1987. *The Efficient Secret: The Cabinet and the Development of Political Parties in Victorian England*. Cambridge: Cambridge University Press.

———. 1997. *Making Votes Count: Strategic Coordination in the World's Electoral Systems*. Cambridge: Cambridge University Press.

Cox, Gary W., and Mathew D. McCubbins. 1993. *Legislative Leviathan: Party Government in the House*. Berkeley: University of California Press.

Crotty, William. 1980. *American Political Parties in Decline*. Boston: Little Brown.

Davidson, R., and J. MacKinnon. 1981. Several Tests for Model Specification in the Presence of Alternative Hypotheses. *Econometrica* 49 (3):781–93.

Davis, Lance. 1965. The Investment Market, 1870–1914: The Evolution of a National Market. *Journal of Economic History* 25:355–99.

Davis, Lance, Jonathan Hughes, and Duncan McDougall. 1961. *American Economic History: The Development of a National Economy.* Homewood, Ill.: Irwin.

Deardorff, Alan. 1994. Overview of the Stolper-Samuelson Theorem. In *The Stolper-Samuelson Theorem: A Golden Jubilee,* edited by Alan Deardorff and Robert Stern, pp. 7–34. Ann Arbor: University of Michigan Press.

Destler, I. M. 1992. *American Trade Politics.* 2d ed. Washington D.C.: Institute for International Economics.

Destler, I. M., and John Odell. 1987. *Anti-Protection: Changing Forces in United States Trade Politics.* Washington, D.C.: Institute for International Economics.

Dickens, W., and L. Katz. 1987. Inter-Industry Wage Differences and Industry Characteristics. In *Unemployment and the Structure of Labor Markets,* edited by K. Lang and J. Leonard. Oxford: Basil Blackwell.

Diebold, William. 1941. *New Directions in Our Trade Policy.* New York: Council on Foreign Relations.

Dobson, J. 1976. *Two Centuries of Tariffs.* Washington, D.C.: International Trade Commission.

Dod, Charles. Various years. *The Parliamentary Companion.* London: Whittaker & Co.

Dunham, Arthur. 1930. *The Anglo-French Treaty of Commerce of 1860 and the Progress of the Industrial Revolution in France.* Ann Arbor: University of Michigan Press.

Dupeux, Georges. 1959. *Le Front Populaire et les elections de 1936.* Paris: A. Colin.

Duverger, Maurice. 1954. *Political Parties: Their Organization and Activities in the Modern State.* New York: Wiley.

Easterbrook, W. T., and Hugh Aitken. 1956. *Canadian Economic History.* Toronto, Ont.: Macmillan.

Edin, Per-Anders, and John Zetterberg. 1992. Interindustry Wage Differentials. *American Economic Review* 82 (5):1341–49.

Eichengreen, B. 1989. The Political Economy of the Smoot-Hawley Tariff. *Research in Economic History* 12:1–43.

Elwitt, Sanford. 1975. *The Making of the Third Republic: Class and Politics in Modern France 1868–1884.* Baton Rouge: Louisiana State University Press.

Epstein, E., and R. Gordon. 1939. Profits of Selected American Industrial Corporations, 1900–1914. *Review of Economic Statistics* 21 (3):122–28.

Ethier, W. J. 1974. Some of the Theorems of International Trade with Many Goods and Factors. *Journal of International Economics* 4:199–206.

Ethier, W. J. 1982. The General Role of Factor Intensity in the Theorems of International Trade. *Economic Letters* 10:337–42.

Ethier, William. 1988. *Modern International Economics.* 2d ed. New York: W. W. Norton.

Fallon, P. R., and P. R. G. Layard. 1975. Capital-Skill Complementarity. *Journal of Political Economy* 83 (2):279–302.

Fohlen, Claude. 1956. *L'industrie textile au temps de Second Empire.* Paris: Plon.

Foner, Eric. 1970. *Free Soil, Free Labor, Free Men: The Ideology of the Republican Party Before the Civil War.* New York: Oxford University Press.

Forster, Ben. 1986. *A Conjunction of Interests: Business, Politics, and Tariffs 1825–1879.* Toronto, Ont.: University of Toronto Press.

France. Assemblee nationale. *Annales de la chambre des deputes. Debats parlementaires.* Paris: Imprimerie du journal officiel.

Frankel, Jeffrey. 1991. Measuring International Capital Mobility: A Review. *American Economic Review* 82:197–202.

Freeman, Richard. 1976. Individual Mobility and Union Voice in the Labor Market. *American Economic Review* 66:361–68.

————. 1980. The Exit-Voice Tradeoff in the Labor Market. *Quarterly Journal of Economics* (June):643–73.

Frieden, Jeffry. 1991. *Debt, Development, and Democracy: Modern Political Economy and Latin America, 1965–1985.* Princeton, N.J.: Princeton University Press.

Friman, H. Richard. 1990. *Patchwork Protectionism: Textile Trade Policy in the United States, Japan, and West Germany.* Ithaca, N.Y.: Cornell University Press.

Gabel, Matthew. 1998. *Interests and Integration: Market Liberalization, Public Opinion, and European Union.* Ann Arbor: University of Michigan Press.

Galambos, Louis. 1979. The American Economy and the Reorganization of the Sources of Knowledge. In *The Organization of Knowledge in Modern America,* edited by A. Olson and J. Voss, pp. 269–82. Baltimore: Johns Hopkins University Press.

Gamble, A. M., and S. A. Walkland. 1974. *The British Party System and Economic Policy, 1945–1983.* Oxford: Clarendon Press.

Ganz, Gabriele. 1977. *Government and Industry: The Provision of Financial Assistance to Industry and Its Control.* Abingdon: Professional Books.

Geroski, P., and A. Jacquemin. 1985. Industrial Change, Barriers to Mobility, and European Industrial Policy. *Economic Policy* 1 (November):170–205.

Ghemawat, Panka, and Barry Nalebuff. 1990. The Devolution of Declining Industries. *Quarterly Journal of Economics* 105:167–87.

Gibbons, R., and L. Katz. 1992. Does Unmeasured Ability Explain Inter-industry Wage Differentials? *Review of Economic Studies* 59:515–35.

Gille, Bertrand. 1964. *La siderurgie française au XIXe siecle.* Geneva: Droz.

Gilligan, Michael. 1997. *Empowering Exporters: Reciprocity and Collective Action in Twentieth Century American Trade Policy.* Ann Arbor: University of Michigan Press.

Glasser, Carrie. 1940. *Wage Differentials: The Case of the Unskilled.* New York: Columbia University Press.

Glezer, L. 1982. *Tariff Politics: Australian Policy-making 1960–1980.* Melbourne: Melbourne University Press.

Goldin, Claudia. 1990. *Understanding the Gender Gap: An Economic History of American Women.* New York: Oxford University Press.

Goldin, Claudia, and Lawrence Katz. 1996. The Origins of Technology-Skill Complementarity. *Quarterly Journal of Economics* 113 (June):683–732.

Goldstein, Judith. 1986. Political Economy of Trade. *American Political Science Review* 80 (1):161–84.

————. 1993. *Ideas, Interests, and American Trade Policy.* Ithaca, N.Y.: Cornell University Press.

Gollan, R. 1955. Trade Unions and Labour Parties. *Historical Studies* 7 (17):17–36.

Golob, Eugene. 1944. *The Méline Tariff: French Agriculture and Nationalist Economic Policy.* New York: Columbia University Press.

Gordon, D., R. Edwards, and M. Reich. 1982. *Segmented Work, Divided Workers: The Historical Transformation of Labor in the United States.* Cambridge: Cambridge University Press.

Gourevitch, Peter. 1986. *Politics in Hard Times: Comparative Responses to International Economic Crises*. Ithaca, N.Y.: Cornell University Press.

Grant, Wyn. 1980. Business Interests and the British Conservative Party. *Government and Opposition* 15 (2):143–61.

Green, D. 1984. Government and Industry in France. *Public Money*. September:27–31.

Gregory, R. 1984. Industry Protection. Australian National University Centre for Economic Policy Research Paper #111. Canberra.

Griliches, Zvi. 1969. Capital-Skill Complementarity. *Review of Economics and Statistics* 51 (4):465–68.

Grossman, Gene, and James Levinsohn. 1989. Import Competition and the Stock Market Return to Capital. *American Economic Review* 79:1065–87.

Guillen, Pierre. 1978. La politique douaniere da la France. *Relations internationales* 16 (Winter):315–31.

Gujurati, Damodar. 1995. *Essentials of Econometrics*. 2d ed. Boston: McGraw-Hill.

Haggard, Stephan. 1988. The Institutional Foundations of Hegemony. In *The State and American Foreign Economic Policy*, edited by G. John Ikenberry, David Lake, and Michael Mastanduno, pp. 91–119. Ithaca, N.Y.: Cornell University Press.

Hall, Peter. 1986. *Governing the Economy: The Politics of State Intervention in Britain and France*. Oxford: Oxford University Press.

Hammermesh, Daniel. 1993. *Labor Demand*. Princeton, N.J.: Princeton University Press.

Hay, Donald, and Derek Morris. 1984. *Unquoted Companies: Their Contribution to the United Kingdom Economy*. London: Macmillan.

Hayward, J. E. S. 1974. Steel. In *Big Business and the State*, edited by Raymond Vernon, pp. 255–71. Cambridge, Mass.: Harvard University Press.

Hechter, K. 1940. *Insurgency: Personalities and the Politics of the Taft Era*. New York: Columbia University Press.

Heckscher, Eli. 1954. *An Economic History of Sweden*. Cambridge, Mass.: Harvard University Press.

Heclo, Hugh, and Henrik Madsen. 1987. *Policy and Politics in Sweden*. Philadelphia: Temple University Press.

Helleiner, Gerald. 1977. Transnational Enterprises in the New Political Economy of U.S. Trade Policy. *Oxford Economic Papers* 29 (1):102–16.

Hibbs, Douglas. 1977. Political Parties and Macroeconomic Policies. *American Political Science Review* 71 (4):1467–87.

Hibbs, Douglas, and Hakan Locking. 1996. Wage Dispersion and Productive Efficiency: Evidence for Sweden. Paper presented at the 92nd Annual Meetings of the American Political Science Association, San Francisco.

Hill, J., and J. Mendez. 1983. Factor Mobility and the General Equilibrium Model of Production. *Journal of International Economics* 15:19–25.

Hiscox, Michael J. 1989. Policy-Making Models and the 25 Percent Tariff Cut. Unpublished honors thesis. University of Sydney. Sydney.

———. 1997. The Trade War at Home: Factor Mobility, International Trade, and Political Coalitions in Democracies. Ph.D. diss., Harvard University.

———. 1998. International Factor Mobility and Trade Politics. Paper presented at the 94th Annual Meeting of the American Political Science Association, Boston.

————. 1999. The Magic Bullet? The RTAA, Institutional Reform, and Trade Liberalization. *International Organization* 53 (4):669–98.

————. 2002. Factor Specificity, Inter-Industry Mobility, and Technological Change: Evidence from Manufacturing Wages and Profits in the U.S. between 1820 and 1990. *Journal of Economic History* 62 (2):1–35.

Holian, David, Timothy Krebs, and Michael Walsh. 1997. Constituency Opinion, Ross Perot, and Roll-Call Behavior in the U.S. House: The Case of NAFTA. *Legislative Studies Quarterly* 22:169–92.

Holmlund, Bertil. 1984. *Labor Mobility: Studies of Labor Turnover and Migration in the Swedish Labor Market*. Stockholm: Industrial Institute for Economic and Social Research.

Hughes, Kent. 1979. *Trade, Taxes, and Transnationals: International Economic Decision Making in Congress*. New York: Praeger.

Hull, Cordell. 1948. *Memoirs of Cordell Hull*. New York: Macmillan.

International Labour Office. Various years. *Yearbook of Labour Statistics*. Geneva: International Labour Office.

Irwin, Douglas. 1995. *Industry or Class Cleavages over Trade Policy? Evidence from the British General Election of 1923*. NBER Working Paper 5170. Cambridge, Mass.: National Bureau of Economic Research.

Jacoby, S., and S. Sharma. 1992. Employment Duration and Industrial Labor Mobility in the United States 1880–1980. *Journal of Economic History* 52 (1):161–79.

James, J. 1976. The Development of a National Money Market. *Journal of Economic History* 36 (December):878–97.

James, John, and Jonathan Skinner. 1985. The Resolution of the Labor Scarcity Paradox. *Journal of Economic History* 45:513–40.

James, Scott, and David Lake. 1989. The Second Face of Hegemony. *International Organization* 43 (1):1–29.

Johnson, D., and Porter, K. 1973. *National Party Platforms*. Urbana: University of Illinois Press.

Johnston, T. L. 1963. *Economic Expansion and Structural Change: A Trade Union Manifesto*. Edited and translated. Report Submitted to the 16th Congress of Landsorganisationen I Sverige. London: George Allen and Unwin Ltd.

Jolly, J. 1977. *Dictionnaire des parlementaires francais*. Paris: Presses universite de France.

Jones, H. G. 1976. *Planning and Productivity in Sweden*. London: Croom Helm.

Jones, Ronald. 1971. A Three-Factor Model in Theory, Trade, and History. In *Trade, Balance of Payments, and Growth*, edited by J. Bhagwati, Ronald Jones, Robert A. Mundell, and Jaroslav Vanek, pp. 3–21. Amsterdam: North-Holland.

Jones, Ronald, and J. Scheinkman. 1977. The Relevance of the Two-Sector Production Model in Trade Theory. *Journal of Political Economy* 85:909–35.

Jupp, J. 1982. *Party Politics, Australia: 1966–1981*. Sydney: Allen and Unwin.

Kahane, Leo. 1996. Congressional Voting Patterns on NAFTA: An Empirical Analysis. *American Journal of Economics and Sociology* 55:395–409.

Katz, Lawrence, and Lawrence Summers. 1989. Industry Rents: Evidence and Implications. *Brookings Papers on Economic Activity: Microeconomics*. Washington, D.C.: Brookings Institution.

Katz, Richard. 1986. Intraparty Preference Voting. In *Electoral Laws and Their Political Consequences*, edited by B. Grofman and A. Lijphart, pp. 85–103. New York: Agathon.

Katzenstein, Peter J. 1985. *Small States in World Markets: Industrial Policy in Europe.* Ithaca, N.Y.: Cornell University Press.

Key, V. O. 1964. *Politics, Parties, and Pressure Groups.* 5th ed. New York: Crowell.

Kim, Sukkoo. 1992. Trends in U.S. Regional Manufacturing Structure, 1860–1987. Ph.D. diss., University of California, Los Angeles.

King, Anthony. 1977. *Britain Says Yes: The 1975 Referendum on the Common Market.* Washington, D.C.: American Institute for Public Policy Research.

King, Gary, Michael Tomz, and Jason Wittenberg. 2000. *Clarify: Software for Interpreting and Presenting Statistical Results,* ver. 1.2.1. Cambridge, Mass.: Harvard University. June 1. *http://gking.harvard.edu/.*

Kirby, M. 1977. *The British Coalmining Industry 1870–1946.* Hamden: Archon Books.

Korpi, W. 1978. *Working Class in Welfare Capitalism.* London: Routledge and Kegan Paul.

Kottman, R. 1968. *Reciprocity and the North Atlantic Triangle.* Ithaca, N.Y.: Cornell University Press.

Krause, Lawrence. 1984. Australia's Comparative Advantage in International Trade. In *The Australian Economy: A View from the North,* edited by Richard Caves and Lawrence Krause, pp. 275–312. Washington, D.C.: Brookings.

Krueger, Alan, and Lawrence Summers. 1987. Reflections on the Inter-industry Wage Structure. In *Unemployment and the Structure of Labor Markets,* edited by K. Lang and J. Leonard, pp. 17–47. Oxford: Basil Blackwell.

———. 1988. Efficiency Wages and the Inter-Industry Wage Structure. *Econometrica* 56 (2):259–93.

Krugman, Paul, and Maurice Obstfeld. 1988. *International Economics: Theory and Policy.* Boston: Little Brown.

Kuznets, Simon, Ann Ratner Miller, and Richard A. Easterlin. 1960. *Population Redistribution and Economic Growth: United States, 1870–1950,* vol. 2: *Analyses of Economic Change.* Philadelphia: American Philosophical Society.

La Nauze, J. 1948. *Political Economy in Australia.* Carlton: Melbourne University Press.

Lake, David. 1988. *Power, Protection, and Free Trade.* Ithaca, N.Y.: Cornell University Press.

Landes, David. 1969. *The Unbound Prometheus: Technological Change and Industrial Development in Western Europe from 1750 to the Present.* Cambridge: Cambridge University Press.

Lange, Peter, and Geoffrey Garrett. 1985. The Politics of Growth. *Journal of Politics* 47 (3):792–827.

LaPalombara, Joseph, and Myron Weiner. 1966. *Political Parties and Political Development.* Princeton, N.J.: Princeton University Press.

Lavergne, Real. 1983. *The Political Economy of U.S. Tariffs.* New York: Academic Press.

Lawrence, Robert, and Barry Bosworth. 1987. Adjusting to Slower Economic Growth: The External Sector. In *The Swedish Economy,* edited by Barry P. Bosworth and Alice M. Rivlin, pp. 55–88. Washington, D.C.: Brookings Institution.

Leamer, Edward. 1984. *Sources of International Comparative Advantage: Theory and Evidence.* Cambridge, Mass.: MIT Press.

Lebergott, Stanley. 1964. *Manpower in Economic Growth: The American Record since 1800.* New York: McGraw-Hill.

Lindbeck, Assar. 1974. *Swedish Economic Policy.* Berkeley: University of California Press.

Lipset, Seymour Martin, and Stein Rokkan. 1967. *Party Systems and Voter Alignments: Cross-National Perspectives.* New York: Free Press.

Lohmann, Susanne, and Sharyn O'Halloran. 1994. Divided Government and U.S. Trade Policy. *International Organization* 48 (4):595–632.

Long, Clarence. 1960. *Wages and Earnings in the United States, 1860–1890.* Princeton, N.J.: Princeton University Press.

Longmate, Norman. 1984. *The Breadstealers: The Fight Against the Corn Laws, 1838–1846.* New York: St. Martin's Press.

Lorwin, Val R. 1954. *The French Labor Movement.* Cambridge, Mass.: Harvard University Press.

Loveday, P., and A. Martin. 1966. *Parliament, Factions, and Parties: The First Thirty Years of Responsible Government in New South Wales, 1856–1889.* London: Cambridge University Press.

Loveday, P., A. Martin, and R. Parker. 1977. *Emergence of the Australian Party System.* Sydney: Hall and Iremonger.

Lowe, Marvin. 1942. *The British Tariff Movement.* Washington, D.C.: American Council on Public Affairs.

Lubenow, W. C. 1988. *Parliamentary Politics and the Home Rule Crisis: The British House of Commons in 1886.* Oxford: Clarendon Press.

Lundberg, Erik. 1985. The Rise and Fall of the Swedish Model. *Journal of Economic Literature* 23 (1):1–36.

Mabbett, Deborah. 1995. *Trade, Employment, and Welfare: A Comparative Study of Trade and Labour Market Policies in Sweden and New Zealand, 1880–1980.* New York: Oxford University Press.

Magee, Stephen. 1980. Three Simple Tests of the Stolper-Samuelson Theorem. In *Issues in International Economics,* edited by Peter Oppenheimer, pp. 138–53. London: Oriel.

Magnus, Philip. 1964. *Gladstone: A Biography.* London: Murray.

Marcus, M. 1967. Firms' Exit Rates and Their Determinants. *Journal of Industrial Economics* 16 (1):10–21.

Margo, R. and G. Villaflor. 1987. The Growth of Wages in Antebellum America: New Evidence. *Journal of Economic History* 47 (4):873–95.

Marks, Stephen. 1993. Economic Interests and Voting on the Omnibus Trade Bill of 1987. *Public Choice* 75:21–42.

Marrison, A. J. 1983. Businessmen, Industries, and Tariff Reform. *Business History* 25 (2):48–78.

Martin, A. 1959. *Members of the Legislative Assembly of New South Wales, 1856–1901.* Canberra: Australian National University Press.

Mayer, Wolfgang. 1984. Endogenous Tariff Formation. *American Economic Review* 74 (5):970–85.

McArthur, J., and S. Marks. 1988. Constituent Interest vs. Legislator Ideology. *Economic Inquiry* 26:461–70.

McCord, Norman. 1958. *The Anti-Corn Law League, 1838–1846.* London: Allen Unwin.

McCalmont, Frederick. 1895. *The Parliamentary Poll Book of All Elections 1832 to 1895.* London: S. E. Stanford.

McDiarmid, Orville. 1946. *Commercial Policy in the Canadian Economy.* Cambridge, Mass.: Harvard University Press.

McDonald, Judith, Anthony Patrick O'Brien, and Colleen Callahan. 1997. Trade Wars: Canada's Reaction to the Smoot-Hawley Tariff. *Journal of Economic History* 57 (4):802–26.

McGillivray, Fiona and Wendy Schiller. 1996. Political Geography of Lobbying. Paper presented at the 92d Annual Meeting of the American Political Science Association, September, San Francisco.

McKenzie, Robert. 1963. *British Political Parties*. 2d ed. London: Heinemann.

McLean, Iain. 1995. Interests and Ideology in the UK Parliament of 1841–47: An Analysis of Rollcall Voting. Paper presented at the 91st Annual Meetings of the American Political Science Association, Chicago.

McLean, Simon. 1895. *The Tariff History of Canada*. Toronto: Warwick Bros. Rutter.

Midford, Paul. 1993. International Trade and Domestic Politics. *International Organization* 47 (4):535–64.

Millar, T. B. 1978. *Australia in Peace and War: External Relations 1788–1977*. Canberra: Australian National University Press.

Milner, Helen V. 1988. *Resisting Protectionism: Global Industries and the Politics of International Trade*. Princeton, N.J.: Princeton University Press.

Milner, Henry. 1989. *Sweden: Social Democracy in Practice*. Oxford: Oxford University Press.

Mincer, Jacob. 1984. Human Capital and Economic Growth. *Economics of Education Review* 3:195–205.

Mitchell, Brian. 1980. *European Historical Statistics, 1750–1975*. 2nd revised edition. New York: Columbia University Press.

———. 1984. *International Historical Statistics: The Americas and Australasia*. Detroit: Gale Research.

———. 1988. *British Historical Statistics*. New York: Cambridge University Press.

Mitchell, Olivia S. 1982. Fringe Benefits and Labor Mobility. *Journal of Human Resources* 17 (2):286–98.

Montgomery, Arthur. 1939. *The Rise of Modern Industry in Sweden*. London: P. S. King.

Morley, J. 1881. *The Life of Richard Cobden*. Vol. 1. Boston: Roberts.

Mulhall, Michael G. 1899. *The Dictionary of Statistics*. 4th ed. London: Routledge Sons.

Mussa, Michael. 1974. Tariffs and the Distribution of Income. *Journal of Political Economy* 82 (6):1191–203.

———. 1982. Imperfect Factor Mobility and the Distribution of Income. *Journal of International Economics* 12 (1):125–41.

Mytelka, Lynn Krieger. 1982. The French Textile Industry. In *The Emerging International Economic Order*, edited by H. Jacobson and D. Sidjanski, pp. 129–66. Beverly Hills, Calif.: Sage.

Nairn, N. B. 1957. Rise of the Trades and Labour Council. *Historical Studies of Australia and New Zealand* 28.

Nairn, Tom. 1972. The Left Against Europe. *New Left Review* 75:5–120.

Naudin, Jean. 1928. *Les accords commerciaux de la France depuis la guerre*. Paris: Recueil Sirey.

Neatby, Blair. 1963. *William Mackenzie King: 1924–1932*. Toronto: University of Toronto Press.

New South Wales Legislative Assembly. 1862. Select Committee on the State of Manufactures and Agriculture in the Colony. *Votes and Proceedings of the New South Wales Legislative Assembly, 1862* Volume 5.

North, Douglass. 1965. The Role of Transportation in the Economic Development of North America. *Les grandes maritimes voies dans le monde XVe—XIXe siècles.* Colloque international d'histoire maritime Vienne. Paris: S.E.V.P.E.N.

North, Douglass, and Robert Paul Thomas. 1973. *The Rise of the Western World.* Cambridge: Cambridge University Press.

O'Brien, Patrick, ed. 1983. *Railways and the Economic Development of Western Europe, 1830–1914.* London: Macmillan.

Odell, K. 1989. The Integration of Regional and Interregional Capital Markets: Evidence from the Pacific Coast, 1883–1913. *Journal of Economic History* 49 (June):297–310.

Oi, Walter Y. 1962. Labor as a Quasi-Fixed Factor. *Journal of Political Economy* 70 (6):538–55.

Olson, Mancur. 1965. *The Logic of Collective Action.* Cambridge, Mass.: Harvard University Press.

———. 1982. *The Rise and Decline of Nations.* New Haven, Conn.: Yale University Press.

Ostrogorski, Moisei. 1902. *Democracy and the Organization of Political Parties.* Trans. F. Clarke. New York: Macmillan.

Palmer, Bryan D. 1983. *Working Class Experience: The Rise and Reconstitution of Canadian Labour, 1800–1980.* Toronto: Butterworth.

Parsons, Donald. 1972. Specific Human Capital: An Application to Quit Rates and Layoff Rates. *Journal of Political Economy* 80 (6):1120–43.

Pastor, Robert. 1980. *Congress and the Politics of U.S. Foreign Economic Policy, 1929–1976.* Berkeley: University of California Press.

Patterson, G. 1968. *The Tariff in the Australian Colonies, 1856–1900.* Melbourne: Cheshire.

Peel, George. 1913. *The Tariff Reformers.* London: Methuen and Co. Ltd.

Pencavel, J. 1970. *An Analysis of the Quit Rate in American Manufacturing.* Princeton, N.J.: Princeton University Press.

Pinchin, Hugh. 1978. *The Regional Impact of the Canadian Tariff.* Ottawa: Economic Council of Canada.

Pincus, Jonathan. 1977. *Pressure Groups and Politics in Antebellum Tariffs.* New York: Columbia University Press.

Polsby, Nelson. 1968. The Institutionalization of the United States House of Representatives. *American Political Science Review* 62:144–69.

Pontusson, Jonas. 1991. Labor, Corporatism, and Industrial Policy: The Swedish Case in Comparative Perspective. *Comparative Politics* 23 (2):163–80.

Pontusson, Jonas, and Peter Swenson. 1993. Markets, Production, Institutions, and Politics: Why Swedish Employers Have Abandoned the Swedish Model. Paper prepared for the 8th Conference of Europeanists, Council of European Studies, Chicago, March.

Pratt, Edwin. 1912. *History of Inland Transport and Communication in England.* London: Paul, Trench, Trubner.

Premfors, R. 1983. Governmental Commissions. *American Behavioral Scientist* 26: 623–42.

Presthus, R. 1973. *Elite Accommodation in Canadian Politics.* Cambridge: Cambridge University Press.

Protheroe, David R. 1980. *Imports and Politics: Trade Decision-Making in Canada 1968–1979.* Montreal: Institute for Research on Public Policy.

Ragan, James F., Jr. 1984. Investigating the Decline in Manufacturing Quit Rates. *Journal of Human Resources* 19:53–71.

Ramey, Valerie, and Matthew Shapiro. 1998. *Displaced Capital: A Study of Aerospace Plant Closings.* NBER Working Paper No. 6775. October. Cambridge, Mass.: National Bureau of Economic Research.

Ratcliffe, Barrie. 1978. The Tariff Reform Campaign in France, 1831–1836. *Journal of European Economic History* 7 (1):61–138.

Ratner, S. 1972. *The Tariff in American History.* New York: Van Nostrand.

Rattigan, A. 1986. *Industry Assistance: The Inside Story.* Melbourne: Melbourne University Press.

Rehn, Gösta. 1985. Swedish Active Labor Market Policy: Retrospect and Prospect. *Industrial Relations* 24 (1):62–89.

Reich, Leonard. 1985. *The Making of American Industrial Research.* Cambridge: Cambridge University Press.

Remini, R. 1958. Martin Van Buren and the Tariff of Abominations. *American Historical Review* 63 July.

Rempel, Richard. 1972. *Unionists Divided: Arthur Balfour, Joseph Chamberlain, and the Unionist Free Traders.* Hamden, Conn.: Archon Books.

Republique française, Ministere des finances et des affairs economiques, Institut national de la statistique et des etudes economiques. Various years. *Annuaire statistique de la France.* Paris: Presses universitaires de France.

Rivlin, Alice M. 1987. Overview. In *The Swedish Economy*, edited by Barry P. Bosworth and Alice M. Rivlin, pp. 1–21. Washington, D.C.: Brookings Institution.

Rogowski, Ronald. 1989. *Commerce and Coalitions: How Trade Affects Domestic Political Alignments.* Princeton, N.J.: Princeton University Press.

———. 1998. Electoral Systems and Vote-Buying: Why PR Works Best When Voters are Loyal, Majoritarian Systems When Voters are Fickle. Unpublished manuscript, University of California, Los Angeles.

Rohde, David. 1989. Something's Happening Here. In *Home Style and Washington Work*, edited by Morris Fiorina and David Rohde, pp. 137–64. Ann Arbor: University of Michigan Press.

Rose, Richard. 1980. *Politics in England: An Interpretation for the 1980s.* 3d ed. Boston: Little, Brown.

Rosenbloom, Joshua. 1989. Is Wage Dispersion a Good Index of Labor Market Integration? A Comment on Rothenberg. *Journal of Economic History* 49 (1): 166–69.

———. 1990. One Market or Many? Labor Market Integration in the Late Nineteenth-Century United States. *Journal of Economic History* 50 (1):85–107.

———. 1994. *Was There a National Labor Market at the End of the Nineteenth Century? Intercity and Interregional Variation in Male Earnings in Manufacturing.* NBER Working Paper Series on Historical Factors in Long Run Growth. No. 61. Cambridge, Mass.: National Bureau of Economic Research.

Rosenthal, Howard L., and Keith T. Poole. 1991. United States Congressional Roll Call Voting Records, 1789–1990. [Computer file]. 2nd release. Ann Arbor, Mich.: Inter-university Consortium for Political and Social Research.

———. 2000. United States Congressional Roll Call Voting Records, 1789–1990: Reformatted Data [Computer file]. 2nd release. Ann Arbor, Mich.: Inter-university Consortium for Political and Social Research [distributor].

Ross, Arthur M. 1958. Do We Have a New Industrial Feudalism? *American Economic Review* 48 (5):903–20.

Russell, D. 1969. *Frederic Bastiat: Ideas and Influence.* New York: Foundation for Economic Education.

Rustow, Dankwart. 1955. *The Politics of Compromise: A Study of Parties and Cabinet Government in Sweden.* Princeton, N.J.: Princeton University Press.

Rydon, J. 1975. *A Biographical Register of the Commonwealth Parliament, 1901–1972.* Canberra: Australian National University Press.

Safran, William. 1985. *The French Polity.* 2d ed. New York: Longman.

Sainsbury, Diane. 1980. *Swedish Social Democratic Ideology and Electoral Politics 1944–1948.* Stockholm: Almqvist Wiksell International.

Samuelson, Paul A. 1971. Ohlin Was Right. *Swedish Journal of Economics* 73 (4):365–84.

Sauvy, Alfred. 1984. *Histoire economique de la France entre les deux guerres.* Paris: Economica.

Sawyer, John E. 1954. The Social Basis of the American System of Manufacturing. *Journal of Economic History* 14 (4):361–79.

Schattschneider, E. E. 1935. *Politics, Pressures, and the Tariff.* Englewood Cliffs, N.J.: Prentice-Hall.

Scherer, F. M. 1980. *Industrial Market Structure and Economic Performance.* 2d ed. Chicago: Rand McNally.

Scheve, Kenneth, and Matthew Slaughter. 1998. *What Determines Individual Trade Policy Preferences?* NBER Working Paper No. 6531. April. Cambridge, Mass.: National Bureau of Economic Research.

———. 2001. *Globalization and the Perceptions of American Workers.* Washington, D.C.: Institute for International Economics.

Schnietz, Karen. 1994. To Delegate or Not to Delegate: Congressional Institutional Choice in the Regulation of Foreign Trade, 1916–1934. Ph.D. diss., University of California, Berkeley.

Schonhardt-Bailey, Cheryl. 1991. Specific Factors, Capital Markets, Portfolio Diversification, and Free Trade. *World Politics* 43 (4):545–69.

Semmel, Bernard. 1960. *Imperialism and Social Reform.* London: Allen and Unwin.

Serle, Geoffrey. 1971. *The Rush to Be Rich: A History of the Colony of Victoria, 1883–89.* Melbourne: Melbourne University Press.

Shepherd, G. 1987. United Kingdom: A Resistance to Change. In *Managing Industrial Change in Western Europe,* edited by F. Duchene and G. Shepherd, pp. 145–77. London: Frances Pinter.

Shonfield, Andrew. 1965. *Modern Capitalism: The Changing Balance of Public and Private Power.* New York: Oxford University Press.

Sjoblom, G. 1985. *The Roles of Political Parties in Denmark and in Sweden 1970–84.* Copenhagen: Institute of Political Studies.

Slichter, S. 1950. Notes on the Structure of Wages. *Review of Economics and Statistics* 32:80–91.

Smith, Michael Stephen. 1980. *Tariff Reform in France, 1860–1900.* Ithaca, N.Y.: Cornell University Press.

Sokoloff, Kenneth L. 1984. Was the Transition from the Artisanal Shop to the Non-mechanized Factory Associated with Gains in Efficiency? *Explorations in Economic History* 21 (4):351–82.

———. 1986. Productivity Growth in Manufacturing during Early Industrialization. In *Long-Term Factors in American Economic Growth,* edited by Stanley L. Engerman and Robert E. Gallman, pp. 679–736. Chicago: University of Chicago Press.

Sokoloff, K., and G. Villaflor. 1992. The Market for Manufacturing Workers during

Early Industrialization: The American Northeast, 1820 to 1860. In *Strategic Factors in Nineteenth Century American Economic History*, edited by C. Goldin and H. Rockoff, pp. 29–65. Chicago: University of Chicago Press.

Stanwood, Edward. 1903. *American Tariff Controversies in the Nineteenth Century.* 2 vol. Boston: Houghton Mifflin.

Statistics Canada. Various years. *Corporation Financial Statistics.* Ottawa: Census and Statistics Office.

Steagall, Jeffrey, and Ken Jennings. 1996. Unions, PAC Contributions, and the NAFTA Vote. *Journal of Labor Research* 17:515–21.

Sternquist, Nils, and Bo Bjurulf. 1970. Party Cohesion and Party Cooperation in the Swedish Parliament in 1964 and 1966. *Scandinavian Political Studies* 5 (12): 12–164.

Stewart, Charles H., III. 1991. Lessons from the Post-Civil War Era. In *The Politics of Divided Government*, edited by Gary W. Cox and Samuel. Kernell, pp. 203–38. Boulder, Colo.: Westview Press.

Stolper, Wolfgang F., and Paul A. Samuelson. 1941. Protection and Real Wages. *Review of Economic Studies* 9 (1):58–73.

Sundquist, James L. 1983. *Dynamics of the Party System: Alignment and Realignment of Political Parties in the United States.* Revised edition. Washington, D.C.: Brookings Institution. 30:379–408.

Sundstrom, W., and J. Rosenbloom. 1993. Occupational Differences in the Dispersion of Wages and Working Hours: Labor Market Integration in the United States, 1890–1903. *Explorations in Economic History* 30:379–408.

Tasca, Henry J. 1938. *The Reciprocal Trade Policy of the United States.* Philadelphia: University of Pennsylvania Press.

Tarbell, I. 1911. *The Tariff in Our Times.* New York: Macmillan.

Taussig, Frank W. 1931. *The Tariff History of the United States.* 8th ed. New York: G. P. Putnam's Sons.

Taylor, George. 1949. *The Transportation Revolution, 1815–1860.* New York: Rinehart.

Terrill, T. 1973. *The Tariff, Politics, and American Foreign Policy, 1874–1901.* Westport, Conn.: Greenwood Press.

Thorburn, Hugh G. ed. 1985. *Party Politics in Canada.* 5th ed. Scarborough, Ont.: Prentice-Hall.

Tosini, Suzanne, and Edward Tower. 1987. The Textile Bill of 1985: The Determinants of Congressional Voting Patterns. *Public Choice* 54:19–25.

Toynbee, Arnold. [1884] 1958. The Classical Definition of the Industrial Revolution. In *The Industrial Revolution in Britain*, edited by Philip A. M. Taylor, pp. 1–6. Lexington, Mass.: Heath.

Tsokhas, K. 1984. *A Class Apart? Businessmen and Australian Politics 1960–1980.* Melbourne: Oxford University Press.

Tucker, Robert C. 1978. *The Marx-Engels Reader.* 2nd ed. New York: W. W. Norton.

Turner, John. 1984. *Businessmen and Politics: Studies of Business Activity in British Politics, 1900–1945.* London: Heinemann.

Turner, Julius, and Edward V. Schneier, Jr. 1970. *Party and Constituency.* Rev. ed. Baltimore: Johns Hopkins University Press.

U.K. Department of Employment, Central Statistical Office. 1971. *British Labour Statistics: Historical Abstract.* London: H.M. Stationery Office.

U.K. Parliament. Various years. *Hansard Parliamentary Debates.*

Underhill, Frank. 1961. *In Search of Canadian Liberalism.* Toronto: Macmillan.

U.S. Congress. Various years. *Annals of Congress.* Washington, D.C.: U.S. Government Printing Office.

U.S. Congress. Various years. *Congressional Globe.* Washington, D.C.: U.S. Government Printing Office.

U.S. Congress. Various years. *Congressional Record.* Washington, D.C.: U.S. Government Printing Office.

U.S. Congress. 1827–1833. *Register of Debates in Congress.* Washington, D.C.: Gales and Seaton.

United Nations. Various years. *Industrial Statistics Yearbook.* New York: Department of Economic and Social Affairs, Statistical Office of the United Nations.

Urquhart, Malcolm C. 1965. *Historical Statistics of Canada.* Cambridge: Cambridge University Press.

U.S. House, Committee on Ways and Means. 1884. *The Morrison Tariff Bill.* Washington, D.C.: Government Printing Office.

U.S. Department of Commerce, Bureau of the Census. 1976. *Historical Statistics of the United States: Colonial Times to 1970.* Washington, D.C.: U.S. Government Printing Office.

U.S. Department of Commerce, Bureau of the Census. 1989. *State Personal Income: 1929–87.* Washington, D.C.: U.S. Government Printing Office.

U.S. Department of Commerce, Bureau of the Census. Various years. *Statistical Abstract of the United States.* Washington, D.C.: U.S. Government Printing Office.

U.S. Department of Labor, Bureau of Labor Statistics. Various years. *Employment and Earnings.* Washington, D.C.: Government Printing Office.

U.S. Securities and Exchange Commission. Various years. *Survey of American Listed Corporations: Corporation Profits.* Washington, D.C.: U.S. Government Printing Office.

Uslaner, Eric. 1998. Let the Chits Fall Where They May? *Legislative Studies Quarterly* 23:347–71.

Verdier, Daniel. 1994. *Democracy and International Trade: Britain, France, and the United States, 1860–1990.* Princeton, N.J.: Princeton University Press.

———. 1995. The Politics of Public Aid to Private Industry. *Comparative Political Studies* 28 (1):3–40.

Verney, Douglas V. 1957. *Parliamentary Reform in Sweden, 1866–1921.* Oxford: Clarendon Press.

Victorian Legislative Assembly. 1865. Select Committee upon Manufactures. *Votes and Proceedings of the Legislative Assembly, 1865* Volume 2, Number D26.

Victorian Legislative Assembly. 1883. Report of the Royal Commission on the Tariff. *Votes and Proceedings of the Legislative Assembly, 1883* Volume 4, Number 50.

Victorian Legislative Assembly. 1894. First Report of the Board of Enquiry. *Votes and Proceedings of the Legislative Assembly, 1894* Volume 2, Number 37.

Ware, N. 1935. *Labor in Modern Industrial Society.* Boston: D.C. Heath.

Wattenberg, Martin P. 1984. *The Decline of American Political Parties, 1952–80.* Cambridge, Mass.: Harvard University Press.

Warhurst, J. 1981. *State Governments and Australian Tariff Policy.* Canberra: Centre for Research on Federal Financial Relations.

Weaver, R. Kent. 1987. Political Foundations of Swedish Economic Policy. In *The*

Swedish Economy, edited by Barry P. Bosworth and Alice M. Rivlin, pp. 289–317. Washington, D.C.: Brookings Institution.

Weeks, Joseph D. 1886. *Report on the Statistics of Wages in Manufacturing Industries with Supplementary Reports*. Washington, D.C.: U.S. Government Printing Office.

Whetham, E. 1974. The Agricultural Act. *Agricultural History Review* 22 (1):36–49.

Whitfield, L. 1950. The Age on Public Affairs from 1861 to 1881. MA thesis. University of Melbourne.

Whitlam, E. G. 1985. *The Whitlam Government, 1972–75*. Melbourne: Penguin.

Wilensky, Harold. 1976. *The "New Corporatism," Centralization, and the Welfare State*. London: Sage.

Wilks, Stephen. 1981. Planning Agreements: The Making of a Paper Tiger. *Public Administration* 59 (Winter):399–419.

Williamson, Jeffrey. 1982. The Structure of Pay in Britain, 1710–1911. *Research in Economic History* 7:1–54.

Williamson, Jeffrey, and Peter Lindert. 1980. *American Inequality: A Macroeconomic History*. New York: Academic Press.

Williamson, Oliver E. 1985. *The Economic Institutions of Capitalism: Firms, Markets, and Relational Contracting*. New York: Free Press.

Winn, Conrad. 1976. *Political Parties in Canada*. New York: McGraw-Hill Reyerson.

Wright, Gordon. 1964. *Rural Revolution in France*. Stanford, Calif.: Stanford University Press.

Young, Stephen. 1978. Industrial Policy in Britain, 1972–1977. In *Planning in Europe*, edited by J. Hayward and O. Narkiewicz, pp. 79–100. London: Croom Helm.

Young, Stephen, and A. V. Lowe. 1974. *Intervention in the Mixed Economy: The Evolution of British Industrial Policy, 1964–72*. London: Croom Helm.

Zebel, Sydney. 1940. Fair Trade: An English Reaction to the Breakdown of the Cobden Treaty System. *Journal of Modern History* 12 (2):161–85.

INDEX

ACMA (Associated Chambers of Manufactures; Australia), 125, 125n.17
Act of Union (Canada, 1840), 104
Adams Compromise Act (U.S., 1832), 49, 178, 181
Adams Party (U.S.), 49, 49nn.9–10, 181
aerospace industry, 27
AFL (American Federation of Labor), 55, 60
AFL-CIO (U.S.), 37, 65, 69, 139
Agrarian Party (Sweden), 35–36, 99, 100, 100n.5, 102–3, 102n, 129
agriculture, 30
AIF (Association de l'industrie française), 86–87, 86n.7
Aldrich, Nelson W., 171
Alfred Herbert Ltd., 81
Alliance for GATT Now, 163n.2
Alt, James, 6, 162
Amalgamated Association of Iron and Steel Workers (U.S.), 55n.25
Amalgamated Shearers' Union (Australia), 121
American Farm Bureau, 65
American Federation of Labor (AFL), 55, 60
American Iron and Steel Association, 55n.25, 57n.27
American Iron and Steel Institute, 57n.27
American Pocket Cutlery Manufacturers, 182
American Protective Tariff League, 59n.30
American Soap Manufacturers' Association, 179
Annuaire statistique de la France (Institute National de la Statistique et des Etudes Economiques), 174
Annual Survey of Manufactures (U.S.), 172–73
Anti–Corn Law League (Britain), 4, 73, 73nn.2–3, 75, 75n.7, 85
Associated Chambers of Manufactures (ACMA; Australia), 125, 125n.17
Association Against a Tariff on Foodstuffs (Sweden), 98
Association de fabrique lyonnaise (France), 87n.8
Association de l'industrie française (AIF), 86–87, 86n.7
Association for the Promotion of Canadian Industry, 106
associations. *See* peak associations
Australia, 114–27; class coalitions in, 10; colonial period, 114–17; federation period, 117–

21, 117–21nn.3–11; industrialization in, 17, 128; interwar period, 121–23, 123n.13, 129; labor skill levels in, 31n.23; land use in, 30; political parties in, xiii, 35–36, 36–37nn.4–5 (*see also specific parties*); postwar period, 123–27, 124–26nn.15–18, 130; protectionism in, 10; research and development in, 32n.26; transportation in, 29–30; voting on trade legislation in, 119–20, 119n.9, 121–22, 126, 127; wages/profits in, 17, 23, 175
Australian Council of Trade Unions, 126
auto industry, 67, 67nn.49–50
automobile domestic content legislation (U.S., 1982), 145

Bain, J., 32n.28
Baldwin, Stanley, 76, 78, 79
Balfour, Arthur James, 78
Barton, Edmund, 120
Bastiat, Frédéric, 85, 85nn.1–2
Bateman, F., 16, 172
Beer, Samuel, 80n
Bennett, Richard, 109–10
Bérégovoy government, 94
Bessemer Steel Association (U.S.), 182
Blair House accord (France and the U.S., 1992), 94–95
Blum, Léon, 91
Board of Enquiry (Australia), 117–18n.4
Bonapartists (French Third Republic), 36n.3
Bordeaux wine makers (France), 85, 87n.8
Boström, Gustav, 98–99
Bosworth, Barry, 27–28
Brawley, Mark, 9n
Brigden Commission (Australia), 122
Britain, 71–82; and Canada, 104–5; class conflict in, rise in, 10; electoral reform in, 4; factor mobility in, 71, 72, 128; free trade and empire, years of, 76–78, 76nn.9–10, 78nn.11–12; industrialization in, 17, 30; interwar period, 78–79, 78–79n.13, 129; labor/capital mobility in, 17; Left-Right trade partisanship in, 7; Napoleonic Wars to Cobden-Chevalier Treaty, 71–75, 73n.5, 73nn.2–3, 75nn.7–8, 128; political parties in, 35 (*see also specific parties*); postwar period, 79–82, 80n, 82n.15, 129; regulation of business/labor in, 29; transportation in, 29–